Torture as Public Policy

Torture as Public Policy

Restoring U.S. Credibility
on the World Stage

James P. Pfiffner

Paradigm Publishers
Boulder • London

Published in the United States by Paradigm Publishers, 3360 Mitchell Lane, Suite E, Boulder, CO 80301 USA.

Paradigm Publishers is the trade name of Birkenkamp & Company, LLC, Dean Birkenkamp, President and Publisher.

Library of Congress Cataloging-in-Publication Data

Pfiffner, James P.
  Torture as public policy : restoring U.S. credibility on the world stage / James P. Pfiffner.
     p. cm.
  Includes bibliographic references and index.
  ISBN 978-1-59451-508-8 (hardcover : alk. paper)
  ISBN 978-1-59451-509-5 (paperback : alk. paper)
  1. Torture—United States. 2. Torture—Government policy—United States.
3. Political prisoners—Abuse of—United States. 4. United States—Foreign public opinion. I. Title.
  HV8599.U6P54 2009
  364.6'7—dc22

                                                                        20090150680

Printed and bound in the United States of America on acid-free paper that meets the standards of the American National Standard for Permanence of Paper for Printed Library Materials.

Designed and typeset by Straight Creek Bookmakers

14 13 12 11 10   1 2 3 4 5

Contents

For my children:
Megan Cyr Pfiffner
Katherine Courtney Pfiffner and
Morgan Meehan Pfiffner

—so that their children may grow up in a United States
that does not encourage or condone torture.

Preface

When I saw the photographs from Abu Ghraib in the spring of 2004, my first reaction was, "This is the United States of America, we are not supposed to do this." My second reaction was that the perpetrators of the torture and humiliation were a bunch of immature kids who were not trained for their job and were acting out their own sadistic fantasies. But the further I looked into this sad episode in our history, the more I realized that the sadism depicted in the photographs was not an isolated incident perpetrated by a few "bad apples." The "apples" were bad all right, but the context within which they performed their sadism was systemic, and it reached all the way up the chain of command. An important part of the barrel was rotten.

This book is the way I dealt (and am dealing) with the sad and unfortunate events during the war on terror that resulted in the systematic torture of detainees. My way of coping with these horrors was to try to understand the events analytically. Why did this happen? How did this happen? Who was responsible? Is torture ever justified? Although it is understandable that, in the immediate aftermath of 9/11, the Bush administration felt that a harsh interrogation policy was necessary, it continued to hew to its policy position for the rest of the administration, even after the photos of Abu Ghraib were made public and it was clear that Iraq had nothing to do with 9/11.

Part of my reaction to the revelations of U.S. torture came from my experience as a soldier in the jungles of Vietnam and Cambodia in 1970. At that time I could imagine the possibility of being captured, and I did not want our enemies to have any excuse to torture me. Of course, a U.S. prohibition of torture does not mean that our enemies will also forswear its use, as John McCain's experience in Vietnam demonstrates. But as he pointed out with respect to Bush administration policy, that is not the point. In his words: "This is not about them. This is about us."

In the past, the United States has been a champion of human rights and an international leader in condemning torture. Adopting the brutality of our enemies undermines the cause of justice throughout the world and severely hampers our ability to use moral suasion to influence the behavior of brutal regimes. It also dulls our revulsion toward torture and enables sadists to think they are acting as patriots. Colin Powell argued that torture would undermine U.S. ideals in a private memorandum to President Bush and in a public letter to members of Congress. The professional Judge Advocate General lawyers in the Pentagon objected to the Bush administration's policy, but they were often not informed of the interrogation policies until they had already been formulated and were faits accompli.

Civilian control of the military is an important principle upon which this nation is based; this is the way it should remain. But the Bush administration failed to heed the warnings of both civilian and military career professionals, and this led to the abandonment of our ideals. U.S. torture policy and its implementation have caused immeasurable harm to our reputation throughout the world; we have been excoriated by our allies and condemned by our enemies. Innumerable terrorists and fighters against the United States have been recruited in reaction to our interrogation policies.

Although torture has probably accompanied most wars in human history, including those of the United States, it is one thing for individuals to violate laws, rules, and policies and engage in torture. It is quite another thing for the President of the United States to override warnings and to suspend the Geneva Conventions. This decision set in motion a chain of policy directives that led to the abuse and torture of detainees. The president approved of meetings of National Security Council principals that made decisions about "enhanced interrogation techniques" to be used on detainees. As John Ashcroft said at one of the meetings, "history will not judge this kindly."

Four years after the atrocities of 9/11, the president publicly urged Congress to pass a law (the Military Commissions Act) that would allow his administration to continue with "the program," which involved interrogation techniques that most people in the world consider to be torture. The president's administration also developed a range of policy directives that were recorded in official memoranda and were circulated through the chain of command, setting the conditions under which torture took place. These were all authoritative policy decisions: thus the title of this book and the impetus for writing it.

Acknowledgments

In writing this book, I have profited greatly from the help and advice of many friends and colleagues. The leadership of the School of Public Policy at George Mason University has established a commitment to scholarship from which I have benefitted. Thanks are due to Dean Kingsley Haynes and Vice Dean Jim Finkelstein, who have built SPP into an impressive home for public policy scholars and teachers. Much of the research for this book was completed when I was at the Institute for Advanced Study at the University of London, and I want to express my gratitude to Deans Nicholas Mann and James Dunkerley for their hospitality when I was their guest at University College as S.T. Lee Professorial Fellow for six months. Many colleagues in the UK gave me helpful advice and invited me to give talks on U.S. interrogation policy and the Iraq War, and I want to thank Sharer Ali, Neils Bjerre-Poulson, Nigel Bowles, Steve Casey, Philip Davies, John Dumbrell, Jose Harris, Jon Herbert, Timothy Lynch, Iwan Morgan, John Owens, Mark Phythian, Jon Roper, Richard Rose, and Colin Talbot.

My editor at Paradigm Publishers, Jennifer Knerr, provided encouragement and brought her considerable professionalism to my benefit in the writing and production of this book. I have also benefitted greatly from colleagues who have taken the time and trouble to read portions of my manuscript and have given me their advice and counsel: Jerry Mayer read several chapters and provided incisive and insightful suggestions. Guy Adams commented on several chapters and allowed me to use a pre-publication portion of his book in my research. Lou Fisher, Michael Genovese, Nancy Kassop, Dick Pious, and Bob Spitzer also read portions of the manuscript and gave me their wise counsel. S.G. Mestrovic read the whole manuscript and brought his impressive knowledge of these issues to bear in helping me improve the book.

Others who have helped me with the research for this book in various ways include Mary Boardman, Lara Brown, Mary Anne Borelli, Spike Bowman, Janine Davidson, Mary Lenn Dixon, George Edwards, Chuck Jones, David Luban, Stuart Malawer, Cathy Rudder, John Ritzert, Ronald Rotunda, Mark Rozell, Herman Schwartz, Louise Shelley, Claire Snyder, James Szymalkak, Fred Timm, Susan Tolchin, Matthew Waxman, Benjamin Wittes, and Joe Zengarle. Although these friends and colleagues are complicit in my thinking about these issues, they should not be implicated in my conclusions.

Finally, my children have been an inspiration for this work, and my wife, Deb, has helped in a myriad of ways, and I owe them more gratitude than I can express.

CHAPTER 1

Introduction

U.S. Detainee Policy

Military necessity does not admit of cruelty—that is, the infliction of suffering for the sake of suffering or for revenge, nor of maiming or wounding except in fight, nor of torture to extort confessions.
> —Lieber Code, Commissioned by President Lincoln[1]

We'll have to work sort of the dark side, if you will. We've got to spend time in the shadows in the intelligence world. A lot of what needs to be done here will have to be done quietly, without any discussion, using sources and methods that are available to our intelligence agencies—if we are going to be successful. That's the world these folks operate in. And, uh so it's going to be vital for us to use any means at our disposal basically, to achieve our objectives.
> —Vice President Cheney[2]

The U.S. government adopted an unprecedented program of coolly calculated dehumanizing abuse and physical torment to extract information. This was a mistake, perhaps a disastrous one. It was a collective failure ... Precisely because this was a collective failure, it is all the more important to comprehend it and learn from it.
> —Philip D. Zelikow, former counsel to Condoleezza Rice[3]

The purpose of this book is to try to explain how the United States came to use torture as a tool of public policy during the administration of George W. Bush. Of course there was no written document that ordered anyone to commit torture. And by the narrow definition of the Bush administration, "torture" was not explicitly part of its policy. Nevertheless, a series of policy directives, operational decisions, and leadership actions predictably led to the encouragement and condoning of interrogation methods that amounted to torture in many cases and the cruel, inhuman, and degrading treatment of detainees[4] in other cases. All such actions violated the Geneva Conventions, which were established in 1949 and which the United States signed in 1955. At the extreme, a number of detainees held by the United States during the war on terror died as they were being brutally treated; that is, they were tortured to death.

In addition to the violence done to individual captives, some of whom were innocent of any wrongdoing or actions hostile to the United States, the interrogation policies of the Bush administration had widespread negative ramifications for the reputation of the United States throughout the world. From its inception in the eighteenth century, the United States has always prided itself on being a special nation. Since the founding of the nation, Americans have considered themselves morally sound, if not superior to other nations in their commitment to liberty and human rights. Despite a history of slavery and some ill-considered foreign interventions, we acted (we told ourselves) from idealistic motives.

After World War II, the United States was one of the leaders that helped set up the regime of international law that was embodied in the Geneva Conventions, established in 1949 and ratified by the United States in 1955. Robert H. Jackson, chief prosecutor in the Nuremberg war trials and later justice of the Supreme Court, articulated the ideals to which the United States and its allies aspired after the atrocities of World War II: "That four great nations, flushed with victory and stung with injury[,] stay the hand of vengeance and voluntarily submit their captive enemies to the judgment of the law is one of the most significant tributes that Power has ever paid to reason."[5]

In recent years, the United States has been quick to condemn other nations that ignored human rights, mistreated their citizens, denied due process of law to suspects, or tortured prisoners. The State Department regularly published accounts of prisoner abuse elsewhere in the world, and used these accounts to urge improvements in human rights in these countries. In particular, the United States condemned the use of torture in Iraq and used the fact of Saddam's horrific torture practices as partial justification for the U.S. invasion of Iraq in 2003. President Bush began that war with idealistic declarations about the God-given rights of all human individuals. Thus it is more than ironic that the United States has used harsh interrogations and torture in its "War on Terror." This irony has not been lost on foreign nations, including our allies and adversaries. This book is an attempt to analyze how aggressive interrogation policies were conceived and implemented, often over the objections of career professionals in the civilian and military services. Only by understanding what actually happened can the United States ensure that such policies are not implemented again.

It was not always this way in the United States. Before the Bush administration, the United States had, from the time of the Revolution, always had strict policies forbidding torture. From the Continental Congress instructions to George Washington, to the Lieber Code of President Lincoln, to the Hague Convention of 1907, to the Geneva Conventions, U.S. policy has always been to treat prisoners humanely. This does not mean that U.S. soldiers never engaged in torture. Probably every war in history has witnessed the torture of enemy soldiers. But these almost-inevitable incidents of sadism and revenge, at least in the United States, have always been against the laws and were committed in spite of U.S. policies, not in accord with them. But U.S. policy changed after 9/11.

After the terrorist atrocities of September 11, 2001, the Bush administration was determined to capture those responsible and prevent future attacks against the United States. The nation was traumatized, and public support for President Bush jumped

35 points in an unprecedented rally-round-the-flag response. In October 2001, anthrax spores were sent through the mail to various U.S. officials. Though it was later determined that they were of U.S. origin, the incidents heightened the fear that the United States was under imminent threat of more terrorist attacks. In this atmosphere of fear, the Bush administration judged that U.S. human intelligence capabilities in the terrorist world were minimal and that one of the few sources of intelligence about potential future attacks could come from exploitation of captured terrorists.

This was a reasonable judgment by the administration, and the United States had had past experience with successfully exploiting captured enemy soldiers for intelligence purposes, particularly during World War II. But instead of using tried and true methods, advocated by the FBI and other professional interrogators, the Bush administration decided to change U.S. policy to allow, condone, and encourage "robust" interrogations as a means to extract "actionable intelligence" from captives. In order to emphasize the challenge facing the United States, President Bush decided to use the frame of "war" to describe the way the United States would pursue the perpetrators of the 9/11 crimes and deal with potential future threats.[6]

The decision to define the challenge facing the United States as war rather than as criminal terrorism had fateful consequences. It elevated the status of the attackers from that of vicious criminals to warriors against the United States, and at the same time it expanded the scope of tactics that the United States could use in fighting the terrorists. Importantly, it also allowed the Bush administration to claim that the president was acting in his constitutional capacity as commander in chief. This frame also allowed U.S. forces to treat captives as terrorists who had abetted war crimes in attacking civilians in the World Trade Towers in New York. The future captives would not be treated as prisoners of war but rather as illegal "enemy combatants"; this designation was used to justify President Bush's suspension of the Geneva Conventions.[7]

More importantly, the captives would not be tried in criminal courts for crimes they had committed, but rather they would be used as sources of intelligence. Thus prosecution for any crimes they might have committed would be secondary to the intelligence they might provide in preventing future attacks. If criminal prosecution in a court of law was not as important as extracting intelligence, then interrogators would not have to be squeamish about the methods they used to get the captives to talk. This perspective led directly to decisions to allow harsh interrogation techniques in the questioning of detainees, or as Vice President Cheney said, "A lot of what needs to be done here will have to be done quietly, without any discussion, using sources and methods that are available to our intelligence agencies ... We'll have to work sort of the dark side ... And so it's going to be vital for us to use any means at our disposal basically, to achieve our objectives."[8]

Administration officials were convinced that the terrorist attacks on the United States amounted to a new type of war against cross-national cells of terrorists not based in one nation-state. In order to defend the United States, the administration had to create a "new paradigm" of defense and could not be hobbled by the "obsolete" strictures of the Geneva Conventions. According to President Bush,

The terrorists who declared war on America represent no nation, they defend no territory, and they wear no uniform.... They operate in the shadows of society ... they conspire in secret and then strike without warning.... In this new war, the most important source of information on where the terrorists are hiding and what they are planning is the terrorists, themselves. Captured terrorists have unique knowledge about how terrorist networks operate ... our security depends on getting this kind of information.[9]

What this meant for detainees held by U.S. personnel was that they would be subjected to "robust" interrogation methods that sometimes amounted to torture. The pressure for "actionable intelligence" began at the top of the chain of command, and Secretary of Defense Rumsfeld authorized a range of techniques that exceeded those allowed by the Geneva Conventions and the Army Field Manual on interrogation. When these policy decisions got down to operational levels at Guantanamo Bay, Cuba, Bagram Air Force Base in Afghanistan, and Abu Ghraib in Iraq, lower level military personnel subjected detainees to abuse, brutality, and torture. The CIA also tortured "high-value" detainees in these locations as well as in "black sites" in foreign countries.

The significance of these changes in policy was momentous. It is one thing for an individual or small group to engage in torture; it is quite another for the government to encourage harsh interrogations and condone torture as a matter of policy. In the first case, when torturers are caught, they are punished in due course. In the latter case, the government gives official license for sadists to engage in inhuman acts. But more insidiously, governmental sanction of torture encourages ordinary soldiers to believe that they are doing their patriotic duty and merely following orders when perpetrating torture on fellow human beings.

Although it is understandable that, immediately after 9/11, President Bush and other U.S. officials felt the acute need to obtain intelligence in any way they could, the continuation of the policies of harsh interrogation for the rest of the administration demonstrated an unwillingness to reexamine the faulty premises of the early policies. By late fall of 2002, it had become clear that harsh and probably illegal interrogation techniques were being used at Guantanamo. FBI and DOD officials had sent urgent messages of concern about the abuse and mistreatment of detainees at Guantanamo up the chain of command.

It also should have been clear that, after months of detention and interrogation of detainees, it was improbable that any detainees had information that could thwart an impending terrorist attack. Once informed terrorists had been captured, al Qaeda would have made changes to future plans that might be compromised by captives under pressure to reveal them. If there had been any "ticking time bombs," al Qaeda plans would have been changed once those knowing about them were captured by the Americans. Of course, information about the structure and regular operations of al Qaeda might have been gained from the continued detention and questioning of terrorists; the question of whether torture was a legitimate tactic to obtain such information should have occurred to leaders in the Bush administration. In addition, there was compelling information from the CIA and Army that many of the detainees at Guantanamo held little or no intelligence value to the United States (discussed in Chapter Four).

Thus the United States slipped into a set of intelligence policies that encouraged and condoned physical abuse, which many times amounted to torture, as a standard way of dealing with captives who were suspected of terrorism.

This introductory chapter will first examine some of the precedents for governmental sanction of torture in the Western world and U.S. policies that prohibited torture. Chapter Two will establish a chain of policy decisions that undercut previous prohibitions of torture and that condoned and encouraged harsh interrogations that resulted in the torture of detainees. Chapter Three will analyze operational changes and personnel assignments that implemented torture policy. Chapter Four will examine the ethical, moral, and behavioral dimensions of torture. Chapter Five will take up the legal prohibitions against torture in U.S. and international law and how the Bush administration circumvented the law. Finally, Chapter Six will look at command responsibility and those who established U.S. torture policies as well as those who spoke out against such policies.

Historical Perspective

While torture has been practiced throughout human history, torture pursuant to law is particularly worrisome because it uses the authority and power of government to justify inhuman behavior. The use of torture under the auspices of the state has a long history in the Western legal tradition. Torture was prescribed in accord with Roman canon law. The nations of continental Europe, from the late Middle Ages through the eighteenth century, used torture as a normal part of the legal process in serious criminal cases.[10] This section will briefly review the use of torture in judicial processes in the West during the Spanish Inquisition and in the continental legal tradition.

Spanish Inquisition: Ecclesiastical Torture

The Spanish Inquisition of the fifteenth century was an ecclesiastical tribunal that has been iconic in the West of the terrors of torture carried out by humans on other human beings through the authority of government. One of the main results of the Inquisition was the unification of Spain, and for that purpose, King Ferdinand and Queen Isabella sought from Pope Sixtus IV the authority to appoint the inquisitors in Spain. Their initial motive was the eradication of Judaism and the assimilation of Jews into Spanish society through their conversion to Catholicism. In handing over to the Spanish monarchs the religious authority to enforce adherence to the Catholic faith in 1478, the Pope, in effect, gave them the power to consolidate their political power in Spain and persecute the Jews.[11]

In the earlier half of the fifteenth century, half of the Jews in Spain had been baptized Catholic under threats of governmental punishment, and they were known as "conversos." Torquemada, the Grand Inquisitor appointed by Ferdinand and Isabella, convinced them that the conversos were a threat to the unity of the country because they were not sincere in their conversion but secretly practiced their Jewish religion, despite the law and their public behavior. What began as the use of governmental power to force religious and political unity in Spain became the anti-Semitic persecution and torture of Jews; heresy became a crime against the state.[12]

The inquisition thrived on secrecy; those who were accused were kept imprisoned secretly for indefinite periods and were not told the charges against them. Their accusers remained anonymous; the accused were presumed guilty and the proof of their guilt was their confessions, extracted under torture. They were assigned lawyers whose purpose was not to defend them of charges but to convince them to confess.[13]

The purpose of the use of torture was to convince victims to confess to heresy and to inform the authorities about others who were also heretics. The shedding of blood was forbidden, and acceptable techniques used to extract confessions included water torture, suspending victims from the ceiling with chains attached to their legs, and stretching them on the rack.[14] The punishment for heresy was death by fire. Those accused who were persuaded to confess before their execution were garroted before their bodies were thrown onto the fire. Those who were obstinate and refused to confess or convert were burned alive.[15]

The parallels with U.S. interrogation policy include the presumption of guilt (President Bush, Vice President Cheney, and Donald Rumsfeld each made public pronouncements that the detainees in Guantanamo were terrorists and the "worst of the worst"). Secrecy was essential to U.S. detainee operations. For years detainees were not allowed to communicate with their relatives. "Ghost prisoners" were hidden from the International Committee of the Red Cross. And the interrogation techniques used on detainees were carefully kept secret from the public by the Bush administration, though the accounts of former detainees were widely publicized.

The emphasis on confessing to terrorism was illustrated by the confessions under duress of the "Tipton Three" to having been in a photograph with Osama bin Laden. The British government later demonstrated that the three were in England at the time the photograph was taken and thus could not have been the people appearing in the photograph. The purpose of "extraordinary rendition" in many cases seemed to be to force from detainees confessions that they were associated with al Qaeda. As in the Inquisition, interrogation techniques did not ordinarily involve the shedding of blood, but the CIA used waterboarding and military personnel suspended prisoners from their hands with feet barely touching the floor in Afghanistan.

Medieval Europe: Judicial Torture

"Judicial torture" is defined by historian John Langbein as "the use of physical coercion by officers of the state in order to gather evidence for judicial proceedings."[16] Torture in the legal system of Roman canon law was not used to punish (not that this never happened), but rather to obtain evidence of guilt for a crime.

Before the Fourth Lateran Council of 1215 the determination of guilt in capital crimes (e.g., serious crimes of murder, rape, treason, and heresy) was by ordeal. That is, the appeal for proof of guilt or innocence was to God, who would protect a person if he was innocent but let him suffer (or drown) if guilty. But the Fourth Lateran

Council ended the use of ordeals to establish guilt. And since God could no longer be considered the infallible judge of guilt or innocence, a new system of proof had to be designed for secular authorities that was sufficient to justify punishing a person with death or maiming. The Roman canon law had a high standard of proof for guilt in a capital crime: either two eyewitnesses or a confession of the accused was necessary. This was a high standard of proof, and circumstantial evidence, being considered too subjective, was insufficient. Out of this need for near-certain proof grew the laws of torture to obtain confessions of suspects.

If the suspect confessed, the proof of guilt was certain enough that fallible human judgment was not the final determination. Thus, absent two eyewitnesses, torture was used to elicit confessions from the accused. The level of probable cause necessary before a person was allowed to be tortured was quite high (for instance, one witness and strong circumstantial evidence). Also, a confession, if it appeared to be made merely to stop the pain, was not sufficient. The person was expected to confess details of the crime that could be independently verified. The confession had to be "voluntary," so the accused had to repeat his confession in court in addition to his confession under torture. The problem was that, if the victim recanted his confession, he was subject to torture again, until he did confess "voluntarily."[17]

This system of legally sanctioned torture lasted into the eighteenth century primarily because an alternative law of proof with the certainty of a confession could not easily be devised. The system was abandoned in the eighteenth century as systems of punishment and incarceration developed for minor crimes. The standard of proof for these crimes was less stringent, and circumstantial evidence could be sufficient to convict a person. Thus the European "law of proof" gradually changed in different countries to accept standards of proof for capital crimes that did not call for the "certainty" of confessions obtained under torture. European society came, during the Enlightenment, to have more confidence in the judgment of human beings, as opposed to the infallible judgment of God. Thus in continental Europe, circumstantial evidence that could convince a judge came to be sufficient for judgment, and torture was no longer needed to prove guilt.[18]

Interestingly, England never developed the routine use of torture in judicial proceedings. The reason was that a primitive trial by jury system for determining guilt had been developing in Britain since the Middle Ages. Trial by the judgment of peers was cited as a right of the barons when they forced King John to sign Magna Carta in 1215.

This is not to say, however, that state-sanctioned torture was unknown in England. From 1540 to 1640, torture was used to investigate crimes of state (treason, spying, heresy), when authorized by the privy council or the monarch. John Langbein has recorded eighty-six documented cases in which the privy council or monarch sanctioned the use of torture for confession or to obtain information about treasonous activity. Most of the cases were conducted in the Tower of London in the Tudor era.[19] Although these cases were legally sanctioned torture, they are relatively few, considering that more than eight hundred executions per year were carried out during these years.[20] With only seven cases of torture carried out during the reigns of James

I and Charles I, torture was declining, and after 1640 no warrants for torture were issued in England.[21] The legal scholar William Blackstone considered torture to be "an engine of state, not of law." Thus in England, torture was officially sanctioned in some cases, but not *legally* sanctioned.[22]

U.S. Treatment of Captured Enemy Soldiers

The United States has had a long record of officially requiring humane treatment of prisoners taken in wartime—from the early years of the Republic, to the Lieber Code of the Civil War, to World War II, and Korea. This policy includes the Philippine and Vietnam wars, both of which included counterinsurgency warfare that involved enemy combatants who did not wear military insignia or bear arms openly.

In 1775 the American colonists were fighting an insurgency war against the British Army. The commander of the revolutionary forces, General George Washington, wrote to the British General Gage to complain about the terrible treatment the British extended to captive soldiers of the Revolutionary Army. In doing so, he contrasted the treatment that British captives were being afforded: "Not only your Officers, and Soldiers have been treated with a Tenderness due to Fellow Citizens, & Brethren; but even those execrable Parricides [traitors to the revolutionary cause] whose Counsels & Aid have deluged their Country with Blood, have been protected from the Fury of a justly enraged People."[23] The Americans were truly engaged in an existential struggle with the British; if they lost they would still be subjects of the British Crown and not an independent country. Yet Washington was not willing to torture prisoners in order to gain intelligence about possible future military attacks by the British.

In 1785, the United States negotiated a treaty with Prussia concerning the mutual treatment of prisoners. The treaty provided that prisoners would not be "put into irons, nor bound, nor otherwise restrained in the use of their limbs." It continued that the state of war did not preclude the need to adhere to constraints on the treatment of captives by captors: "The state of war is precisely that for which [the protections] are provided, and during which they are to be as sacredly observed as the most acknowledged articles in the law of nature or nations."[24]

During the Civil War, another existential threat to the United States, President Lincoln was committed to the humane treatment of captives held by the Union Army. In 1863, Lincoln issued a set of instructions regarding the conduct of Union soldiers toward Confederate combatants. The rules of warfare were developed by Francis Lieber, a scholar of the law of war. Section 16 of the Code provides that "military necessity does not admit of cruelty—that is, the infliction of suffering for the sake of suffering or for revenge, nor of maiming or wounding except in fight, nor of torture to extort confessions." Section 80 provides that "the modern law of war permits no longer the use of any violence against prisoners in order to extort the desired information, or to punish them for having given false information."[25]

During the war in the Philippines, U.S. forces used torture in interrogations and argued that since the enemy did not comply with civilized norms of warfare, the United States was not obligated to treat them humanely. However, at the court martial trial of Major Edwin F. Glenn, the judge decided that this justification was not sufficient. "The [necessity] defense fails completely, inasmuch as it is attempted to establish the principle that a belligerent who is at war with a savage or semi-civilized enemy may conduct his operations in violation of the rules of civilized war. This no modern State will admit for an instant.... "[26]

In World War II the United States carefully conformed to the 1929 Geneva Convention (precursor to the 1949 Geneva Conventions) with respect to German and Italian prisoners of war, more than four hundred thousand of whom were held in the United States. In the forward to a book about German POWs, three hundred eighty thousand of whom were kept in a prison camp at Camp Hearne, Texas, former German POW Willie Nellessen commented on the civility of his U.S. guards. "Our captors minded the [Geneva Convention] rules as long as the war lasted and we were impressed by the tolerance shown by the American officers, guards, and farmers. It all was somewhat unusual for us." He went on to explain that he was able to further his education in the program at Camp Hearne, which gave him the background necessary to be trained in banking after the war, and he eventually became chairman of the board of a bank. He concluded, "I am grateful both to God and the Americans who stood guard at Camp Hearne during those terrible last two years of the war."[27]

Even more impressively, U.S. Forces adhered to the 1929 Geneva Conventions when holding Japanese prisoners of war despite brutal treatment of captured U.S. soldiers by the Japanese. During the Korean War, the United States had not yet signed the 1949 Geneva Conventions, but General Douglas MacArthur required that his troops conform to the provisions of the Conventions. By the time of the Vietnam War, the United States had signed the Geneva Conventions, and despite the failure of North Vietnam to treat U.S. prisoners humanely, the United States officially applied the standards of the Geneva Conventions to captured North Vietnamese troops as well as to the Viet Cong guerillas, even though the Viet Cong did not conform to the requirements of uniformed combatants.[28]

The fact that the United States officially adhered to the principle of treating captured enemy soldiers humanely throughout its history up to the Bush administration does not mean that U.S. troops never committed any atrocities or that torture never occurred. During wartime it is impossible to eliminate all acts of barbarism. The difference is that it was official U.S. policy throughout all previous U.S. wars that prisoners be treated humanely, even if the spirit of the law was not always honored. In past U.S. wars, soldiers who tortured enemy captives did so in spite of official policy; after 9/11, they acted in conformance to Bush administration policy (even though some of their actions admittedly went beyond policy guidance).[29]

Overview of the Book

The next chapter establishes the policymaking chain that led to the abuse and torture of detainees at Guantanamo Bay, Cuba; Bagram Air Force Base, Afghanistan; Abu Ghraib, Iraq; and in secret CIA "black sites." Policy can be established in a number of ways, and this chapter will focus on formal decisions and legal memoranda concerning the status of detainees and how they were to be treated. The key decisions included President Bush's Military Order of December 13, 2001, and his decision to suspend the Geneva Conventions in dealing with al Qaeda. Donald Rumsfeld issued memoranda on December 2, 2002, and April 16, 2003, which authorized the use of techniques that went beyond those allowed by then-existing Army regulations. Several legal memoranda, particularly the "torture memo," signed by Jay S. Bybee, paved the way for U.S. policies to allow and condone harsh interrogation methods that often amounted to torture. The chapter will also document the objections to these policies registered by civilian and military officials who risked their careers in order to make their concerns known to their governmental superiors.

Chapter Three will take up the implementation of the policies described in Chapter Two. Implementation included the choice of personnel to command Guantanamo and Abu Ghraib as well as the standard operating procedures established to deal with detainees. The chapter will examine the techniques that were authorized and how they were actually utilized in military prisons. Formal reports by investigations established in the Defense Department documented the way detainees were treated, and the actions of guards will be correlated with the techniques authorized in the memoranda. Of course, some actions, including murder, went well beyond the authorized techniques, and distinctions will be made between methods clearly authorized by official policy, techniques that were inhumane but did not amount to torture, and criminal acts that were not authorized by any administration policy. The chapter will also examine the interrogation technique known as "waterboarding" and the practice of "extraordinary rendition," in which U.S. officials sent detainees to other countries in order to have them interrogated by foreign interrogators using torture beyond what U.S. personnel were willing to use.

In Chapter Four, ethical and sociological aspects of torture will be examined. Those who defend torture often use the extreme hypothetical scenario of the "ticking time bomb" to attempt to establish that under some circumstances a policy of torture is justified. The premises and consequences of the ticking bomb scenario will be analyzed, and the argument will be made that, under careful examination, the logic of the argument breaks down. Critics of torture policy often assume that torture, aside from its morality, is an effective way to extract accurate information from terrorists. That assumption is undermined by a range of scientific analyses and the experience of many interrogators, which will be examined. The chapter argues that once torture is set in policy, it metastasizes beyond its original bounds and undermines the professionalism of any governmental unit that practices it. Finally, the chapter will take up the cases of a number of individuals who were apprehended and tortured by mistake: the "wrong man problem."

Torture is forbidden by the Geneva Conventions, U.S. law, military regulations, and customary international law. But the Bush administration went to considerable lengths to create a legal framework that would protect them and the interrogators from prosecution for crimes. The legal arguments of key administration documents will be analyzed, and it will be argued that their reasoning was tenuous and faulty.

In 2005, the Detainee Treatment Act was passed, and it outlawed torture by U.S. personnel throughout the world. After determining that he did not have the votes necessary to keep a veto of the Detainee Treatment Act from being overridden by Congress, President Bush convinced Congress to pass the Military Commissions Act, which allowed him to redefine the meaning of Common Article 3 of the Geneva Conventions. This allowed President Bush to secretly authorize harsh interrogation techniques that the CIA would be allowed to use on suspected terrorists. Finally, the Supreme Court decisions that rejected the Bush administration's claims regarding habeas corpus will be analyzed.

The final chapter of the book will take up command responsibility. The principles of command responsibility were firmly established in tribunals after World War II in which some German and Japanese military leaders were prosecuted and convicted of war crimes. Command responsibility entails a superior–subordinate relationship, the knowledge of a war crime, and the failure to prevent or punish such an act. These criteria will be applied to persons in the chain of command of those who committed acts of torture. Throughout the making of U.S. policy on interrogation for suspects of terrorism, many civilian and military officials objected to the new policies that condoned harsh treatment and torture of detainees. Many of these officials warned their superiors that the policies were illegal, immoral, and counterproductive; yet these warnings were suppressed or ignored. The chapter will document these warnings and the reactions of Bush administration officials to them.

Finally, it will be argued that the criminal prosecution of U.S. officials who encouraged or condoned torture would be counterproductive to the full investigation and airing of the Bush administration's policies and actions during the war on terror. The United States will not be able to get beyond this sad episode in its history unless the policies and actions of U.S. personnel are fully exposed and confronted. Only then will the United States be able to understand how the abuse and torture were allowed to occur, and with "a decent Respect to the Opinions of Mankind" regain our reputation as a nation that upholds the rule of law and that will not condone torture.

CHAPTER 2

Policymaking on Torture

What took place at Guantanamo is a matter of public record today, and the investigations turned up nothing that suggested that there was any policy in the department other than humane treatment.

—Donald Rumsfeld[1]

We thought they [Guantanamo detainees] were POWs. We always did. We were overruled ... essentially by the President of the United States.

—Colonel Manuel Supervielle (Retired)[2]

Abuse of detainees has never been, is not, and will never be the policy of this government.

—White House spokesman Tony Fratto[3]

Immediately after the trauma of 9/11, the administration was prepared to do anything it could in order to prevent another attack. In addition to the immediate military actions and the launching of Operation Enduring Freedom in Afghanistan, policy decisions had to be made for the internment of enemy personnel, and more importantly, to extract from them intelligence that might help prevent another terrorist attack on the United States. In order to get that intelligence, Bush administration officials felt that harsh interrogation techniques would be necessary and that legal protection had to be assured for those who might later be accused of torture. In late 2001 the administration set out to make the necessary changes in policy and legal interpretation.

Public policies can be formal or informal. In formal policymaking, authoritative government officials explicitly make decisions about what course of action the government will follow. In addition to public law, those policies can be issued in the executive branch through executive orders, military orders, memoranda, or verbal commands. Formal policymaking will be the subject of this chapter. Informal policies can be encouraged or enforced through public pronouncements, behavioral patterns, verbal feedback, and bureaucratic rewards or punishments. These types of informal, behavioral policies will be taken up in the next chapters on the operational administration of abuse and torture and the behavioral dynamics of torture.

Authoritative, legal opinions can also constitute policymaking. If executive branch officials want to take some actions that are potentially against the law, the law is the official public policy limiting the actions. If authoritative legal opinions are issued, especially by the Justice Department's Office of Legal Counsel (OLC), whose opinions are binding on the executive branch, the legal memoranda constitute policy. Authoritative OLC opinions make public policy in the sense that they allow or disallow certain actions. Thus the OLC legal opinions that enabled interrogators to use techniques previously forbidden by law are, in effect, policy, even though they did not mandate particular actions. They formally allowed previously forbidden interrogation techniques to be used. In their zeal to protect the country and ensure that they were not blamed for any future attack, administration officials allowed the law to set the only limits on what they would do. As former Bush appointee and OLC director, Jack Goldsmith, put it, "the question 'What should we do?' so often collapsed into the question 'What can we lawfully do?' ... And it is why what the lawyers said about where those edges were ended up defining the contours of the policy."[4]

This chapter will examine the key Bush administration policy decisions that led to the abuse and torture at Guantanamo, Bagram Air Force Base, and Abu Ghraib, as well as at secret CIA "black sites" in several countries. The first decision was President Bush's Military Order of November 13, 2001, which authorized military commissions, defined enemy combatants, and set the conditions of their imprisonment. This decision was supported by an OLC memorandum that claimed plenary powers for the president during war time. The second key decision was the suspension of the Geneva Agreements. President Bush ordered that suspension on February 7, 2002, lifting the limits on what could be done to detainees by interrogators. The third key decision was made by Secretary of Defense Rumsfeld on December 2, 2002; it allowed military interrogators to use techniques that were not allowed by the Army Field Manual on interrogation. Rumsfeld's decision was supported by the "Torture Memo" of August 1, 2002, which will also be examined along with a second opinion issued on the same day that specified techniques that the CIA could use with high-value detainees. Finally, Donald Rumsfeld rescinded his decision on techniques, and on April 16 issued an order that authorized another set of techniques that went beyond the clear limits in the Army Field Manual 34–52. The conclusion will tie together these separate actions that came to constitute a policy that allowed torture to occur in American prisons.

President Bush's Military Order of November 13, 2001

Immediately after 9/11, John Yoo, with David Addington's help, began to sketch out a legal regime that would maximize presidential power. Their framework was based on the premise that in a time of war, the authority of the president expanded in any way it seemed necessary to protect the country. The first major declaration was Yoo's memo of September 25. Yoo asserted that the president had the authority to retaliate against not only perpetrators of terrorism, but against any foreign state "suspected" of supporting terrorists, and that he could use military force preemptively against terrorist organizations or states "whether or not they can be linked to the specific terrorist incidents of September 11." His memo concluded that "the President has the plenary constitutional power to take such military actions as he deems necessary and appropriate" to respond to 9/11. Furthermore, Congress cannot "place any limits on the President's determinations as to any terrorist threat, the amount of military force to be used in response, or the method, timing, and nature of the response. These decisions, under our Constitution, are for the President alone to make and are unreviewable."[5]

When captives began to accumulate in Afghanistan, the more important prisoners had to be housed where the United States could control them and keep them off the battlefield, but more importantly, in the administration's judgment, they had to be exploited for any intelligence they might have about possible future attacks on the United States. The administration chose the U.S. military installation at Guantanamo Bay, Cuba, to house the prisoners because it was close to the United States, yet not officially part of U.S. territory, and thus (they reasoned) outside the jurisdiction of the U.S. court system. (Later the administration's reasoning was declared to be faulty by the Supreme Court.)

On November 13, 2001, President Bush issued a military order that declared that, in accord with his commander-in-chief authority and in light of the national emergency created by the terrorist attacks of 9/11, suspected terrorists could be detained and put on trial for violations of the laws of war.[6] The order applied to non-U.S. citizens who were members of al Qaeda or "engaged in, aided or abetted" it or people who "knowingly harbored" them. The order called for the secretary of defense to detain such persons, treat them humanely, provide them with the necessities of life, honor their religious beliefs, and have them "detained in accordance with such other conditions as the Secretary of Defense may prescribe."[7]

The president's military order preempted an ongoing interagency working group that had been examining the legal implications of how to handle detainees who might have been members of the Taliban or al Qaeda. It was led by Pierre Prosper, who was ambassador at large for war crimes, and who had successfully prosecuted war crimes in Rwanda, including genocide, in the United Nation's International Criminal Tribunal.[8] But according to deputy White House counsel Timothy E. Flanigan, David Addington felt it would be useful to demonstrate that the president was not dependent on "legal bureaucrats" and could make decisions "without their blessing—and without the interminable process that goes along with getting that blessing."[9] National Security Advisor Rice and Secretary of State Colin Powell knew that the Prosper Committee was working on the issue and thought that they would have some input when the order was drafted. But in late October Vice President Cheney felt that the process was taking too long and he short-circuited the process and ignored the Prosper committee work.

For purposes of detainees, the most important aspect of the military order was the establishment of the category of "unlawful enemy combatant," which the Bush administration would use in order to exclude suspected terrorists or fighters against

U.S. forces from the protections of the Geneva Convention rules about the treatment of prisoners of war or others captured in the administration's war on terror. One might expect that such an important and far-reaching order would involve consultation with the national security advisor, the secretaries of state and defense, or military lawyers from the Judge Advocate General Corp. But Vice President Cheney gave strict instructions that others in the White House and cabinet be bypassed and not informed until President Bush signed the order.

The order was drafted by David Addington, the vice president's lawyer, and was purposefully kept secret from the rest of the administration. Addington succinctly expressed his attitude toward consultation: "Fuck the interagency process."[10] One of the few lawyers who did see the draft said that it "was very closely held because it was coming right from the top." The decision to write the draft without respect to the Geneva Conventions (a treaty) or Uniform Code of Military Justice (enacted in law) was based on a legal memorandum written by John Yoo on November 6. When asked why the secretary of state (the State Department has jurisdiction over treaties) was not shown the draft, Yoo said "The issue we dealt with was: Can the president do it constitutionally? State—they wouldn't have views on that."[11]

On November 13, 2001, Cheney personally took the draft document to President Bush in his private dining room to clear it with him. Powell, Rice, and Rice's deputy John Bellinger thought that the Prosper committee was still working on the policy and did not know that Cheney was in the process of finalizing it. After Bush's concurrence, Cheney made sure that no one else could make any last minute objections by giving it to his aides David Addington and Tim Flannigan, who took it to associate White House counsel Berenson, who was not told that it came from Cheney. Berenson took it to the staff secretary, Stuart Bowen, Jr., who was told not to let other White House staffers see it and to prepare it for the president's signature. Despite Bowen's objections that other relevant staffers had not seen the document, he was told that it was too sensitive for others to see and that the president was waiting to sign it. Cheney then took the document back to the Oval Office, where the president signed it immediately. White House aides who were present at the signing said they did not know that the vice president had been involved in the drafting of the memo.[12]

On the evening of November 13, when CNN broadcast that the military order had been signed by the president, Colin Powell exclaimed "What the hell just happened?"[13] and National Security Advisor Rice sent an aide to find out about the order because she had not been informed, much less consulted.

The Military Commissions order was important because it created the new category of "enemy combatant" to avoid the "prisoner of war" category that would have invoked the Geneva Conventions. People could be labeled enemy combatants at the president's discretion. In accord with the president's decision, made the next month, to suspend the Geneva Conventions, enemy combatants would not be entitled to the protections of the Geneva rules, either for prisoners of war or for others held at the mercy of opposing forces. This determination led to the abuse and torture of detainees.

One of the ostensible purposes of vetting important decision with White House staffers and members of the Cabinet who might be involved with implementing orders is that they might know something that the vice president or his lawyers do not know about the issue. Vice President Cheney had been successful in excluding from the decision process anyone who might have disagreed with his draft of the order; he got his way, but the decision led to a flawed legal framework for dealing with detainees in the war on terror. The consequences of excluding outside input on the draft came when the Supreme Court, in *Hamdan v. Rumsfeld,* struck down the military commissions plans because they were not set up in accord with U.S. law or the Uniform Code of Military Justice.[14] The lack of a regular, legal process for prosecuting suspected terrorists continued to be problematic for the rest of the Bush administration.

Suspending the Geneva Conventions

Detainees began to arrive at Guantanamo on January 11, 2002, and the administration needed a legal regime under which they could be interrogated. The legal regime for Army interrogations was the Army Field Manual for Interrogations FM 34–52 (1992), which was based on the rules for the treatment of enemy captives required by the Geneva Conventions. The FBI also had developed interrogation protocols that complied with the Geneva restrictions and U.S. law. The FBI approach was designed to gradually establish a rapport with suspects and carefully document all evidence so that it would stand up in court and the suspect could, if guilty, be prosecuted successfully in court. This approach to interrogation had also worked effectively in World War II.

The Bush administration, however, was impatient and wanted to exploit the detainees for intelligence purposes rather than gather evidence for future prosecution. But they feared that if the detainees were treated strictly according to the accepted rules of war, the Geneva Conventions, they could not be forced to give up intelligence quickly enough to prevent future attacks. Thus the administration decided to use an intelligence exploitation (rather than a criminal justice) framework in the treatment of detainees; the interrogation purposes were considered to be more important than merely keeping enemy personnel off the battlefield or prosecuting them for any crimes they might have committed.

In order to use the harsh interrogation methods that President Bush thought would be necessary in the war on terror, it would be necessary to get around laws and regulations on the treatment of prisoners. A range of national and international laws prohibited torture or cruel and degrading treatment of prisoners, and these restrictions potentially stood in the way of the administration's plans for aggressive intelligence gathering from captured persons suspected of terrorism. The first, and most fundamental, restraints on harsh interrogations were based on the Geneva Conventions that were formulated in 1949 and ratified by the United States in 1955. This analysis will explain the arguments upon which President Bush relied in deciding to suspend the Geneva Conventions for members of al Qaeda and the Taliban. Following sections will examine how administration lawyers and policymakers developed a range of harsh interrogation techniques that had hitherto been forbidden but which could now be employed in the war on terror.

Top members of the Bush administration thought that terrorists did not deserve to be treated according to the Geneva rules because they did not represent a state that had signed the agreement. In addition, they were terrorists who did not act according to the rules of war. Accordingly, John Yoo, at the Office of Legal Counsel, working with David Addington, wrote legal memoranda arguing that the United States was not bound by the strictures of Geneva. Yoo's memo of January 9, 2002, concluded that the Geneva Conventions did not protect members of al Qaeda, because they were non-state actors, did not respect the rules of war, and had not signed the Geneva Accords. In addition, the war on terror was a new type of war that was not between traditional nation-states. Yoo argued that the drafters of the Geneva Convention "could not have" contemplated a conflict between a nation-state and a "transnational terrorist organization."[15] He thus concluded that the Geneva Conventions should not apply to the treatment of al Qaeda prisoners. In a public statement on January 11, Secretary of Defense Rumsfeld said that the Guantanamo detainees would be "handled not as prisoners of war, because they're not, but as unlawful combatants [who] do not have any rights under the Geneva Convention."[16]

State Department Counsel William Taft replied to Yoo's memo, arguing that "Both the most important factual assumptions on which your draft is based and its legal analysis are seriously flawed ... In previous conflicts, the United States has dealt with tens of thousands of detainees without repudiating its obligations. I have no doubt we can do so here."[17] Taft considered the issue to be in the process of policy development prior to its being considered by the NSC principals, but on January 18, when Secretary Powell was in Asia, Taft learned that the president had determined that the Justice Department's interpretation would be administration policy.[18]

Although General Tommy Franks had initially ordered U.S. troops to conduct themselves in accord with the Geneva Conventions, Secretary Rumsfeld overrode his order when on January 19 he instructed Chairman of the Joint Chiefs of Staff General Myers that Geneva POW status did not extend to members of al Qaeda or to the Taliban. Myers sent the decision to Guantanamo.[19] The Judge Advocate Generals of the services (JAGs), however, were not consulted about the decisions.[20] That is, those who, because of their training and years of experience, were among the most informed and qualified lawyers on the laws of war, were excluded from being consulted on this important decision. The reason they were left out of the loop was that they might have raised objections about the legal reasoning or the policy implications of this decision. Administration lawyers were careful to maximize the chances that their preferred policies would be adopted without change. As David Addington reportedly said, "Don't bring the TJAGs into the process, they aren't reliable."[21]

General Tommy Franks then confirmed the decision in a January 24, 2002, memo: "With the war on terrorism at full speed, the ability to obtain accurate and timely information about the capabilities, intentions, and activities of foreign powers, organizations, or persons may be at odds with the Laws of War and other training our military personnel received."[22] Franks seemed to be well aware that he was conveying to his troops the message that their training in the Geneva Conventions would no longer restrict their actions with respect to captives. This amounted to an invitation to ignore training on interrogation and engage in techniques formerly forbidden because intelligence was necessary and the war on terrorism was at "full speed."

President Bush, however, had not yet made a formal decision about U.S. policy with respect to Geneva. Before that decision, the issue was considered by Secretary of Defense Rumsfeld in preparation for his advice to President Bush. In late January, Chairman of the Joint Chiefs of Staff General Myers and Douglas Feith, Deputy Secretary of Defense for Policy (the number three person in the Pentagon hierarchy) went to Rumsfeld's office to advise him. Before getting to Rumsfeld's office General Myers expressed to Feith his strong conviction that the United States had to comply with the Geneva Conventions. "I feel very strongly about this, and if Rumsfeld doesn't defend the Geneva Conventions, I'll contradict him in front of the President!"[23] When they talked with Rumsfeld, Feith seemed to agree with Myers, saying: "Obeying the Geneva Conventions is not optional. The U.S. Constitution says there are two things that are the supreme law of the land—statutes and treaties." According to Feith, Geneva was a "treaty in force" and as such was part of the "supreme Law of the Land. Compliance was *mandatory,* not optional" (emphasis in original).[24] Myers added that compliance with Geneva was part of "our military culture," and said "We train our people to obey the Geneva Conventions, it's not even a matter of whether it is reciprocated—it's a matter of who we are."[25]

Myers might have thought that Feith was arguing for the application of Geneva in the war on terror, but that was not Feith's purpose. Feith's reasoning was that soldiers of signatory nations were due treatment in accord with the Geneva Conventions, but if others received the same treatment, there would be no incentive for states to sign the conventions. Since al Qaeda was not a nation-state that had signed the agreements, granting its members treatment in accord with Geneva would in fact undermine the Geneva Treaty by granting privileges to those who had not signed the treaty.[26] Feith thought that Geneva did apply to the Taliban, since Afghanistan had signed the treaty, but that insofar as the Taliban fighters did not wear uniforms and sometimes hid among civilians, they were not entitled to POW status.[27] Rumsfeld accepted Feith's interpretation of how the United States should treat the Geneva Conventions.

The consequence of Feith's reasoning was that no one at Guantanamo was entitled to be treated according to the Geneva Conventions. When asked if this was his reasoning, he replied "Oh yes, sure. Absolutely. That's the point."[28] Thus it might seem that General Myers was misled by Feith's argument that the United States was bound by the Geneva Conventions. According to one military observer, Myers was "well and truly hoodwinked."[29] In addition, when asked if the decision to suspend the Geneva Conventions was intended to preclude constraints on interrogations in the war on terrorism, Feith responded, "absolutely."[30]

On January 22, OLC Director Jay S. Bybee signed a memo making a legal argument that Geneva did not protect al Qaeda or the Taliban and that the U.S. War Crimes Act (which incorporated Geneva rules) thus would not apply to U.S. interrogation personnel.[31] On January 25, a memo from the president's counsel, Alberto Gonzales, reaffirmed the reasoning of the OCL memo and recommended that Geneva Convention III on Treatment of Prisoners of War should not apply to al Qaeda and Taliban prisoners. He reasoned that the war on terrorism was "a new kind of war" and that the "new paradigm renders obsolete Geneva's strict limitations on questioning of enemy prisoners.... " Gonzales argued that exempting captured al Qaeda and Taliban prisoners from Geneva Convention protections would preclude the prosecution of U.S. soldiers under the U.S. War Crimes Act. "A determination that GPW is not applicable to the Taliban would mean that Section 2441 [of the War Crimes Act] would not apply to actions taken with respect to the Taliban."[32]

Although Powell felt that the proper place to make a formal recommendation to the president on such an important issue was in a principals meeting of the NSC, he asked Rice for a personal meeting with the president to discuss the issue. Treaty issues, particularly the abandoning of such an important international agreement, were in the jurisdiction of the State Department, but the decision had been made without Powell's advice and without any formal, high-level discussion of the issues. Powell met with the president on January 21 and said that he told the president: "I wanted everybody covered, whether Taliban, al-Qaeda or whatever, and I think the case was there for that."[33]

In a memo of January 26, 2002, Powell presciently objected to the reasoning of the Justice Department and the President's Counsel. He argued that the drawbacks of deciding not to apply the Geneva Conventions outweighed the advantages because "it will reverse over a century of policy ... and undermine the protections of the law of war for our troops, both in this specific conflict and in general; It has a high cost in terms of negative international reaction.... It will undermine public support among critical allies."[34] Powell also noted that applying the Convention "maintains POW status for U.S. forces ... and generally supports the U.S. objective of ensuring its forces are accorded protection under the Convention." The memo also addressed the intended applicability of the Convention to non-traditional conflicts: "[T]he GPW was intended to cover all types of armed conflict and did not by its terms limit its application."[35]

Bush disagreed with Powell, but reluctantly called an NSC meeting for January 28.[36] But before the meeting, a memorandum drafted by David Addington that Alberto Gonzales sent to the president was leaked to the *Washington Times*. The memo refuted Powell's arguments in advance of the NSC meeting and argued that the "new paradigm" of non-state warfare rendered obsolete the Geneva Conventions and that the OLC judgment was definitive. Powell was upset at the preemptive strike by the White House to undermine his position at the upcoming NSC meeting. According to Powell, the memo was leaked "in order to try to screw me" and "blow me out of the water."[37]

Despite Powell's arguments, and in accord with the Office of Legal Counsel and his counsel's recommendations, President Bush signed a memorandum on February 7, 2002, that stated: "Pursuant to my authority as Commander in Chief ... I determine that none of the provisions of Geneva apply to our conflict with al Qaeda in Afghanistan or elsewhere throughout the world because, among other reasons, al Qaeda is not a High Contracting Party to Geneva." The memo argued that the Geneva Convention applies only to states and "assumes the existence of 'regular' armed forces fighting on behalf of states," and that "terrorism ushers in a new paradigm," that "requires new thinking in the law of war." The memo also stated that "As a matter of policy, the United States Armed Forces shall continue to treat detainees humanely and, *to the extent appropriate and consistent with military necessity,* in a manner consistent with the principles of Geneva (emphasis added)."[38] This determination allowed the use of aggressive techniques of interrogation used by the CIA and military intelligence at Guantanamo that were later, in the fall of 2003, transferred by Major General Geoffrey Miller to the prison at Abu Ghraib.[39] The changes in policy regarding the status of prisoners at Guantanamo upset top level military lawyers in the Judge Advocate General Corps, including lawyers in the Chairman of the Joint Chiefs of Staff's office.[40]

The purpose of the suspension of the Geneva Conventions by the administration was to ensure that prisoners in Guantanamo did not have to be treated according to the Geneva rules. Thus interrogators could apply harsh interrogation techniques to gain intelligence about terrorist activities. In addition, the U.S. War Crimes statute (which referenced the Geneva rules) would not apply to interrogators.

The impact of the abandonment of the Geneva Conventions for the war on terrorism was emphasized by General Sanchez, head of U.S. forces in Iraq (after his retirement):

> This presidential memorandum constitutes a watershed even in U.S. military history. Essentially, it set aside all of the legal constraints, training guidelines, and rules of interrogation that formed the U.S. Army's foundation for the treatment of prisoners on the battlefield since the Geneva Conventions were revised and ratified in 1949.[41]

The irony in this evaluation by Sanchez was that the Bush administration publicly and explicitly acknowledged that the Geneva Conventions did apply to Iraq because it was a signatory to the treaty, as was the United States. That crucial distinction was lost on U.S. forces in Iraq, and Sanchez's actions demonstrate how difficult it is to limit torture and harsh interrogation tactics once they are authorized. Sanchez knew better than anyone how influential this policy decision by the White House became. He himself issued a memorandum in October of 2003 authorizing the use of illegal interrogation practices in Iraq.

Authorizing "Alternative" Methods of Interrogation

The third major policy change affecting interrogations was Secretary Rumsfeld's approval of a list of interrogation techniques available to U.S. forces. That policy decision was based on the "Torture Memo" of August 1, 2002, and was signed by the head of the Office of Legal Counsel, Jay S. Bybee, though it was probably composed by David Addington and John Yoo. The Bybee memo provided the legal basis for the interrogation techniques that were developed over the summer of 2002 and final-ized in the fall. They were forwarded to Secretary Rumsfeld, who authorized the use of most of them on December 2, 2002. A second memo of the same date (Bybee II) specified interrogation techniques that the CIA could use in its interrogation of high value detainees. This section will first examine the legal reasoning of the Bybee memo, then the development of the interrogation techniques, and finally the policy process that led to the approval of those techniques by Donald Rumsfeld. The second Bybee memo, for the CIA, will be examined in the next chapter.

The "Torture Memo" of August 1, 2002

In the summer of 2002 officials at the White House and in the Pentagon were becom-ing frustrated because of the lack of "actionable intelligence" coming from detainees at Guantanamo. They had begun to explore means to break the will of captives by the use of harsh techniques that had been used by the Chinese and North Koreans in the Cold War. Even though President Bush had suspended the Geneva Conventions in January, U.S. law and other international laws forbade the use of harsh techniques that might approach torture. So John Yoo in the Office of Legal Counsel (OLC) in the Department of Justice, with the help of David Addington in the vice president's office, worked on a legal framework that would protect U.S. personnel from prosecu-tion for using harsh interrogation techniques. Opinions of the OLC are considered authoritative in the government and represent the official executive branch inter-pretation of the law. Thus an opinion by OLC could authorize actions by executive branch agencies and protect them from criminal prosecution.[42]

The controversial nature of the OLC judgment about the definition of torture and the authority of the president as commander in chief was reflected in the unwillingness of Yoo and his close colleagues to let others outside their narrow circle read and com-ment on the opinion. As explained by the subsequent head of OLC, Bush appointee Jack Goldsmith: "Many important legal decisions in the Bush administration, by contrast, were made by a very small and largely like-minded group of lawyers, and announced, if at all, without outside consultation. This led to ... legal and political errors that became very costly to the administration down the road."[43]

The normal process for OLC opinions is to circulate them to agencies of the gov-ernment that have expertise or policy interest in the subject of the memo. When Yoo was drafting the August 1 memorandum, the White House told him not to show the opinion to lawyers in the State Department, which was considered too soft and which might have raised objections to the legal reasoning.[44] The OLC supposedly wanted to prevent leaks, but Goldsmith suspected that in fact "it was done to control outcomes in the opinions and minimize resistance to them."[45]

On August 1, 2002, Jay Bybee, director of OLC, signed the memorandum (the Bybee memo is also known as the "torture memo") upon which Yoo and others had been working.[46] The memo made several far-reaching arguments. It argued that, according to U.S. law, torture was a legal term that was very narrowly defined. Part I of the Bybee memo construed the definition of torture narrowly and elevated the threshold of "severe pain" necessary to amount to torture. "We conclude that certain acts may be cruel, inhuman, or degrading, but still not produce pain and suffering of the requisite intensity to fall within Section 2340A's proscription against torture … Physical pain amounting to torture must be equivalent in intensity to the pain accompanying serious physical injury, such as organ failure, impairment of bodily function, or even death."[47] Geneva Convention Common Article 3 prohibits cruel, inhuman, and degrading treatment of prisoners, as well as torture. But the Geneva rules had already been suspended by the president six months before the Bybee memo was written, and were no longer relevant to Yoo's analysis.

The memo's narrow definition of torture allowed for a wide range of brutal actions that do not meet the exacting requirements specified in the memo. The memo specifically excludes from torture "cruel, inhuman, or degrading treatment or punishment," some examples of which are specified, such as wall standing, hooding, noise, sleep deprivation, and deprivation of food and drink. But the memo did specify that some practices would be torture, such as severe beatings with clubs, threats of imminent death, threats of removing extremities, burning, electrical shocks to genitalia, rape, and sexual assault.[48]

According to the memo, for the law to apply, the torturer must have the "specific intent to inflict severe pain" and it must be his "precise objective … Thus, even if the defendant knows that severe pain will result from his actions, if causing such harm is not his objective, he lacks the requisite specific intent *even though the defendant did not act in good faith*" (emphasis added).[49] Thus one could inflict pain that amounted to torture, but not be guilty of torture if the main objective was, for instance, to extract information rather than to cause pain.[50] This is legal sophistry.

With respect to the Convention Against Torture (CAT), ratified by the United States, the Bybee memo concluded that Section 2340A of Title 18, which was enacted to implement the CAT, "reaches only the most heinous acts," and thus left room for the types of techniques that were being considered in the summer and fall of 2002.[51] Finally, the memo argued that any U.S. person accused of torture who was acting pursuant to the orders of the commander in chief could defend against the charge by arguing, among other things, "the right to self-defense," since "the nation itself is under attack."[52]

In addition to arguing that U.S. and international law did not limit the types of interrogation techniques being considered, the Bybee memo argued that the president's authority as commander in chief allowed him to order any treatment he thought appropriate for suspected terrorists. Jack Goldsmith characterized the Bush administration approach to presidential power as having "a theological significance," involving "open chest-thumping about the importance of maintaining and expanding executive power."[53] The Bybee memo was intended to expand significantly executive authority.

Section V of the memo argued that the president's commander-in-chief authority can overcome any law. "[T]he President enjoys complete discretion in the exercise of his Commander-in-Chief authority and in conducting operations against hostile forces."[54] Thus "[a]ny effort to apply Section 2340A in a manner that interferes with the President's direction of such core war matters as the detention and interrogation of enemy combatants thus would be unconstitutional."[55] It argued further that any other effort by Congress to limit the interrogation of enemy combatants would be unconstitutional.[56]

According to John Yoo, Congress cannot "tie the President's hands in regard to torture as an interrogation technique ... It's the core of the Commander-in-Chief function. They can't prevent the President from ordering torture."[57] According to this argument, Congress cannot regulate presidential actions when he is acting as commander in chief, and any law, such as the torture law, "must be construed as not applying to interrogations undertaken pursuant to his Commander-in-Chief authority."[58] Jack Goldsmith, head of OLC after Bybee, explained: "The Bush administration has operated on an entirely different concept of power that relies on minimal deliberation, unilateral action, and legalistic defense."[59]

The use of the commander-in-chief clause to defend against a charge of torture directly connects the president with the acts of torture. A contractor, CIA agent, or soldier cannot invoke the commander-in-chief authority; only the president can. Bush administration arguments that the president is not bound by the law thus make a direct connection between the actions of possible torturers and the president by arguing that it is the president who is not bound by the law. The administration argued, in effect, that the president, when acting as commander in chief, is above the law because no public law (whether signed by a president or not) can impinge on the president's authority with respect to the interrogation of enemy combatants.

On the same day, August, 1, 2002, a second Bybee memo established a separate policy track for the CIA.[60] The memo specified interrogation techniques that could be used by the CIA on high-value detainees. The memo was based on the president's commander-in-chief authority as analyzed in the previous (Bybee I) memo. Bybee II dealt only with one detainee, Abu Zubaydah, and it specified techniques that could be used to compel him to divulge information about any future planned attacks or other information about al Qaeda. The CIA judged that the danger of another attack was real and that very harsh methods were necessary to get Zubaydah to talk. The techniques approved in the Bybee II memo (including sleep deprivation and waterboarding) were much harsher than those allowed by the Army Field Manual, and they will be examined in Chapter Three. CIA and other interrogators considered the 2002 memo to be a "golden shield" for them if they were later accused of breaking the law.[61]

When Jack Goldsmith was appointed by President Bush to head the OLC, he began to examine OLC opinions, and he became concerned about their lack of professionalism. Goldsmith thought that the reasoning in the Bybee memo was so flawed that he took the very unusual step of formally withdrawing it in the fall of 2004. He later wrote that the memo was "legally flawed, tendentious in substance and tone, and overbroad.... "[62] He summarized the import of the August 1 memo: "violent acts aren't necessarily torture; if you do torture, you probably have a defense; and even if you don't have a defense, the torture law doesn't apply if you act under color of presidential authority."[63] Goldsmith said that the Bybee II memo, which approved techniques for the CIA, was "vetted at the highest circles of government."[64] Thus the president and vice president were directly involved in setting the legal framework for the harsh interrogation of detainees.

Some administration officials implied that the OLC memo was merely academic analysis and did not constitute administration policy. But Milton Bearden, who worked in the CIA for thirty years, said about the Bybee memo: "It doesn't matter what distribution that memo had or how tightly it was controlled. That kind of thinking will permeate the system by word of mouth. Anyone who suggests that this and other official memos on this subject didn't have an impact, doesn't know how these things work on the ground."[65]

The memo specified interrogation techniques that could be used by the CIA on high value detainees. The memo was based on the president's commander in chief authority as analyzed in the previous (Bybee I) memo. Bybee II dealt only with one detainee, Abu Zubaydah, and it specified techniques that could be used to compel him to divulge information about any future planned attacks and other information about al Qaeda. The CIA judged that the danger of another attack was real and that very harsh methods were necessary to get Zubaydah to talk.

The December 2, 2002, Techniques Memorandum

President Bush's first key decision was to create the category of enemy combatants in his November 13 military order. The purpose of President Bush's second key decision that suspended the Geneva Conventions was to set U.S. interrogation policy free from the moorings of the Geneva constraints on the treatment of detainees. The "Torture Memo" of August 1, 2002, argued that in interrogating detainees in the war on terrorism, U.S. personnel were not bound by U.S. law, treaties, international law, or customary international law (explained in Chapter Five). When acting on orders from the president in the role of commander in chief, it claimed, U.S. personnel were immunized from any legal prosecution for breaking any laws authorized by the president (with the exception of acts of egregious torture) during interrogation.

The third key policy decision was Secretary Rumsfeld's decision on December 2, 2002, to allow military personnel at Guantanamo to use interrogation techniques that went beyond those authorized in Army Field Manual 34–52 (1992). This decision set interrogators free from the constraints of the Uniform Code of Military Justice (with respect to interrogations) and their training in the treatment of prisoners. The Bybee II memo, which has just been released to the public, authorized the CIA to use specific techniques in interrogation, including waterboarding, that went beyond those permitted to military personnel.

The Search for Additional Interrogation Techniques

After the decision had been made to use the U.S. base at Guantanamo to house prisoners captured in Afghanistan, detainees began to arrive in early 2002. Initially,

Joint Task Force 160 prepared the camp to receive prisoners from Afghanistan. JTF 160, with two thousand troops, was commanded by Marine Brigadier General Michael Lehnert, whose approach was to run the prison camp according to the Geneva Conventions and the Uniform Code of Military Justice. Although told that the Geneva Conventions did not officially apply, he decided that standard operating procedures for treating prisoners would be followed. Head of detention Colonel Terry Carrico said, "The Geneva Conventions don't officially apply. But they do apply."[66]

General Lehnert saw his main mission as housing and caring for the prisoners and keeping them off the battlefield. Near the end of January, however, Secretary Rumsfeld established firmly that the main mission of Guantanamo was producing intelligence. So in February 2002, Rumsfeld appointed Major General Michael Dunlavey to be head of the newly established Joint Task Force 170, which ran intelligence and interrogations at Guantanamo. Dunlavey was selected because he was a tough, experienced soldier and his mission from Rumsfeld was to "maximize the intelligence production."[67] Rumsfeld was so concerned with intelligence that Dunlavey was told to report directly to him, rather than going through the usual chain of command by reporting through the head of the U.S. Southern Command. Dunlavey himself declared: "I got my marching orders from the President of the United States."[68]

Dunlavey's approach to the prisoners contrasted with Lehnert's adherence to Geneva principles, and conditions for the detainees began to deteriorate as interrogation for intelligence became the primary mission of the facility. Detainees were kept in isolation and force fed when they refused to eat; obtaining intelligence came to outweigh plans to try them for war crimes.[69]

In March 2002, Brigadier General Rick Baccus of the Rhode Island National Guard replaced General Lehnert as head of Joint Task Force–160 and took charge of prisoners at Guantanamo. His background was in military police in the National Guard rather than in running prisons, and he ran the treatment of detainees "by the book." That is, he strictly enforced the Geneva regulations about the treatment of detainees and even posted copies of the Geneva rules at the prison camp. But as time passed without intelligence breakthroughs, the Bush administration became impatient and began to put pressure on the interrogators at Guantanamo. Dunlavey and Baccus clashed over the treatment of prisoners, and Baccus was replaced on October 9, 2002, just before a memo requesting additional interrogation techniques went forward from Guantanamo.

By May 2002, General Dunlavey had come to the conclusion that up to half of the detainees at Gitmo contained no intelligence value.[70] Nevertheless, the Bush administration was frustrated by the inability of interrogators to produce useful intelligence by using the traditional techniques of Army FM 34–52, especially from "high-value" detainees such as Mohammed al-Qahtani, who they thought might have been the "twentieth hijacker" and, in Dunlavey's words, "may have been the key to the survival of the United States."[71] Pressure from Washington continued in the form of Rumsfeld "snowflakes" (memoranda), and Dunlavey felt the urgency, which in his words, "must have been all the way to the White House."[72] There was a search for new techniques that might be successful where the traditional techniques had failed.

The Bush administration maintained that the initiative for the abusive techniques originated from the military leadership at Guantanamo. On June 22, 2004, Alberto Gonzales held a press conference in the Old Executive Office Building to release a number of documents related to prisoner abuse. At the press conference, Daniel J. Dell'Orto said that when it was discovered that Mohammed al Qahtani was a high-value detainee who might have information about al Qaeda, it was Guantanamo personnel who initiated the search for interrogation techniques beyond those allowed by Army regulations.

> And so it is concluded at Guantanamo that it may be time to inquire as to whether there may be more flexibility in the type of techniques we use on him. And so on the 11th of October of 2002, Guantanamo generated a request to the Commander of Southern Command and that additional techniques beyond those in the field manual be approved for use against high-value detainees.... That request makes its way up to the Commander of South Com ... General Hill forwards those to the Joint Staff.... And on the 2nd of December, 2002, the Secretary of Defense approves.[73]

In his attempt to deflect blame for Guantanamo interrogation policies from high-level administration officials, Dell'Orto reversed the direction of influence. Pressure for more intelligence came from the top, and the initiative to use Survival Evasion Resistance and Escape (SERE) techniques on detainees originated in the General Counsel's office at DOD.

As early as July 2002, Richard Shiffrin, deputy general counsel for DOD, requested that the chief of staff for the Joint Personnel Recovery Agency, which administered SERE training, send information on resistance techniques.[74] The training was known as Survival Evasion Resistance and Escape (SERE) and was administered in several locations in the United States. The techniques used on U.S. soldiers were based on techniques known to have been used by the Soviets, the Chinese, and the North Koreans and included (among many others) stress positions, forced nudity, hooding, sleep deprivation, humiliation, loud noises (music), extremes of temperature, face and body slaps, and waterboarding. During SERE training, doctors and psychologists were available to assure that permanent damage was not done to U.S. trainees.[75] The purpose of SERE training, however, is not to elicit information during interrogations, but rather to allow U.S. soldiers to experience the type of treatment they might encounter if they were captured by an enemy who did not respect the Geneva Conventions and to give them the physical and psychological means to resist such treatment. The Communist use of the SERE techniques was intended to force false confessions from U.S. personnel; the Bush administration intended to use them for interrogation purposes, for which they were not designed.

On July 25 and 26, Lieutenant Colonel Baumgartner forwarded information to the DOD general counsel's office. The memos listed both psychological and physical pressures used in SERE training, including slapping, stress positions, waterboarding,[76] shaking and manhandling, cramped confinement ("the little box"), and immersion in water. The purposes of these techniques were "to instill fear and despair," "to instill humiliation or cause insult," "to demonstrate self-imposed pressure," and "to punish."

> Other tactics to induce control, dependence, compliance and cooperation included: isolation/solitary confinement, "induced physical weakness and exhaustion, degradation, sensory deprivation (if deprived of sensory input, the brain will experience visual, auditory, and/or tactile hallucinations), sensory overload (exposure to bright, flashing lights, loud music, annoying/irritation sounds, etc.), disruption of sleep and biorhythms, manipulation of diet (in order to have a negative impact on the subject's general health and emotional state)."[77]

A two-page attachment noted that the justification for using the SERE techniques was to obtain quickly information about potential terrorist attacks, and that using these coercive techniques was seen as an alternative to "the more time-consuming conventional interrogation process." The attachment from JPRA, however, warned that "the error inherent in this line of thinking is the assumption that, through torture, the interrogator can extract reliable and accurate information. History and a consideration of human behavior would appear to refute this assumption." The memo concluded: "The application of *extreme* physical and/or psychological duress (torture) has some serious operational deficits, most notably the potential to result in unreliable information" (emphasis in original).[78] In the middle of September, JPRA SERE trainers came to Fort Bragg, NC, to train personnel from Guantanamo in SERE techniques.[79]

The most important source of legitimacy for the exploration of new techniques came from the visit in late September 2002 to the interrogation facilities at Guantanamo by several lawyers from Washington, including Alberto Gonzales, David Addington, William J. (Jim) Haynes, and John Rizzo, who "brought ideas down with them which had been given from sources in D.C.," according to Dunlavey.[80] The lawyers discussed techniques with the Gitmo personnel, and it was clear that they spoke with authority. After all, these were the lawyers for the president, the vice president, the secretary of defense, and the CIA. There was no doubt about their intense personal interest in extracting more intelligence from the detainees. In addition, Donald Rumsfeld was "directly and regularly involved," according to Dunlavey.[81]

Two of the lawyers, Addington and Gonzales, had helped on the August 1 memo before they visited Gitmo.[82] And John Rizzo had requested the Bybee II memo for authority to use CIA-specified techniques, so they all felt that they knew that just about any techniques were legally covered by the OLC memos of August 2002, as long as they did not cause pain that approached organ failure or death. According to Lieutenant Colonel Diane Beaver, the visit from the lawyers reinforced the message that they should do "whatever needed to be done" in order to extract intelligence from the prisoners.[83] Dave Becker, chief of the DOD Interrogation Control Element (ICE), said that the aggressive techniques requested in October 2002 were "a direct result of the pressure we felt from Washington to obtain intelligence and the lack of policy guidance being issued by Washington."[84]

In October 2002, the military leadership sought help and advice from the CIA about techniques that might be used to extract more useful intelligence from detainees. At a meeting at Guantanamo on October 2, ten DOD officials met with CIA counter-terrorism lawyer Jonathan M. Fredman about the effectiveness of certain interrogation techniques. Fredman said that the legal definition of torture "is basically subject to perception," and that in "rare instances, aggressive techniques have proven very helpful." With respect to waterboarding, he said, "If a well-trained individual is used to perform this technique, it can feel like you're drowning." Care had to be taken in applying the techniques, however. "If the detainee dies, you're doing it wrong."[85]

At one point in the meeting, when it was suggested that sleep deprivation was not allowed, Lieutenant Colonel Beaver interjected, "Yes we can—with approval." She also said, "We may need to curb the harsher operations while ICRC [International Committee of the Red Cross] is around. It is better not to expose them to any controversial techniques. We must have the support of the DOD." When Dave Becker said that there were "many reports from Bagram about sleep deprivation being used," Beaver replied: "True, but officially it is not happening. It is not being reported officially. The ICRC is a serious concern."[86]

The meetings with administration lawyers and others from Washington culminated in a list of techniques that was finalized by Lieutenant Colonel Jerald Phifer on October 11. The list did not originate with specific requests from interrogators at Guantanamo; rather, it was developed over several weeks with administration lawyers who visited from Washington. According to Dunlavey, the lawyers "brought ideas with them which had been given from sources in D.C." He said that Secretary Rumsfeld was "directly and regularly involved." He added that the pressure for results "must have been all the way to the White House."[87]

The list was sent up the chain of command for permission to implement. Phifer noted that the "current guidelines for interrogation procedures at GTMO limit the ability of interrogators to counter advanced resistance." The request listed the generally non-controversial techniques in "Category I," including yelling, deception, use of multiple interrogators, and deceiving the detainee about interrogator identity. "Category II" techniques were more controversial and were not permitted by the Army Field Manual 34–52: stress positions for four hours, falsified documents, isolation for thirty days, changing detainee environment, light and sound stimuli, hooding, twenty-hour interrogations, nudity, and exploiting phobias (e.g., dogs). The third set of techniques went beyond the others, and were to be used only on the most difficult detainees: threats of death to detainee and his family, use of cold temperatures or water, waterboarding, and "mild, non injurious contact such as grabbing, poking" and "light pushing."[88] The actual application of these techniques, as will be documented in Chapter Three, resulted in brutality far beyond the euphemistic words used in these memos.

Before passing the request to his superior at SouthCom, General Dunlavey wanted "top cover," so he told Staff Judge Advocate Diane Beaver to provide him with justification for the legality of the techniques. Beaver was not an expert in international law, and so she requested help from lawyers at SouthCom and the JCS, but she got no response or help with legal analysis.[89] Beaver used the research sources available to her and concluded: "I ... agree that the proposed strategies do not violate applicable federal law." Note her choice of the word "agree," which indicated that she was supporting a judgment already made by Dunlavey rather than advising him de novo.[90] Her brief concluded that, despite international and domestic law, and in light of President Bush's decision that the Geneva Conventions do not apply at Guantanamo, the proposed techniques are "all legally permissible so long as there is an important governmental objective, and it is not done for the purpose of causing harm or with the intent to cause prolonged harm."[91] Thus Beaver recommended that the proposed methods be approved, but that the methods in Categories II and III "undergo a legal review prior to their commencement."[92] Though Beaver had some doubts about the legality of some of the techniques, she explained that President Bush had set aside the Geneva Conventions, and "It was not my job to second guess the President."[93]

With Beaver's legal justification, Dunleavy forwarded his recommendation to General James T. Hill, commander of SouthCom (as of August 2002), who received the memo on October 11. Hill felt uneasy with the broad scope of the recommended techniques, and did not forward his recommendation to DOD for two weeks. When he did send the memo to Chair of the Joint Chiefs General Myers on October 25, he stated, "Our respective staffs, the Office of the Secretary of Defense, and Joint Task Force 170 have been trying to identify counter-resistant techniques that we can lawfully employ."[94] His memo thus indicated that OSD had already been working on what techniques could be used and that the request had not come from the Guantanamo personnel unexpectedly, but was part of an ongoing series of discussions including the Joint Chiefs of Staff and the Office of the Secretary of Defense. This is significant because later, administration accounts indicated that Secretary Rumsfeld was merely responding to requests from below when he authorized new techniques. The administration's deliberate obfuscation of the chain of events indicates that, despite the Bybee memo, they knew they were at the edge of breaking the law.

The techniques had been considered by administration lawyers and OSD personnel who were aware of the range of methods that were considered and requested. Just as Beaver had recommended further legal review of the techniques, Hill also was concerned about the legality of the recommended techniques. He thus did not "recommend" adoption of the techniques, but rather stated, "I am forwarding" the proposals. He said that he believed that the methods in Categories I and II were "legal and humane," but he was uncertain whether the methods in Category III were legal, particularly death threats to the detainee and his family. Hill did not know about the lawyer visits to Gitmo and thus the implication that the techniques had already been approved, in effect, by the August 1 OLC memo. Hill later said that there should have been "a major policy discussion on this and everybody ought to be involved."[95] His overall judgment on the proposed techniques was that "there were many techniques in there that I would not have used under any circumstances ... I would not authorize. Never."[96]

When Myers received the memo from Hill, he asked for comments from a few members of the Joint Staff, but he did not include the TJAGs (Judge Advocate

Generals), who later complained that they did not have a chance to comment on it.[97] Some military lawyers who had access to the memo, however, raised their concerns in early November 2002. Air Force Colonel Richburg wrote that "the Air Force has serious concerns regarding the legality of many of the proposed techniques, particularly those under Category III," which might constitute criminal conduct. He also noted that use of the techniques "might preclude the ability to prosecute the individuals interrogated," because the evidence obtained would not be admissible in a prosecution.[98]

A memo from the chief legal advisor to the DOD Criminal Investigative Task Force at Guantanamo, Major Sam W. McCahon, judged that "CITF personnel who are aware of the use or abuse of certain techniques may be exposed to liability under the Uniform Code of Military Justice (UCMJ) for failing to intercede or report incidents," and wrote that "both the utility and legality of applying certain techniques identified in the memorandum listed above are, in my opinion, questionable."[99] A memo from the Headquarters of the Department of the Army said, "Employing many of the suggested techniques would create a PA [public affairs] nightmare … If we mistreat detainees, we will quickly lose the moral highground [sic] and public support will erode. The techniques noted above will not read well in the *New York Times* or the *Cairo Times*. Additionally, many of the techniques arguably violate the torture and inhumane treatment provisions of the ICC."[100] The Marine Corps noted that some of the Category II and III techniques "arguably violate federal law, and would expose our service members to possible prosecution."[101]

When these opinions were received at the office of the chair of the joint chiefs of staff, the legal advisor to the chair, Rear Admiral Jane Dalton, prepared to have the memo stalled out for a full legal analysis. But her efforts were cut short by General Counsel Haynes. According to Dalton, "Jim [Haynes] pulled this away; we never had a chance to complete the assessment."[102] Haynes said that he "did not believe it was necessary to coordinate with the TJAGs."[103] Myers later concluded that the memo had not been staffed out properly.[104]

On December 30, 2002, SERE training specialist John F. Rankin traveled to Guantanamo and conducted training at Camp Delta. The purpose of the trip was to provide interrogators with "the theory and application of the physical pressures utilized during our training. . . . " The class included an "in-depth class on Biderman's Principles." The Biderman principles were developed by Alfred D. Biderman, who was working for the U.S. Air Force and was trying to explain why U.S. prisoners held in North Korea during the Korean war confessed to atrocities that they clearly did not commit, such as using germ warfare against the North Koreans. In his interviews of the former POWs, he developed a table of a set of techniques that the Chinese interrogators used in order to get American airmen to confess to atrocities. The title of his compilation was "Communist Attempts to Elicit False Confessions from Air Force Prisoners of War." The SERE chart was copied from Biderman's chart, although the title was changed to "Coercive Management Techniques."[105]

The irony here is that the techniques being taught to Guantanamo personnel were the distillation of Chinese attempts to get U.S. airmen to confess falsely to atrocities.

The chart was developed to describe Chinese methods; the methods were used to train U.S. soldiers to resist coercive interrogation techniques that might be used by enemies. The techniques were then taught at Guantanamo to train U.S. personnel how to use those counter-resistance techniques to coerce detainees to give up information or confess to their activities with al-Qaeda.[106] General Miller was impressed and pleased with the training.

After his experience with interrogation in Iraq, the director of SERE training at Fairchild Air Force Base in Washington State, Colonel Steven Kleinman, concluded that SERE techniques were not appropriate in intelligence collection for several reasons:

> First, many of the methods used in SERE training are based on what was once known as the Communist Interrogation Model, a system designed to physically and psychologically debilitate a detainee as a means of gaining compliance. Second, that model's primary objective was to compel a prisoner to generate propaganda not intelligence. Third, it was expressly designed to mirror a program that employed methods of interrogation considered by the West to be violations of the Geneva Conventions.[107]

Despite the warnings of military lawyers and the recommendations of Beaver and Hill to seek further legal analysis, the SERE techniques were taught in Guantanamo and Abu Ghraib.

The training by SERE program specialists, sought and approved by General Miller, constitutes policy guidance. The use of the SERE techniques and interrogation strategies were legitimated by official, authoritative military trainers. This helps explain the use of these techniques, even though not all of them were specifically approved in Rumsfeld's memos of 2002 and 2003.

The Haynes-Rumsfeld Memo of December 2, 2002

When DOD General Counsel Haynes received the memo with the request for the use of extraordinary techniques, he wrote an "Action Memo" to Secretary Rumsfeld on November 27. In describing his preparation for the memo, Haynes said that he had discussed the matter with Douglas Feith and General Myers, and said "I believe that all join in my recommendation that, as a mater of policy, you authorize" all techniques in Categories I and II and the fourth technique (mild, non-injurious grabbing, poking, and pushing) in Category III (noting that "all Category III techniques may be legally available"). For such a momentous decision to abandon the adherence to long-standing Army policy and the UCMJ, it is strange that Haynes did not require a more thorough written review of the legal issues than that provided by the relatively low-level Lieutenant Colonel Beaver at Guantanamo. He clearly ignored the recommendations by Beaver and General Hill that more legal analysis was necessary to consider the Category II and III techniques, and he stopped Admiral Dalton from conducting a legal analysis for the Joint Chiefs of Staff.[108] For an administration so careful about the legal ratification of its actions, this was unusual, particularly given the strongly expressed reservations by the military services whose personnel would be applying the techniques.

Why did Haynes and Rumsfeld have such confidence that they could reverse decades of military law and practice without further legal analysis and advice? The probable explanation of Haynes's confidence in his recommendation to Rumsfeld was that he had read the Bybee memo and felt that the OLC had provided an authoritative legal justification for the inapplicability of international and domestic law to actions taken pursuant to orders from the commander in chief.[109] The Bybee memo was kept secret from most members of the government, and it thus appeared on the surface that Beaver was the primary source of legal justification for Rumsfeld's decision to allow the use of additional techniques. This may have been intentional—in order to blame Beaver if legal challenges were raised later.

The action memo provided spaces for Rumsfeld's initials for "Approve," "Disapprove," or "Other." On December 2, 2002, Rumsfeld signed the Approval space.

Notably, General Myers did *not* initial the Haynes memo to indicate that he had concurred.[110] On the memo itself, Rumsfeld penned the comment: "However, I stand for 8–10 hours a day. Why is standing limited to 4 hours?" This comment was either made seriously or in jest. If it was serious, it indicates how naïve Rumsfeld was about the nature of standing in stress positions when used for torture or interrogation purposes. If it was made in jest, it shows an amazing casualness about the serious pain inflicted upon detainees by U.S. personnel. If the intense pain of stress positions must be legitimately inflicted upon persons, one would think that the torture would be undertaken with grim determination rather than the flippancy indicated by Rumsfeld's comment. According to Lawrence Wilkerson, chief of staff to Colin Powell at the time, Rumsfeld's handwritten appendage to the December 2 memo sent the message that anything goes in the interrogation of suspected terrorists; it said "Carte blanche, guys."[111]

On December 18, after Rumsfeld provided his authority to use the techniques, the Guantanamo JFT formulated SERE Standard Operating Procedures for interrogations. The methods included "degradation tactics," including slaps and "stripping"; "Physical Debilitation Tactics," including various stress positions; and "Demonstrate Omnipotence Tactics," such as "Manhandling" and "Walling."[112] Most of these SOPs authorized techniques beyond those in Rumsfeld's memos, but some were based on the SERE training, which in turn was based on Chinese torture techniques.

Thus, according to the SOP, in addition to the Rumsfeld techniques, Guantanamo personnel were authorized to use the "degradation" tactics of slapping and nudity on detainees. They were authorized to use stress positions to break detainees and they could "demonstrate omnipotence" by "manhandling" and "walling" prisoners. These techniques clearly led to brutality that seriously injured many detainees. The combination of the SOP memo and the SERE training constituted official policy for interrogations at Guantanamo. Notably, not all of these techniques were mentioned in the December 2, 2002, Rumsfeld memo or its replacement on April 16, 2003. The purpose of the SOP SERE techniques was to "break real detainees during interrogation operation."[113]

The immediate concern of administration officials and Dunlavey was the high-value detainee Mohamed al-Qahtani, who was believed to be the "twentieth hijacker," and who was believed to have possible knowledge of potential future attacks on the United States. After he had made the formal request for authority to use the additional techniques, Dunlavey was replaced at Guantanamo by General Geoffrey Miller on November 8. The plans for the interrogation of al-Qahtani, using the eighteen new techniques, were finalized on November 12, and General Hill said that Rumsfeld had been "personally involved" in their preparation. General Miller said he got a VOCO (vocal command) from Rumsfeld to use the techniques, and actual interrogation began on November 23, well before Rumsfeld's December 2 memo formally approving the new techniques. According to Miller, he had authorization to use them. "It was an order that came down through the SECDEF."[114] This illustrates the combination of official, formal policy directives combined with the less formal, but still authoritative, training and SOPs that lent official sanction to the abuse and torture of detainees.

Rumsfeld Rescinds the Memo and Approves a New Set of Techniques

This section will explain the actions leading up to Rumsfeld's second set of authorized techniques. Both the policy authorizations and the use of the techniques at Guantanamo upset military and civilian professionals, who expressed their objections, leading to the withdrawal of Rumsfeld's December 2, 2002, memo. After rescinding his memo, Rumsfeld created a working group to recommend to him interrogation techniques that would be legal. The working group, dominated by administration allies, reported on April 4, 2003, recommending a set of techniques, and on April 16, Rumsfeld issued a new set of authorized interrogation techniques.

Civilian Professional Objections

Career civilian professionals working for the DOD became concerned in Fall 2002 about the harsh nature of the techniques being used on detainees at Guantanamo. They thought that many of the techniques were illegal and wrong. They also judged that the illegality of the techniques was exacerbated because they were being administered by young, inexperienced guards and interrogators rather than professionals who actually did have experience in interrogation.

Lowell Jacoby, director of the Defense Intelligence Agency, said that the use of the new techniques was a "painful experience" for him professionally because they violated traditional norms and his agency's culture, but that he had no choice but to implement them. When asked later by a member of Congress why, in light of his concerns about use of the techniques, he did not resign his office, he replied: "Madam, I received a lawful order, it came down from the National Security Council and it was an order relayed to me by the Deputy Secretary of Defense, my job was to execute lawful orders."[115]

In November 2002, the FBI senior counsel for national security law, Spike Bowman, expressed concern over the way that al-Qahtani was being treated, since he had been held in isolation for more than a month, was deprived of sleep, was threatened with dogs, and was hallucinating. Bowman was concerned about the legality of the treatment, but also concerned that the treatment was compromising the possibility of eliciting good information. But he was told that the treatment had been approved by Secretary Rumsfeld (this was before the VOCO, voice command). He said that with sleep deprivation, "If you do it for a week, you're going to come out with a guy on the other end who doesn't know what he's talking about."[116] Bowman was shocked at the lack of training of military interrogators, calling them a "bunch of young soldiers who don't have a clue about interrogation."[117] On November 27, other members of the FBI sent a memo to Washington concluding that ten of the eighteen techniques (e.g., hooding, twenty-four-hour interrogations, stress positions, dogs, removal of clothing) were unlawful.[118]

Mark Fallon, deputy commander of the DOD Criminal Investigation Task Force, wrote in an e-mail about the October 2002 CIA briefing of Guantanamo personnel that many of the techniques discussed "seem to stretch beyond the bounds of legal propriety. Talk of 'wet towel treatment' which results in the lymphatic gland reacting as if you are suffocating, would in my opinion, shock the conscience of any legal body looking at using the results of the interrogations or possibly even the interrogators. Someone needs to be considering how history will look back at this."[119]

Mike Gelles, chief psychologist of the Naval Criminal Investigation Service (NCIS), headed an interagency team of psychologists and psychiatrists. The "behavior consultation team" (BSCT or "biscuits") noted that the military interrogators were eighteen- or nineteen-year-old soldiers with only six weeks' training, and that they were merely "pulling techniques off a list" that came from Washington, rather than engaging in professional interrogation.[120] Gelles said that the behavior included harsh physical contact, stress positions, and humiliation by female personnel. He brought along logs of the interrogations to verify his report when he spoke with Alberto Mora. These actions were being applied by young soldiers who had little training or experience with interrogations.

David Brant, head of NCIS, objected to the use of the additional techniques and said: "If they are going to start doing this we're not going to be in the same room as them." Brant concluded that the abuse was not merely rogue actions by untrained personnel but that the techniques had been approved at a "high level" in Washington.[121] "I don't want my agents in on this type of crap."[122] Brant said that he did not want his agents to condone or participate in any abuse: "No slapping, deprivation of water, heat, dogs, psychological abuse. It was pretty basic, black and white to me."[123] Their participation would taint any future prosecutions of detainees, besides, he said, "It just ain't right."[124] Thus both Gelles and Brant pulled their agents away from Dunlavey's interrogation team.[125]

Brant and Gelles were so upset by what they observed that they went to see Alberto Mora, general counsel for the Navy, on December 18 in order to express their concerns about the treatment of detainees and particularly with "force drift." That is, young, inexperienced interrogators, when using force, "came to believe that if some force is good then more is even better."[126]

Alberto Mora Objections

General Counsel to the Navy Alberto Mora's mother, Klara, came to the United States to escape the impending takeover of Hungary by the Soviet Union; one of his great uncles died in a Nazi concentration camp, and another was hung after being tortured by the Nazis. Klara married Mora's father, a Cuban, and together with their son, they fled Cuba just before Castro's government was about to imprison them because they planned to leave for the United States. Mora was a conservative who was appointed by President Bush and who supported the invasion of Iraq.[127] After listening to the accounts of Brant and Gelles, Mora was disturbed about what he had heard; he felt strongly about torture and the rule of law. "I was appalled by the whole thing. It was clearly abusive, and it was clearly contrary to everything we were ever taught about American values."[128] "The Constitution recognizes that man has an inherent right, not bestowed by the state or laws, to personal dignity, including the right to be free of cruelty ... People who went through things like [his family had] tend to have very strong views about the rule of law, totalitarianism, and America." In Mora's world view, "the law is sacred."[129]

After talking with Brant and Gelles, Mora obtained a copy of Rumsfeld's December 2 memo that authorized the use of hooding, isolation, sensory deprivation, stress positions, and use of phobias. Mora found the legal analysis of the issues by Lieutenant Colonel Beaver to be "a wholly inadequate analysis of the law"; it argued that cruel, inhuman, and degrading treatments were allowed, and there were no limits set on the use of the various techniques.[130] Mora concluded that several of the interrogation techniques approved by the memorandum "whether applied singly or in combination, could produce effects reaching the level of torture."[131]

Mora's conclusion was that using such techniques could well be illegal and that the Rumsfeld memo authorizing it could be "almost incalculably harmful to U.S. foreign, military, and legal policies." Mora went to see Rumsfeld's counsel, Haynes, on December 20 and "expressed surprise that the Secretary had been allowed to sign it."[132] The techniques could amount to torture and were "completely unbounded"; that is, no clear limits were set on their use. After Haynes agreed to take into account Mora's views, Mora left Haynes's office feeling that the memo reflected shoddy and hasty legal work and that it would quickly be rectified.

When Mora returned in January from a Christmas vacation, NCIS Director Brant told him that the maltreatment at Guantanamo was unabated, and Mora began to think that the policy allowing abuse had been consciously adopted. On January 9, Mora returned to Haynes's office to show him a memo drafted by Navy JAG lawyers analyzing the interrogation techniques and argued that such abuse could not be condoned without "profoundly altering [the] core values and character" of the U.S. military.[133] He told Haynes that "the coercive interrogations in Guantanamo were not committed by rogue elements of the military acting without authority," but were authorized "by the highest DOD authorities, including the Secretary of Defense." He said that it could even "damage the Presidency" and that Haynes should "Protect your client" (i.e., Secretary Rumsfeld and by implication, the President).[134]

When it appeared that there was no change in policy, Mora returned to confront Haynes a third time. He had drafted a harsh memo to Haynes and Dalton (counsel to JCS) arguing that most category II and III techniques were cruel and unusual and possibly torture, which was illegal under national and international law. He said that he "strongly non-concurred" with the authorization of these techniques. Mora later called to tell Haynes that he would sign the memo, thus making it part of the official record and leaving a paper trail if interrogation policy changes were not made.[135]

After these interventions by Mora, Haynes convinced Rumsfeld that the legal justifications of the abuse policy were questionable and that the consequent interrogation actions might amount to torture. Consequently, Rumsfeld rescinded the December 2 memo on January 15, 2003. Mora thought that he had won an important victory for American justice, but two days later Rumsfeld appointed a "working group" of Pentagon lawyers to examine the issues anew. This group included the judge advocate generals of the services, who should have been consulted before the December 2 memo had been approved. The working group would also allow input from the service lawyers who were skeptical of the use of abusive interrogation techniques. Despite the objections of the service lawyers, the working group recommended that Rumsfeld authorize a new range of abusive techniques.

The Defense Lawyers Working Group

The working group was chaired by General Counsel of the Air Force Mary Walker, who was committed to Haynes's and the administration's interpretation of the law. By the time they met, she had received a draft memo written by John Yoo of OLC, and the group was instructed that its report had to conform to the legal reasoning in the memo. The Yoo memo was finalized on March 14, and it closely tracked the reasoning he (with others) had set forth in the Bybee I memo of August 1, 2002. There was only one copy of the draft Yoo memo, and it was kept in Mary Walker's office.[136] During February and March, the military members of the group expressed concern that they were bound to accept as dispositive the OLC (John Yoo's) interpretation of the law.

Major General Jack Rives, Deputy JAG of the Air Force, noted that the legal opinions of OLC "were relied on almost exclusively," and Army JAG Major General Thomas J. Romig said that the legal analysis of OLC was "incorporated into the subject draft Report and forms, almost exclusively, the legal framework for the Report's Conclusions."[137] Marine Corps Staff Judge Advocate Kevin M. Sandkuhler said that "OLC does not represent the services; thus, understandably, concern for the service members is not reflected in their opinion … We nonetheless recommend that the working group product accurately portray the services' concerns that the authorization of aggressive counter-resistance techniques will adversely impact" the "pride, discipline, and Self-Respect" and "Criminal and Civil Liability" of members of the military services.[138]

The draft working group report was dated March 6, 2003, and closely tracked the Yoo memo in its legal reasoning and conclusions that the techniques did not amount to torture and that any law constraining the president's treatment of detainees would violate the Constitution's commander-in-chief authority.[139] The service JAGs objected to the draft conclusions of the working group report.[140] General Rives noted that the "more extreme interrogation techniques, on their face, amount to violations of domestic criminal law and the UCMJ" and would place "the interrogators and the chain of command at risk of criminal accusations domestically." More broadly, Rives argued that

> use of the more extreme interrogation techniques simply is not how the U.S. armed forces have operated in recent history. We have taken the legal and moral "high ground" in the conduct of our military operations regardless of how others may operate. Our forces are trained in this legal and moral mindset beginning the day they enter active duty. It should be noted that law of armed conflict and code of conduct training have been mandated by Congress and emphasized since the Viet Nam conflict when our POWs were subjected to torture by their captors.[141]

General Romig said "the 'bottom line' defense proffered by OLC is an exceptionally broad concept of 'necessity.' This defense is based upon the premise that any existing federal statutory provision or international obligation is unconstitutional per se, where it otherwise prohibits conduct viewed by the President, acting in his capacity as Commander-in-Chief." Such an argument would, in Romig's judgment, put soldiers at "substantial risk of criminal prosecution or personal liability arising from a civil lawsuit."[142]

Mora considered the process of the working group unnecessarily rushed and the draft report to be "deeply flawed." He judged the Yoo memo, upon which it was based, to have been written with "seeming sophistication" but thought that it was "profoundly in error" on the legality of cruel, inhuman, and degrading treatment of prisoners. Mora talked with John Yoo, whose legal reasoning the working group was bound to follow, in the Pentagon on February 6, 2003. When he asked Yoo: "Are you saying the President has the authority to order torture?" Yoo answered, "yes."[143] Mora thought that Yoo's conclusions were particularly dangerous because an opinion by OLC was considered legally binding.[144]

Consequently, Mora told Haynes to "never let [the Working Group Report] see the light of day."[145] In March 2003, the working group was thanked by Rumsfeld and dismissed with no indication of his own conclusions. In June 2003, Mora read in the newspaper that Haynes had sent a letter in response to an inquiry from Senator Patrick Leahy stating that it was the policy of DOD not to use torture or to subject prisoners to cruel, inhuman, or degrading treatment. In Mora's mind, this expressed what the policy of the United States ought to be, and he assumed that, since he received no copy for his concurrence, the working group report was never finalized. Only later did Mora learn that the working group report had been finalized in April 2003 and that it had been briefed to SouthCom Commander Hill and JTF GTMO Commander Miller and was thus official DOD policy.[146]

The final working group report was in fact issued on April 4, 2003, and it contained the legal and constitutional reasoning of the draft report. It applied its legal and constitutional reasoning to a list of thirty-five specific techniques and recommended that

Secretary Rumsfeld approve 1 through 26 for use on unlawful combatants outside the United States; it recommended that techniques 27 through 35 be "conducted at strategic interrogation facilities; where there is a good basis to believe that the detainee possesses critical intelligence," provided that the interrogators are trained and that medical assistance is available.[147] (The techniques will be explained and analyzed in the next chapter.)

Techniques 1 through 17 were standard interrogation methods authorized by existing law and Army regulations that were not controversial. Techniques 18 through 34 were more extreme and could amount to torture depending on how they were applied: scenery down, hooding, mild physical contact, dietary manipulation, environmental manipulation, sleep adjustment, false flag, and threat of transfer.[148] Techniques 27 through 35 were "more aggressive counter-resistance techniques" that were to be used on detainees who were extremely resistant to techniques 1 to 26 and were believed to have vital information. They included: isolation, prolonged interrogation (twenty hours per day), prolonged standing (non-stress) for four hours per twenty-four, sleep deprivation (not to exceed four days in succession), face slap/stomach slap, removal of clothing, and increasing anxiety by use of aversions (e.g., dogs).[149]

On April 16, 2003, Secretary Rumsfeld approved the use of techniques 1 through 27; the only technique approved from the most extreme methods was isolation. Techniques 18 to 27 went beyond those accepted in FM 32–54 and could amount to torture. Rumsfeld added, "If, in your view, you require additional interrogation techniques for a particular detainee, you should provide me, via the Chairman of the Joint Chiefs of Staff, a written request describing the proposed technique, recommended safeguards, and the rationale for applying it with an identified detainee."[150] The April 16 memo was briefed to General Miller at Guantanamo, but Mora did not hear of it for a year.

In sum, the request for new techniques that went from Dunlavey to Hill on October 11 and from Hill to Myers on October 25, who passed it on to Haynes, and from Haynes to Rumsfeld on November 27, and which was signed by Rumsfeld on December 2, did not merely originate spontaneously out of the frustration of lower-level interrogators. Rather the request grew out of "tremendous pressure" (Dunlavey's words) from Washington for more intelligence, with Rumsfeld's direct and regular involvement, and it came with the participation of the very top lawyers of the Bush administration.[151]

Given the Bush administration's rejection of explicit objections and warnings from civilian DOD personnel at Guantanamo, the objections of military lawyers to the draft working group report, and the impassioned remonstrances of Alberto Mora, there can be no doubt that the official policy of the administration was to use the harsh interrogation techniques that resulted in the torture of detainees.

White House Approval of Interrogation Techniques for Guantanamo

In 2002, the CIA asked the top officials in the Bush administration for written approval of the interrogation techniques the CIA had been using on suspected terrorists.[152]

The CIA may have been concerned that blame for use of the techniques would be leveled against the CIA, and they wanted to have written proof that the CIA was not a "rogue agency" that was perpetrating torture on its own. One lawyer who had been in the CIA general counsel office in 2004, A. John Radsan, said that "the question was whether we had enough 'top cover.'" In response to a request from CIA Director Tenet, on July 17, 2002, National Security Adviser Rice verbally authorized the CIA to use harsh interrogation techniques, subject to a determination by the Justice Department's Office of Legal Counsel that the techniques were legal.[153]

On August 1, 2002, along with a memo stating that the president had the constitutional authority to order harsh interrogations (Bybee I), the Office of Legal Counsel issued a second opinion (Bybee II) that authorized the CIA to use a specific set of interrogation techniques on high-value detainees, like Abu Zubaydah.[154] These techniques included slamming detainees against the wall (walling), cramped confinement, stress positions, sleep deprivation, and waterboarding. Although most of these techniques had commonly been considered torture, the memo argued that when administered carefully, they did not reach the level of pain and suffering that would be necessary to constitute torture.

In April 2004, photos of the Abu Ghraib abuse of detainees became public, and in June of 2004 Tenet again asked for written approval of the techniques. Perhaps he was worried that since President Bush and Secretary Rumsfeld had publicly denounced the actions of the guards at Abu Ghraib, he needed explicit approval of the CIA's continuing use of harsh interrogation techniques. One former CIA official said that the interrogations resulted in useful information, but the CIA felt that "we don't want to continue unless you tell us in writing that it's not only legal but is the policy of the administration."[155] Another possible reason for renewed doubts on the part of the CIA may have been that the Office of Legal Counsel, which had legally cleared the harsh interrogation tactics, was now headed by Jack Goldsmith, who was much more skeptical of the legal reasoning that the OLC issued under his predecessor, Jay S. Bybee.

These concerns of the CIA strongly indicate that they had serious doubts about the legal justification of the interrogation techniques they were using. Despite these concerns, the Bush administration issued the authorizations because it clearly wanted the CIA to continue using the techniques.

In April 2008, it was disclosed that the National Security Council's "Principals Committee" met in the White House Situation Room a number of times to discuss which "enhanced interrogation techniques" would be used on specific high-value detainees. The meetings were chaired by National Security Adviser Condoleezza Rice, and included Vice President Cheney, Secretary of Defense Donald Rumsfeld, Secretary of State Colin Powell, Attorney General John Ashcroft, and CIA Director George Tenet. The meetings commenced after top al Qaeda operative Abu Zubaydah was captured in Pakistan by the CIA in the spring of 2002. The CIA wanted to employ harsh techniques, including waterboarding, to interrogate him and they briefed members of the Principals Committee. Zubaydah was subjected to waterboarding in August 2002. As in other high-level meetings about the legality and implementation of harsh interrogation techniques, lawyers from the State Department and the military services were explicitly excluded.[156]

In 2008, when he was asked about the meetings, President Bush said, "yes, I'm aware our national security team met on this issue. And I approved."[157] He added that he had told the country that he had approved of the enhanced interrogation techniques. "And I also told them it was legal. We had legal opinions that enabled us to do it."[158] At one meeting Attorney General Ashcroft stepped back from the immediate discussion to ask, "Why are we talking about this in the White House? History will not judge this kindly."[159]

Evidently, John Yoo must have convinced the NSC principals that the discretion to torture is "the core of the commander-in-chief function. [Congress] can't prevent the president from ordering torture." Congress or public law cannot "tie the president's hands in regard to torture as an interrogation technique."[160]

In a statement for the Senate Armed Services Committee, Secretary of State Rice said that the SERE methods, including waterboarding, that were discussed in the White House meetings "had been deemed not to cause significant physical or psychological harm." Her NSC counsel at that time, John B. Bellinger III, said that he "expressed concern that the proposed CIA interrogation techniques comply with applicable U.S. law, including our international obligations."[161]

If there was any doubt that the harsh interrogation techniques, including water-boarding, were approved at the highest levels of the U.S. government, including President Bush and Vice President Cheney, these meetings of the NSC principals in the White House eliminates those doubts. The official policy of the U.S. Government was to employ harsh techniques of interrogation, some of which constituted torture, such as waterboarding, to extract intelligence from detainees in the war on terror.

Conclusion

The pattern that emerges from the policy decisions described above is one of policy direction from the top, secrecy, and deception. The draft military order was closely held by a few lawyers around the vice president who ordered that it be kept secret from National Security Adviser Rice and Secretary of State Powell. It was signed by President Bush without the advice of the military officers who were tasked with implementing it. The policy decision to suspend the Geneva Conventions in early 2002 was prepared in secret and not distributed to those who normally would sign off on such an important step, particularly State Department lawyers. When Gonzales recommended suspending Geneva to the president, Secretary of State Powell was out of the country. After Powell was able to convince President Bush to discuss the matter at an NSC meeting, a refuting memo was leaked to the *Washington Times* to undermine his position. President Bush signed the executive order.

The "Torture Memo" of August 1, 2002 (Bybee I), written by Yoo, Addington, and Gonzales, was not sent to the State Department for comment, and it was kept secret from most of the government. It was not cleared with the TJAGs, the top military lawyers who had worked with military law throughout their careers. Its authoritative judgment that harsh interrogation techniques would not amount to torture unless they led to pain equivalent to organ failure or death amounted to a secret policy. A small group of lawyers in the White House and their loyalists in the Pentagon knew about the policy, but not those who were responsible for legal policy in the military, the general counsels to the services, or the judge advocates general. The second torture memo (Bybee II) specified which harsh techniques could be used by the CIA, and it was kept secret until April 2009.

The December 2, 2002, memo signed by Secretary Rumsfeld did not merely arise from the interrogators at Guantanamo. The highest ranking lawyers in the Bush administration traveled to Guantanamo to help develop the recommended techniques. They did so with the knowledge of the Bybee memo of August 1 that justified abusive treatment and pain short of organ failure and that claimed that the president was not bound by laws that affected his treatment of prisoners. The memo was sent to the Pentagon with recommendations from Lieutenant Colonel Beaver and General Hill that more legal analysis be completed before any final decision was made. DOD General Counsel Haynes, rejecting that advice, did not ask for analysis or input from the military service counsels or the TJAGs. He spoke with only two people (that we know of) about it before forwarding it to Rumsfeld with a recommendation for his signature. The memo was kept secret from most of the military counsels and TJAGs.

When Rumsfeld's memo of December 2, 2002, was finally discovered by Mora, he waged an intense campaign in December 2002 and January 2003 to have it reconsidered. When it was finally rescinded, after Mora's threat to go on the record with a strongly dissenting memo, Rumsfeld appointed a working group headed by an ally who rushed the process in order to ratify Rumsfeld's techniques. The outcome was seriously constrained by the requirement to conform the report to the draft Yoo memo of March 14, 2003. The final report was *not* signed off on by or even disclosed to all members of the working group. But its conclusion led Rumsfeld to authorize most of the techniques that had been in the December 2, 2002, memo, in addition to others.

In reflecting on his attempts to bring Defense Department policy within more traditional interpretations of the law, Mora concluded:

> If cruelty is no longer declared unlawful, but instead is applied as a matter of policy, it alters the fundamental relationship of man to government. It destroys the whole notion of individual rights. The Constitution recognizes that man has an inherent right, not bestowed by the state or laws, to personal dignity, including the right to be free of cruelty. It applies to all human beings, not just in America—even those designated as "unlawful enemy combatants." If you make this exception, the whole Constitution crumbles. It's a transformative issue.[162]

Referring to his personal ancestry, Mora concluded: "No Hungarian after Communism, or Cuban after Castro, is not aware that human rights are incompatible with cruelty. The debate here isn't only how to protect the country. It's how to protect our values."[163]

The torture and mistreatment of detainees in the war on terror and in the Iraq war gravely affected the prestige of the United States throughout the world, in the eyes of its allies and adversaries. The policy decisions that led to that outcome were often made without the type of consultation within the Bush administration or the broader government that might have ensured that all important likely consequences of the decisions were fully explored. When career officials were informed, administration policymakers often excluded or ignored the considered opinion of those who were experts in international law and legal policy, and the decisions were often made against the advice of those in the military who would have to carry those policies out.

CHAPTER 3

Operations

The Implementation of Policy

It's [waterboarding] a no-brainer for me.... We don't torture.... But the fact is, you can have a fairly robust interrogation program without torture, and we need to be able to do that.

—Vice President Cheney[1]

Although the CIA program authorizes waterboard use only in narrow circumstances ... the waterboard may be used on as many as five days during a 30 day approval period.... The CIA used the waterboard 'at least 83 times during August, 2002' in the interrogation of Zubaydah ... and 183 times during March 2003 in the interrogation of KSM....

—OLC Director Steven Bradbury[2]

If the detainee dies, you're doing it wrong.

—CIA lawyer Jonathan Fredman[3]

This chapter will explain how the policy decisions documented in the previous chapter were implemented in operational terms at Guantanamo,Cuba; Bagram Air Force Base, Afghanistan; and Abu Ghraib, Iraq. Bush administration officials denied that there was any policy of harsh interrogation that led to abuse and torture at Guantanamo, and thus the practices at the three different sites were unconnected. But in reality, the practices at Guantanamo, in the words of the Schlesinger Report, "migrated" to Bagram and Abu Ghraib through military leadership, exchange of personnel, and through training in SERE techniques. Thus the abuse and torture at Abu Ghraib and Bagram in the fall of 2003 had their roots in the interrogation practices at Guantanamo in the fall of 2002.

After the operation of interrogations in the detainment centers is described, the chapter will take up the specific techniques that were authorized through official DOD memoranda. It will then link the actual behavior of U.S. personnel in the mistreatment of detainees to the authorized interrogation techniques. Most interrogations were probably done according to Army Field Manual regulations and were thus in accord with the Geneva Conventions. Many, however, were abusive and linked to techniques that were officially authorized, though forbidden by the Geneva Conventions. The most horrific actions on the part of U.S. personnel went well beyond even the authorized techniques and constituted criminal behavior. Some of these actions were prosecuted, and some soldiers went to jail for them. Finally, the chapter will explain the practice of "extraordinary rendition," in which persons suspected of terrorism have been sent for interrogation to countries that are known for their practice of torture during interrogation.

Guantanamo

In December 2001, a significant number of people had been taken into U.S. custody in Afghanistan, and the United States had to decide where to locate them and what to do with them. The U.S. base at Guantanamo was chosen as, in Rumsfeld's words, "the least worst place" to hold detainees.[4] On January 11, 2002, the first twenty prisoners were flown in from Afghanistan, and several hundred followed over the next year or so. Before the flight, the detainees were stripped, put in orange jump suits, and handcuffed to a metal belt and leg irons.[5] Blackened goggles were placed over their eyes, ear covers were put on their ears, and medical masks were placed over their mouths. In the plane they were shackled to metal bolts in the floor; they were in diapers and were not allowed to use a toilet for the full flight.[6]

When they arrived at Guantanamo, they were forced to kneel on the tarmac for hours before they were processed and sent to Camp X-Ray. They were then placed in wire mesh cages about 2 by 2 meters square.[7] The cages were open to the elements and thus very hot in the sun and wet and cold in the rain. In April 2002, they were transferred to Camp Delta, a more permanent set of prison cells.

The detainees were characterized by U.S. officials as the very worst and most dedicated terrorists. Vice President Cheney spoke about the types of terrorists they expected to keep in Guantanamo, and provided reasons for why they did not deserve to be treated well: "The basic proposition is that somebody who comes into the United States of American illegally, who conducts a terrorist operation killing thousands of innocent Americans ... is not a lawful combatant. They don't deserve to be treated as a prisoner of war."[8] Cheney's statement strongly implied that the detainees were all directly connected to the atrocities of 9/11. Of course, the people who did in fact come to the United States and who conducted the 9/11 atrocities were all dead. Cheney presumably meant to imply that those who were fighting against coalition forces in Afghanistan were the equivalent of the actual terrorists who perpetrated 9/11. General Myers, chair of the Joint Chiefs of Staff, characterized the detainees being flown to Guantanamo as people who would "gnaw through hydraulic lines in the back of a C-17 to bring it down."[9]

On January 27, 2002, Secretary of Defense Donald Rumsfeld said, just before he left for Guantanamo: "These are among the most dangerous, best trained vicious killers on the face of the earth. And that means that the people taking care of these detainees and managing their transfer have to be just exceedingly careful for two reasons. One, for their own protection, but also so these people don't get loose back out on the street and kill more people. This is a very, very serious business and it ought to be treated in that manner ... They are not POWs, they will not be determined to be POWs.... "[10] President Bush, in talking about the detainees at Guantanamo in July of 2003, declared: "The only thing I know *for certain* is that these are bad people."[11] (emphasis added) In 2005, he again stated: "They're dangerous and they're still around, and they'll kill in a moment's notice."[12] Vice President Cheney said: "These are the worst of a very bad lot ... They are very dangerous. They are devoted to killing millions of Americans, innocent Americans, if they can, and they are perfectly prepared to die in the effort."[13]

Statements like these, coming from those who were the most authoritative government officials in the nation and who should have been the most knowledgeable about the war on terror, were likely to dispose U.S. personnel to treat the detainees as if they were complicit in the 9/11 atrocities and actively seeking to kill American civilians. In combination with official changes in policy, these leadership cues set the conditions that led to the abuse and torture of those detained by U.S. forces. Despite these characterizations of the detainees, many detainees were clearly not guilty of fighting against the United States, nor were they threats.

The reason Guantanamo was chosen was that it was relatively close to the United States, and the administration reasoned that since it was not technically U.S. territory, it would not fall under the jurisdiction of U.S. courts. (That reasoning was later rejected by the Supreme Court, which reasoned that despite the technical sovereignty that Cuba claimed, the United States in fact had complete control of the base for a century and would continue to control it indefinitely, and it thus had to be treated as under the control of the United States.) A total of about 780 detainees were at Guantanamo at some time, and the peak prison population was 680 in 2003. Most transfers to Guantanamo ended in 2004. By 2008, the population had dropped to about 250.[14] The detainees came from forty different countries, but most of them (about 65 percent) came from Afghanistan, Saudi Arabia, and Yemen.[15]

After the detainees had been at Guantanamo for about a month, the leadership of Joint Task Force (JTF) 160 began to doubt the intelligence value of many of them. According to Marine Major Timothy Nichols, some of the detainees had "some moderate intelligence value. A larger group had less than moderate intelligence value. But most had none."[16] Certainly, most tactical intelligence had become lost or moot, since the detainees had spent weeks in Afghanistan and a month at Guantanamo after their capture. Former Secretary of the Army Thomas White said that up to a third of the detainees had no intelligence value.[17] (For a more detailed analysis of the population of inmates at Guantanamo and their likely intelligence value, see the "Wrong Man" section of Chapter Four.)

In the late summer of 2002, the CIA sent to Guantanamo an expert on Islamic extremism who was a fluent speaker of Arabic, to report on the types of detainees incarcerated there. After interviewing detainees, he concluded that about one third of the detainees were not connected to terrorist threats against the United States and did not have any intelligence value. Although some of the detainees were certainly dangerous to the United States, many "were just caught in a dragnet. They were not fighters, they were not doing jihad. They should not have been there."[18] A detailed study of Pentagon records by Seton Hall scholars in 2005 found that only 5 percent of those apprehended in Afghanistan were actually captured by U.S. personnel, and only 8 percent of them were categorized as fighting for al Qaeda.[19]

Benjamin Wittes, in his analysis of the CSRT records, organized the detainees into three categories: those who admit they had or would fight the United States or its allies, those who were associated with al Qaeda or the Taliban in some way (e.g., staying in a guest house or training camp), and those who denied any wrongdoing or did not make any claim at all. Wittes argued that those in the first category did present a credible threat to U.S. interests; those in the second category may have had some connection with the Taliban or al Qaeda but were low level and of little intelligence value; those in the third category had plausible explanations that their capture was mistaken or there was little evidence against them.[20] The analyses of the CSRT files of the Seton Hall group, the West Point group, and Wittes were made after about four hundred detainees had been released.

The broader point here is that a large portion of the detainees brought to Guantanamo did not pose a threat to the United States and had little or no intelligence value. The clearly erroneous statements by Bush, Cheney, and Rumsfeld were thus grossly misleading and contributed to the abuse of prisoners at Guantanamo. There is also no doubt that some of the detainees had fought against the United States in Afghanistan and potentially did pose a threat. Accounts of specific individuals who were wrongly imprisoned, the "wrong man problem," will be presented in Chapter Four.

Reports of the conditions under which Guantanamo detainees were kept and the way they were treated have caused considerable controversy. Military spokespersons have consistently asserted that the prisoners were treated humanely and in the spirit of the Geneva rules. But reports by former detainees tell a different story. In a statement to the Senate Armed Services Committee, Shafiq Rasul reported that he underwent many hours of interrogation, and often he was not allowed to go to the toilet and thus had to undergo the humiliation of urinating in his clothes in the interrogation room. He, and many others, were subject to "short shackling" in which they were forced to squat down and their hands were chained between their legs and fastened to a bolt in the floor. In this position, prisoners could not stand or sit but could only crouch with their legs bent, and they were left for hours at a time. The awkward stress position had to be kept, because if the person fell over, the manacles would dig into his wrists. This can cause severe pain in the legs and back. When left in this position the air conditioning would be turned up until detainees were very cold. They were often, at the same time, subjected to extremely bright strobe lights and very loud music. Occasionally they would be threatened with military working dogs.[21]

Accounts such as this were repeated by other former detainees.[22] For instance, Tarek Dergoul explained how detainees who did not want to be interrogated were extracted from their cells by "Extreme Reaction Forces," which was referred to by the guards and prisoners as "ERFing." Five guards with full riot gear and face masks came to his cell. "They pepper-sprayed me in the face, and I started vomiting … They pinned me down and attacked me, poking their fingers in my eyes, and forced my head into the toilet pan and flushed. They tied me up like a beast and then they were kneeling on me, kicking and punching."[23] Dergoul said that this had happened to him four or five times.

In a testimony before a congressional committee, Murat Kurnaz explained that he was a Turkish citizen who had lived in Germany. He went to Pakistan to study Islam and was horrified by the events of 9/11; he thought that, according to the Koran, "it is never permissible to kill yourself, or to kill women and children" and that "Osama bin Laden is perverting Islam by killing people in the name of Islam." In Pakistan he had a return ticket to Germany, where he was to be married, but he was arrested by the Pakistani police and handed over to U.S. forces in Afghanistan. An interrogator told him that the United States paid a $3,000 bounty for him.[24]

In Kandahar he was beaten repeatedly, electrically shocked through his feet, his head was held under water, and he was chained and hung by his hands for long periods of time. He was transferred to Guantanamo, where he was kept from sleeping and denied food for long periods. He was kept in solitary confinement and subjected to extremes of heat and cold. In addition, he was humiliated religiously and sexually, as well as beaten many times. He did not have a lawyer at his CSRT hearing, which determined that, since his former friend Selcuk Bilgin was a suicide bomber, he was probably guilty of terrorism. He was eventually released to Germany, but almost five years of his life were spent in U.S. prisons in Afghanistan and Guantanamo.[25]

Jumah al Dossari (Detainee Number 261) was arrested when he went to Afghanistan in 2001. The U.S. government maintained that he was a terrorist who had gone to Afghanistan to fight with the Taliban against the United States. Dossari maintains that he went to Afghanistan to report on the progress of a mosque that was being built with Saudi funds.[26] When the United States began to bomb Afghanistan, he fled to Pakistan, but he was picked up by Pakistani forces and given to the United States. When he was taken to Kandahar, he was beaten and kept in an open tent in the winter; he was burned with a cigarette that was put out on his wrist. When he arrived at Guantanamo, he was kept in Camp X-Ray and beaten so badly that he spent three days in intensive care. He said that even more difficult than the physical beatings were his several months in solitary confinement after he attempted suicide. He had no clothes except a pair of shorts, and his only bed was a dirty plastic mat. The air-conditioning was constantly on high, and he had to use the water in his toilet for drinking and washing.

After two and a half years, allegations were made that he went to Afghanistan in 1989 for military training, that he was at Tora Bora, and that he recruited for the Taliban, all of which he denied. He was not shown any evidence against him nor did he have a lawyer. He was in despair and attempted suicide several times, once breaking a vertebra. Eventually, he got to see an attorney every few months. He said that he is not bitter about Americans in general, and once after he was beaten at Camp X-Ray, a female guard told him surreptitiously, "I'm sorry for what happened to you. You're a human being just like us."[27] In 2007, after five and a half years in Guantanamo, Dossari was released to the Saudi government.

Although the above statements by former detainees may be seen as self-serving, the similarity of many different accounts at different times leads to the conclusion that the essence of the various accounts is reasonably accurate. It also tracks closely with the U.S. military investigations that are detailed below.

If one thinks that the account of the former detainees might be exaggerated, here is the account of a U.S. soldier, Sean Baker, who had been dressed in an orange jump suit and played the role of a detainee for the training purpose of practicing ERFing (extractions from cells). Baker was at Guantanamo as a military police soldier, but the guards in training thought that he was a detainee.

> They grabbed my arms, my legs, twisted me up and unfortunately one of the individuals got up on my back from behind and put pressure down on me while I was face down. Then he—the same individual—reached around and began to choke me and press my head down against the steel floor. After several seconds—twenty to thirty seconds—I began to panic and I gave the code word I was supposed to give to stop the exercise, which was "red" ... That individual slammed my head against the floor and continued to choke me. Somehow I got enough air. I muttered out, "I'm a US soldier. I'm a US soldier."[28]

Baker ended up at Walter Reed military hospital for forty-eight days, where he was treated for traumatic brain injury. He was then released from the military.

Most of the above brutality did not have much to do with interrogations, which was the major reason for keeping prisoners at Guantanamo. Interrogations at Guantanamo could also be brutal, and accounts of them have been written by many former inmates. But the most credible accounts of harsh interrogations were made by FBI agents who were assigned to Guantanamo to interrogate detainees about al Qaeda. The FBI approach to interrogation was nonviolent and based on building a rapport with the subject in order to get him to reveal secrets. In the summer and fall of 2002, FBI agents often clashed with General Dunlavey about the best way to elicit information from an unwilling detainee. FBI agents were initially allowed to interrogate detainees with their nonviolent methods, but military personnel became impatient, and the FBI agents were withdrawn so that the military could take over and use physical force.

The important change in interrogation practice came in the spring and summer of 2002, when the DOD leadership was not getting the information they thought was being concealed by detainees. In February, Rumsfeld assigned General Dunlavey to head intelligence and pressured him to produce results. In the fall of 2002, the memo requesting new techniques beyond those in the Army Field Manual was sent up the chain of command. In November, General Dunlavey was replaced by General Geoffrey Miller, whose specialty was artillery and who had no experience with interrogation. Miller instructed his interrogators to get tough with detainees who were not cooperative. The FBI continued to object to the harsh techniques, which they thought were ineffective and possibly illegal.

In one meeting abut interrogation methods, a lieutenant colonel claimed that the harsh interrogation practices had resulted in valuable information obtained from al Qahtani, and thus the techniques worked. After the lieutenant colonel had spoken, the FBI unit chief said: "Look, everything you've gotten thus far is what the FBI gave you on al Qahtani from its paper investigation."[29] The meeting then ended because of the controversy between the FBI representative and the military officer. Despite the torture and abuse of al Qahtani, very little useful intelligence was gathered, and no "ticking time bomb" was discovered.[30]

According to the Church Report, twenty-four thousand interrogation sessions were conducted at Guantanamo from 2002 to March 2005.[31] As of February 2009, approximately sixty detainees were cleared to be released, but were still at Guantanamo. About sixty might be prosecuted, though evidence was not firm. And twenty-one detainees would be charged with crimes. A total of 779 people were incarcerated at Guantanamo; three were convicted of crimes, and two of these were released.[32]

Bagram Air Force Base, Afghanistan

Bagram Theater Internment Facility is located at Bagram Air Force Base; the sheet metal building was converted from a Soviet air plane repair facility. Its purpose was to provide a central holding facility where persons captured in Afghanistan could be held and interrogated.

Chris Mackey (a pseudonym) was in the Army reserve, was called to active duty, and learned Arabic before being deployed to Bagram Air Force Base in Afghanistan in the fall of 2001. Mackey was in the Military Intelligence Corps and in charge of interrogating prisoners who might have information related to the Taliban or al Qaeda. Mackey was determined to adhere to the rules of Geneva, even though the president decided they did not apply to members of al Qaeda or the Taliban.

Mackey knew the techniques approved by the Army in its field manual and was scrupulous about observing them. His book *The Interrogators* chronicles his tour in Afghanistan from the fall of 2001 to the summer of 2002. "I had an unshakable conviction that we should follow the rules to the letter: no physical touching, no stress positions, no 'dagger on the table' threats, and no deprivation of sleep."[33] He was able to keep his resolution in overseeing the interrogations during the time that he was there. He had to admit, however, that "by the time we left Afghanistan, we had come to embrace methods we would not have countenanced at the beginning of the war."[34] He said that when he and his fellow interrogators were replaced in the summer of 2002, the new personnel "took to monstering with alacrity.... What was an ending point for us was a starting point for them."[35]

While Mackey was in Afghanistan, Bush administration lawyers were working on expanding the legal framework for interrogation. During the summer of 2002, the "alternative" techniques using SERE training as a template were being developed at Guantanamo. It was during late 2002 that the serious abuse and torture began at Bagram Air Force Base.

Mackey was thoroughly disgusted when he learned about the actions of U.S. personnel at Abu Ghraib and Afghanistan after he left. "The reason the United States should not torture prisoners is not because it doesn't work. It is simply because it is wrong. It dehumanizes us, undermines our cause, and, over the long term breeds more enemies of the United States than coercive interrogation methods will ever allow us to capture."[36]

Even though Secretary Rumsfeld's approval of techniques was specifically intended for use at Guantanamo, his December 2, 2002, memo's influence and authority spread to Afghanistan. The memo was sent to the officer in charge of intelligence at Bagram Air Base in Afghanistan, who saw a PowerPoint presentation of the techniques approved in the Rumsfeld memo.[37]

From October 2001 to December 2002, the policy in Afghanistan was officially set by the Army Field Manual FM 34–52 (1992), as recounted by Chris Mackey above. But the changes in techniques at Guantanamo were quickly adopted at ("migrated to") Bagram Air Force Base, and U.S. personnel began using some of the techniques that were allowed in the Rumsfeld memo of December 2, 2002. An SOP had been developed at Bagram that, according to the DOD IG, had been "influenced by the counterresistance memorandum that the Secretary of Defense approved on December 2, 2002," which included "yelling, loud music, and light control, environmental manipulation, sleep deprivation/adjustment, stress positions, twenty-hour interrogations, and controlled fear (muzzled dogs)...."[38] After the deaths of detainees, a new policy was issued in March 2003, which reflected the working group recommendations of interrogation techniques that were officially authorized by Rumsfeld in April 2003.[39]

At that time Captain Carolyn Wood was in charge of the A/519 Military Intelligence unit at Bagram and had seen the list of aggressive techniques authorized in the December 2, 2002, memo. She subsequently developed "non-doctrinal, non-field manual approaches and practices" of interrogation.[40] She was posted to Abu Ghraib in August 2003 as interrogation officer in charge at Abu Ghraib. The Fay/Jones Report later found that she failed to train and supervise her troops and prevent the abuse that happened when she was in charge.[41] According to the Fay/Jones Report, Captain Wood created a chart, "Interrogation Rules of Engagement," to specify which techniques were authorized. These techniques "clearly came from documents and personnel in Afghanistan and Guantanamo." And the "practices were accepted as SOP by newly-arrived interrogators at Abu Ghraib."[42]

According to the Schlesinger Report, methods that were intended for use only at Guantanamo, e.g., stress positions, isolation up to thirty days, removal of clothing, isolation for long periods, stress positions, use of dogs, sleep and light deprivation, came to be used.[43] These techniques were not authorized by Rumsfeld but were "approved and promulgated by the senior command in the theater."[44] In order to assure that the methods being used were authorized, U.S. intelligence officers sent a memo listing the techniques to Central Command in Florida on January 24, 2003. When there was no reply, either positive or negative, the command in Afghanistan assumed that there was no objection and that the techniques were allowable.[45]

Bagram was also the site of the torture and death of several detainees. In December 2002, a taxi driver named Dilwar was imprisoned, and was beaten so brutally that a coroner testified that his legs had been "pulpified."[46] American officials later admitted that he was innocent of fighting Americans. Another prisoner, held by the CIA, died of hypothermia after having been left in a cold cell without any clothes. A third prisoner named Habibulla was beaten brutally and died when he was hung by his wrists.[47]

Abu Ghraib

After U.S. forces had invaded Iraq in March of 2003 and had defeated the military forces of Saddam Hussein, the notorious prison at Abu Ghraib, which had been the center for much of Saddam's torture and killing, was looted and stripped of any useful building materials. The U.S. occupying authority knew of its reputation as the center for the extreme torture and killing of many Iraqis and other prisoners by Saddam Hussein, but CPA head Paul Bremer explained that there was no other facility in the country that was reasonably intact and that could be used to hold thousands of prisoners. So he, "with great reluctance," ordered the prison to be renovated for use by the United States, and he planned to set aside the "execution rooms" as a museum to remind people of the brutality of Saddam's regime.[48]

On June 30, 2003, Brigadier General Janice Karpinski took command of the 800th Military Police Brigade, which was in charge of all military prisons in Iraq, and on August 4, Abu Ghraib was opened for use by U.S. military police. Karpinski said that the initial policy was the Geneva Conventions, and they were posted on the walls of the cell block of Abu Ghraib.[49] Karpinski spent most of her time in Baghdad and did not take hands-on control of Abu Ghraib.

In August, Undersecretary of Defense for Intelligence Stephen Cambone had his deputy, Lieutenant General William (Jerry) Boykin, organize a visit by Guantanamo commander Major General Geoffrey Miller to Abu Ghraib with a view toward improving its operation and increasing the collection of intelligence about the uprising against U.S. forces. Miller took along one of his "Tiger Teams" of interrogators and recommended that, as had been done at Guantanamo, military police (MPs) should be actively involved in intelligence collection by "setting the conditions" for prisoner interrogation by military intelligence troops (and CIA and contractor personnel).

At the end of Miller's inspection of Abu Ghraib, according to General Karpinski, he told the soldiers there: "The first thing I noticed is that you're treating the prisoners too well. You have to take control, and they have to know that you're in control. You have to treat the prisoners like dogs.[50] General Karpinski said that she objected to Miller's assertion of authority and his intention to "Gitmo-ize" the facility for which she was officially responsible. His response, according to her, was, "You can do this my way, or we can do it the hard way."[51] The subsequent changes in the methods of interrogation, according to Colonel Thomas Pappas, Commander of the 205th Intelligence Brigade, were "enacted as the result of a specific visit by Maj. Gen. Geoffrey Miller."[52] Karpinski said that Secretary Rumsfeld had issued a memorandum detailing which techniques could be used specifically at Abu Ghraib. She said that she did not see the memos when she was in Iraq, but she did personally see them, as signed by Rumsfeld, after the abuses at Abu Ghraib had been revealed.[53]

Although Miller maintained that it was necessary to provide a safe and humane environment, his assessment also stated that "it is essential that the guard force be actively engaged in setting the conditions for successful exploitation of the internees."[54] Miller decided that one key to intelligence extraction was to combine the efforts of military intelligence (MI) interrogators with the military police (MP) function of housing and caring for detainees. The problem with General Miller transferring the interrogation techniques and other procedures from Guantanamo to Abu Ghraib, according to the Taguba Report, was that the two detention facilities had different functions and different types of detainees. Guantanamo was intended to hold members of al Qaeda who potentially had information related to possible future terrorist attacks on the United States, while Abu Ghraib held large numbers of "Iraqi criminals" and individuals involved in the uprising against U.S. forces. In addition, according to Army doctrine, the role of MPs should remain distinct from that of military intelligence personnel.[55]

Miller brought to Iraq Rumsfeld's April 16 authorization to use methods beyond those in the Army Field Manual, and in the fall of 2003 officially took control of Abu Ghraib. According to the Schlesinger Report, "Interrogators and lists of techniques circulated from Guantanamo and Afghanistan to Iraq."[56] In addition, SERE instructors went to Iraq in September 2003 to assist in interrogations.[57] In October, November, and December of 2003, U.S. personnel engaged in the now notorious abuses that resulted in the humiliation, injury, and death of prisoners.

The number of detainees soon began to overwhelm the capacity of the prison, and by October 2003 there were seven thousand prisoners.[58] The prison was grossly undermanned, and the MPs were operating under very harsh conditions. In the fall of 2003, most of the prisoners were common criminals.[59] The lack of personnel and resources played an important role in creating the conditions that allowed the abuse and torture to occur. The low-level MPs were overworked, ill trained, and without proper supplies to carry out their mission. The stress created by these conditions contributed to the unacceptable behavior of the guards, though it does not excuse it.

At the beginning of August 2003, the formal policy for interrogation at Abu Ghraib was the Geneva Conventions explained in the standard Army Field Manual.[60] But later that month, Captain William Ponce, Jr., issued a memo that said, "The gloves are coming off gentlemen, regarding these detainees ... Col. Boltz has made it clear that we want these individuals broken. Casualties are mounting and we need to start gathering info to help protect our fellow soldiers from any further attacks."[61] The memo asked for a list of techniques that would make interrogations more "effective." In Iraq, special mission unit forces used SOPs from Afghanistan, and they were subsequently made SOP for all U.S. forces in Iraq.[62]

After Miller's visit in early September, according to Karpinski, Colonel Thomas Pappas, commander of the 205th Military Intelligence Brigade, formally asked General Sanchez to "escalate" the level of interrogations.[63] In a memo dated September 14, 2003, General Sanchez authorized specific interrogation techniques. The transmittal memo stated that the "Counter-Resistance Policy" was "modeled on the one implemented for interrogations conducted at Guantanamo Bay," but modified to take into account the Geneva Conventions, and he instructed: "My intent is to implement this policy immediately."[64]

General Sanchez, commander of CJTF-7, was aware that the Geneva Conventions applied in Iraq, but using the reasoning in President Bush's February 7 policy memo, concluded that tougher methods than allowed for prisoners of war could be used on "unlawful combatants" who were captured and interrogated. On October 15, the 372nd Military Policy Company was put in charge of Abu Ghraib; its members were mostly Army reserves who were not trained to be prison guards.

Despite the stipulation in Rumsfeld's memo that the techniques beyond FM 34–52 were limited to unlawful combatants held at Guantanamo, Commanding General Sanchez on September 14 authorized the use of twelve techniques beyond the Army field manual, including dietary manipulation, environmental manipulation (change of temperature), sleep adjustment, isolation for thirty days (for more than thirty days it must be briefed to the MI commander), presence of military working dogs (muzzled), sleep management (but with four hours of sleep per twenty-four hour period), loud music and light control ("used to create fear"), stress positions (limited to one hour). The memo ordered a number of safeguards and medical attention to detainees subjected to the techniques. Despite the carefully limited instructions for use of the techniques, the operational environment made it likely that the safeguards and limits would be ignored.[65]

When officials at U.S. Central Command in Florida became aware of how the practices authorized by Sanchez were being used at Abu Ghraib, they warned Sanchez, and on October 12 he rescinded some of the tactics on the list and insisted that the use of some of them required his direct approval. These included the use of dogs, more than thirty days isolation, and maintaining stress positions for forty-five minutes. At the same time, an "Interrogation Rules of Engagement" memo of October 9 said that "at no time will detainees be treated inhumanely nor maliciously humiliated."[66] The Schlesinger Report found that Lieutenant General Sanchez's command, "reasoning from the President's memorandum of February 7, 2002," believed that the presence of "unlawful combatants" justified more aggressive interrogation techniques.[67] Schlesinger also concluded that these changes caused confusion among U.S. personnel at Abu Ghraib as to which techniques were acceptable and which were not.[68]

Military Intelligence officer Colonel Thomas Pappas was officially given control of Abu Ghraib on November 19, 2003, which formalized the replacement of military police control with military intelligence control. General Karpinski said that Pappas was living at Abu Ghraib well before the official change of control and had effective control of Abu Ghraib, and that she did not have control in the fall of 2003.[69] This change from MP control of the prison to MI control was criticized by the Taguba Report as being "not doctrinally sound" and confused the roles and missions of the two different types of units: the MPs to hold and care for prisoners and MI to extract as much information as possible.[70] It was during the October–December period that the abuses at Abu Ghraib were photographed.

MPs reported that in the fall of 2003, military intelligence personnel encouraged them to abuse the detainees and praised them when they did. For instance, the MI personnel were quoted as saying, "Loosen this guy up for us. Make sure he has a bad night. Make sure he gets the treatment." When they did what MI wanted, they were praised: "Good job, they're breaking down real fast. They answer every question. They're giving out good information. Keep up the good work."[71] When asked about the abusive techniques, one MP said, "I witnessed prisoners in the MI hold section, wing 1A, being made to do various things that I would question morally. In Wing 1A we were told that they had different rules and different SOP for treatment. I never saw a set of rules or SOP for that section, just word of mouth."[72] Taguba found that the MPs at Abu Ghraib "had received no training in detention/internee operations," and that they had little or no instruction on the Geneva rules for prisoners of war, which officially did apply to the Iraq conflict.[73]

In addition to military personnel, CIA and contract employees also participated in the interrogation and abuse of detainees. In late spring of 2003, CIA personnel killed a man (Jamadi) suspected of fighting in the insurgency by beating him and then tying his arms behind his back and hanging him from his arms. A forensic pathologist concluded "asphyxia is what he died from—as in a crucifixion."[74] The CIA was implicated in at least three additional deaths of detainees in Iraq.

From the above accounts, the connections between Guantanamo, Bagram, and Abu Ghraib become clearer. General Miller was sent from Guantanamo to Abu Ghraib to make recommendations for more effective extraction of intelligence. Miller pushed General Karpinski aside, recommended that detainees be treated "like dogs," and recommended that MPs become actively engaged in "setting the conditions" for more effective interrogations by military intelligence personnel. He was put in charge of Abu Ghraib in October 2003 and thus was able to implement his recommendations. His actions were reinforced by General Sanchez, who authorized harsh techniques in September 2003, though some were withdrawn a month later. Personnel were transferred from Afghanistan and brought with them knowledge of the techniques they were employing against detainees. The combination of these changes, the lack of training of MPs, and the harsh conditions that guards lived with led to the abuse and torture that were recorded in the photographs of abuse seen around the world. The Schlesinger Report summed it up: "Interrogators and lists of techniques circulated from Guantanamo and Afghanistan to Iraq."[75]

Colonel Steven M. Kleinman, a colonel in the Air Force and director of the SERE training at Fairchild AFB in Washington State, concluded that intense pressure for actionable intelligence led interrogators to treat all detainees as if they were complicit and had valuable intelligence. After his experience in Iraq with SERE instructors, he admitted that "in far too many cases, we simply erred in pressing interrogation and interrogators beyond the edge of the envelope. As a result, interrogation was no longer an intelligence collection method; rather, it had morphed into a form of punishment for those who wouldn't cooperate."[76]

Authorized Techniques of Military Interrogation

Many of the incidents of documented abuse and torture of detainees occurred after explicit changes in policy and the migration of techniques from Guantanamo to Bagram to Iraq. Some of these incidents can be traced, directly or indirectly, to techniques approved by official memoranda. Many of the incidents of abuse resulted from the severe or excessive application of approved techniques that ignored the limitations noted on the official memos. But some of the reports of torture, abuse, and deaths resulted from illegal behavior that was not in accord with official policy but was criminal behavior on the part of U.S. personnel.

This section will examine the interrogation techniques that were explicitly authorized by policy directives. It will begin with the methods authorized by the traditional Army Field Manual (FM 34–52, 1992), which were designed to conform to the Geneva Conventions. It will then consider the additional techniques authorized by Secretary Rumsfeld in December 2002, and after he rescinded those, the ones he approved in April 2003. Although these methods were formally approved by the Secretary of Defense, the actual training of interrogators in Guantanamo and Abu Ghraib also included SERE techniques that were designed to train U.S. personnel to resist enemy pressure to elicit false confessions. The following section will look at the actual implementation of the techniques.

Army Field Manual 34–52 (1992)

The U.S. Army Field Manual (1992), *Intelligence Interrogation*, in conformance with the Geneva Conventions, listed seventeen techniques that could be used by military interrogators.[77] These techniques may not be gentle, but none of them (unless taken to extremes) came close to torture.

The manual lists the categories of persons who are protected by the Geneva Conventions of 1949. In addition to "enemy prisoners of war" and "captured insurgents," it lists "other captured, detained, or retained persons." This last category covers all persons under U.S. military control. It further specifies that "captured insurgents and other detained personnel whose status is not clear, such as suspected terrorists, are entitled to PW (Prisoner of War) protection until their precise status has been determined by competent authority." These are the requirements that President Bush intended to eliminate by declaring that suspected members of al Qaeda were "illegal enemy combatants" and thus not entitled to any Geneva protections.

Field Manual 34–52 (p. 1–8) further explains that the Geneva Conventions and U.S. policy "expressly prohibit acts of violence or intimidation, including physical or mental torture, threats, insults, or exposure to inhumane treatment as a means of or aid to interrogation.... Use of torture and other illegal methods is a poor technique that yields unreliable results, may damage subsequent collection efforts, and can induce the source to say what he thinks the interrogator wants to hear." It specifies as torture (among other things): forcing a person into "abnormal positions for prolonged periods of time," "food deprivation," "any form of beating," "mock executions," "abnormal sleep deprivation," and "threatening or implying" torture to the detainee or his family. U.S. soldiers subjected detainees in the war on terror to all of these prohibited techniques.

The approved techniques in FM 34–52, all in accord with the Geneva Conventions, include:

    A. "Asking straightforward questions"
    B. "Incentive/Removal of Incentive"
    C. Playing on "Emotional Love" of a detainee for an individual or group
    D. Playing on "Emotional Hate" of a detainee for an individual or group
    E. "Fear Up Harsh"
    F. "Fear Up Mild"
    G. "Reduced Fear"
    H. "Pride and Ego Up"
    I. "Pride and Ego Down"
    J. "Futility"
    K. "We Know All"
    L. "Establish Your Identity" (pretend you think the detainee is someone else)
    M. "Repetition Approach"
    N. "File and Dossier" (pretend there is an incriminating file which must be corrected)
    O. "Mutt and Jeff" (good cop, bad cop ploy)
    P. "Rapid Fire" (of questions)
    Q. "Silence"

Requested Techniques and Rumsfeld Approval

When the standard FM 34–52 techniques did not result in sufficient intelligence, further techniques were developed.[78] As explained previously, the techniques that went beyond those authorized in the Army Field Manual 34–52 were developed in the summer and fall of 2002. The list of these techniques was the result of interaction between administration officials in Washington and the command at Guantanamo.[79] The following methods were included on the Phifer memo of October 11, 2002, that went to General Hill at SouthCom, and two weeks later to Richard

Myers, chair of the JCS.[80] DOD General Counsel Haynes then took them to Donald Rumsfeld, recommending his approval of all of them except Numbers 1, 2, and 3 of Category III.

Category I:

1. "Yelling at the detainee."
2. "Techniques of deception." ("multiple interrogator" and "interrogator identity")

Category II:

1. "The use of stress positions (like standing) for a maximum of four hours."
2. "The use of falsified documents or reports."
3. "Use of isolation facility for up to 30 days. Extensions beyond the initial 30 days must be approved by commanding general."
4. "Change of 'environment' for interrogation."
5. "Deprivation of light and auditory stimuli."
6. "The detainee may also have a hood placed over his head ... (not to restrict breathing)."
7. "The use of 20 hour interrogations."
8. "The removal of all comfort items (including religious items)."
9. "Switching the detainee from hot rations to MREs." (meals ready to eat)
10. "Removal of Clothing."
11. "Forced grooming (shaving of facial hair, etc.)."
12. "Using detainees (sic) individual phobias (such as fear of dogs) to induce stress."

Category III:

1. "The use of scenarios designed to convince the detainee that death or severely painful consequences are imminent for him and/or his family." [not approved on December 2]
2. "Exposure to cold weather or water (with appropriate medical monitoring)." [not approved]
3. "Use of a wet towel and dripping water to induce the misperception of suffocation." [not approved]
4. "Use of mild, non-injurious physical contact such as grabbing, poking in the chest with the finger, and light pushing." [approved by Rumsfeld]

On November 27, 2002, DOD counsel Haynes recommended that Secretary Rumsfeld approve all techniques in categories I and II, and only number 4 from III (mild, non-injurious physical contact). Rumsfeld approved Haynes's recommendations on December 2, 2002. [81]

After great concern about the legality of the methods was expressed to Rumsfeld, particularly through Navy General Counsel Alberto Mora's conversations with Rumsfeld's counsel Haynes, the above approval memo was rescinded by Rumsfeld on January 15, 2003. Rumsfeld then appointed a working group to examine the legality of the techniques. The working group issued a report on April 4, 2003, and based on that memorandum, Rumsfeld authorized the following techniques on April 16, 2003.

Techniques Recommended by Working Group on April 4, 2003

After rescinding his previous memo, Rumsfeld appointed the working group to recommend techniques that would be legal. He insisted that the working group restrict its analysis to the legal framework laid out in a draft memorandum by John Yoo, which was based on the Bybee I memo of August 1, 2002. The working group reported its findings to Rumsfeld (without informing many of the career lawyers who were initially included in the group) on April 4, 2003.

In its April 4, 2003, memo the working group recommended approval of Techniques 1–26. Techniques 1–17 were from the Army Field Manual 34–52, as listed above.[82] Additional techniques recommended:

18. "Change of Scenery Up"
19. "Change of Scenery Down"
20. "Hooding"
21. "Mild Physical Contact"
22. "Dietary Manipulation" (with "no intended deprivation of food or water")
23. "Environmental Manipulation" ("e.g., adjusting temperature")
24. "Sleep Adjustment" ("This technique is NOT sleep deprivation")
25. "False Flag" (pretending that a detainee will be interrogated by people from other countries)
26. "Threat of Transfer"
27. "Isolation"

It then recommended that the following techniques be approved, but to be "conducted at strategic interrogation facilities; where there is a good basis to believe that the detainee possesses critical intelligence ... " (among other limitations):[83]

28. "Use of Prolonged Interrogations" (e.g., twenty hours per day)
29. "Forced Grooming"
30. "Prolonged Standing" (in "normal position" for four hours per twenty-four)
31. "Sleep Deprivation"
32. "Physical Training"
33. "Face Slap/Stomach Slap"
34. "Removal of Clothing"
35. "Increasing Anxiety by Use of Aversions"

Techniques Approved by Secretary Rumsfeld on April 16, 2002

The following are the techniques (R–X) that Rumsfeld approved on April 16[84] (note that the numbering has been changed to lettering). Letters A–Q (numbers 1–17 were straight from FM 34–52). Letters R–X were selected from the recommended numbers 18–35 that the working group submitted on April 4, 2003.

R. "Change of Scenery Up"
S. "Change of Scenery Down"
T. "Dietary Manipulation" (with "no intended deprivation of food or water")
U. "Environmental Manipulation" ("e.g., adjusting temperature")
V. "Sleep Adjustment" ("This technique is NOT sleep deprivation")
W. "False Flag" (pretending that he will be interrogated by people from other countries)
X. "Isolation" (not known to have been done for interrogation "for more than 30 days")

The Rumsfeld memo notes that the techniques must be used with safeguards and that they apply only to "unlawful combatants held at Guantanamo Bay, Cuba. Techniques "are usually used" in combination. Detainees were to be "treated humanely and, to the extent appropriate with military necessity, in a manner consistent with the principles of the Geneva Conventions." If "you require additional interrogation techniques for a particular detainee, you should" send a written request to the secretary of defense.

Survival Evasion Resistance and Escape (SERE) Techniques

The following SERE techniques were developed to train U.S. personnel to resist pressure from enemy interrogators to divulge information or make false confessions. In December 2002, the deputy counsel at DOD requested a list of SERE techniques from the U.S. trainers. The following list is copied verbatim from TAB 16 of the documents that Senator Levin obtained for hearings on abuse and torture in 2008 (the list begins with number 3).[85]

3. Degradation Tactics
   a. Shoulder Slap
   b. Insult Slap
   c. Stomach Slap
   d. Stripping
4. Physical Debilitation Tactics
   a. Stress Positions
      1. Head Rest Index Finger Position
      2. Kneeling Position
      3. Worship-the-Gods

    4. Sitting Position
    5. Standing Position
  3. Demonstrate Omnipotence Tactics (sic, number 3 repeated)
    a. Manhandling
    b Walling

Despite the lists authorized by Rumsfeld, these more brutal techniques constituted official guidance, since they were requested by the Office of the Counsel of the Secretary of defense and given to U.S. interrogators.

Reports of the Techniques in Operation

The following incidents of abuse and torture, all listed above and documented below, could be seen as derived from the SERE training techniques, the Rumsfeld memos, or clearly criminal conduct. Accounts of the use of these techniques are documented in the reports that are summarized after the three lists. The names in parentheses refer to which reports document the techniques.

Rumsfeld Memos (December 2 and April 16)

- slapping (Taguba, Fay)
- hooded and naked detainee on box with wires attached: stress position (Tabuga)
- use of "military working dogs (without muzzles)" (Taguba, Fay, FBI, Jones)
- "prolonged solitary confinement in cells devoid of daylight" (ICRC)
- detainee kept "naked in totally empty concrete cells and in total darkness"
- (ICRC, Fay)
- "isolation and deprivation of sleep" (Fay, Jones)
- "isolation up to 30 days" (Schlesinger)
- "stress positions" (Schmidt-Furlow, Schlesinger)
- "prolonged short shackling in stress positions" (FBI)
- "extreme temperature" (Fay)
- "20 hour interrogations" (Schmidt-Furlow)

SERE Techniques:

- forced nudity (Taguba)
- videotaping naked detainees in sexual positions (Tabuga)
- "sexual taunting by females" (FBI, Schmidt-Furlow)
- "mistreatment of Koran" (FBI)
- "forced physical training" (Schmidt-Furlow)
- "light deprivation" (Schlesinger)

Clearly Criminal and Not Authorized in Any Way:

- "male MP guard having sex with a female detainee" (Taguba)
- "pouring phosphoric liquid on detainees" (Taguba)
- "beating detainees with a broom handle" (Tabuba)
- "sodomizing a detainee with chemical light" (Taguba)
- "withholding medical care" (FBI)
- "deprivation of food and water" (FBI)
- "brutal beating" (FBI)
- "intentional violent or sexual abuse" (Jones)

Homicides

A variety of sources put the number of deaths of detainees in U.S. custody between 2002 and 2005 at more than 100. One compilation from public sources puts the total number of deaths as 112, with 45 of those attributed to homicide, primarily in Iraq. Thirty-six were due to mortar attacks on prisons, and 20 were due to natural causes.[86] As of March 2005, the Army reported that 26 deaths were being investigated for possible criminal prosecution. Eleven deaths were judged to be justifiable homicides, and others died of natural causes, according to the Army.[87] Some of the homicides were preceded by abuse and torture; that is, the detainees were tortured to death.

A former U.S. official familiar with the interrogation program said: "It can look antiseptic on a piece of paper, when it's a legal checklist. It seems clinical. It doesn't sound so much. You have to have the imagination to visualize it graphically and in combination, over time, to understand how this all would work in reality. The totality is just staggering."[88] The above observation was borne out by official military reports on abuse and torture. The following reports summarize some of the abuses discovered by U.S. military officials, FBI agents, the Department of Justice Inspector General, and the International Committee of the Red Cross.

Taguba Report

After photographic evidence of abuse of prisoners was reported in early January 2004, Major General Antonio M. Taguba was assigned on January 31, 2004, to investigate the abuses, and he submitted his report on February 26. His report was based on interviews of fifty witnesses, examination of all of the available photographs, the Criminal Investigations Division (CID) reports and interviews, and on-site visits to Abu Ghraib.

General Taguba concluded that at Abu Ghraib, "numerous incidents of sadistic, blatant, and wanton criminal abuses were inflicted on several detainees. This systemic and illegal abuse of detainees was intentionally perpetrated by several members of the military police guard force."[89] The types of "intentional abuse of detainees by military police" documented included:

Punching, slapping, and kicking detainees; jumping on their naked feet; Videotaping and photographing naked male and female detainees; Forcibly arranging detainees in various sexually explicit positions for photographing; ... Forcing groups of male detainees to masturbate themselves while being photographed and videotaped; Arranging naked male detainees in a pile and then jumping on them; Positioning a naked detainee on a MRE Box, with a sandbag on his head, and attaching wires to his fingers, toes, and penis to simulate electric torture; ... A male MP guard having sex with a female detainee; Using military working dogs (without muzzles) to intimidate and frighten detainees, and in at least one case biting and severely injuring a detainee; Taking photographs of dead Iraqi detainees.[90]

In addition, Taguba also concluded that the U.S. soldiers were guilty of: "Breaking chemical lights and pouring the phosphoric liquid on detainees; Pouring cold water on naked detainees; Beating detainees with a broom handle and a chair; ... Sodomizing a detainee with chemical light and perhaps a broom stick."[91]

Taguba concluded that abuse of prisoners was often done at the request of military intelligence personnel and "Other US Government Agency's (OGA) interrogators" (i.e., CIA) in order to "set physical and mental conditions for favorable interrogation of witnesses."[92] That is, MPs were expected to make life miserable for detainees so that when they were interrogated by military intelligence personnel, they would be more likely to break down more quickly and answer questions. General Taguba was ordered to investigate the actions of MP personnel and did not report on the actions of military intelligence personnel during actual interrogation of detainees.

The photographs made public in the spring of 2004 were taken by MP personnel and recorded only the "softening up" actions of the guards. There were no photos released of interrogation techniques used on detainees in order to extract information.

Fay Report

While the Taguba Report focused on the behavior of the military police at Abu Ghraib, the Fay Report investigated the behavior of the 205th Military Intelligence Brigade.[93] General Fay specifically identified forty-four instances of alleged detainee abuse that were committed by soldiers and civilian contractors at Abu Ghraib. The physical abuse involved slapping, kicking, restricting breathing, dislocating the shoulder of a detainee, and other harsh treatment. Dogs were used to "threaten and terrify detainees," and dogs were released in the cells with juvenile detainees. Clothes were taken away from detainees, with their nakedness used to shame them and increase their vulnerability; in addition, they were left naked in cells during severely cold weather. Detainees were forced into simulated sexual positions with other detainees. Although there are legitimate uses of isolation, Fay concluded that isolation and deprivation of sleep were used in inappropriate ways at Abu Ghraib. Fay reports a death at Abu Ghraib as well as several alleged sexual assaults. The forty-four specific incidents are listed and described in the final pages of the report.

Army Inspector General Report

In July 2004, the Army released the report of its inspector general, Lieutenant General Paul T. Mikolashek. His team examined 125 reports of possible abuses at 16 detention centers and concluded that 94 of them involved misconduct and that 20 resulted in deaths. His conclusion was that the abuses resulted from the "unauthorized actions taken by a few individuals, coupled with the failure of a few leaders to provide adequate monitoring, supervision and leadership over those soldiers ... these abuses, while regrettable, are aberrations."[94] The bulk of his report, however, might lead one to the conclusion that the problems were systemic (as Taguba concluded) rather than individual.

General Mikolashek cited as contributing to the abuses the psychological dynamics when one person has complete control over another, the lack of adequate training, ambiguous instructions concerning interrogations, and an uncertain command structure. But in addition, he said, "In the few cases involving the progression to more serious abuse by Soldiers, tolerance of behavior by any level of the chain of command, even if minor, led to an increase in the frequency and intensity of abuse." He concluded that "in a high-stress, high pressures combat environment, soldiers and subordinate leaders require clear, unambiguous guidance well within established parameters that they did not have in the policies we reviewed."[95] The argument of this book is that the abuses were systemic rather than idiosyncratic. That is, the abuse and torture by low-ranking individuals took place in the broader context of authorized techniques not allowed by the Army Field Manual, of lack of training, inadequate resources, confusing policy changes, permissive guidance, and leadership failure.

Other Army Reports

One Army document related an account of hostage-taking by a soldier in Iraq: "Personnel at the ICE regularly see detainees who are in essence hostages. They are normally arrested by Coalition Forces because they are family of individuals who have been targeted by a brigade based on accusations that may or may not be true...." The original purpose, however, was soon lost, and "in reality, these detainees are transferred to Abu Ghraib prison and become lost in the Coalition detention system."[96] In another instance at Abu Ghraib, a seventeen-year-old boy was used as leverage to "break" a general who was his father. After enduring a fourteen-hour interrogation, during which the victim "had not been broken," U.S. personnel got his son wet, put mud on him, and "drove him around in the back of a Humvee." The general was then allowed to see his son from a distance. After seeing his son shivering, cold, and being mistreated, the general "broke."[97]

FBI Reports

FBI personnel continued to be dubious of the efficacy and legality of the military methods of interrogation and reported their observations to FBI headquarters. The descriptions of harsh treatment by former detainees were often corroborated by FBI witnesses. The Inspector General's Office of the Department of Justice did a thorough investigation of FBI behavior at Guantanamo; they interviewed 230 witnesses, administered a survey to one thousand FBI employees who had been at Guantanamo, and reviewed more than five hundred thousand pages of documents.

The OIG reported that one or more FBI agents personally observed the harsh interrogation of detainees by military personnel or contract employees. The incidents included the following: brutal beating, a female interrogator bending back the thumbs of a detainee and squeezing his genitals, prolonged short shackling in stress positions (overnight) while subjected to strobe lighting and loud music in 90–95 degree heat or cold air-conditioning, sleep disruption, extreme temperature, use of military working dogs, isolation, sexual taunting by females, mistreatment of the Koran, flashing lights and loud music, duct tape over a detainee's eyes and mouth, forced shaving, withholding medical care, forced extractions (ERFing) by seven-man teams, placing women's clothes on detainee's head, deprivation of food and water, removal of clothes, and other techniques of brutality.[98]

The FBI concerns were expressed to top levels of the Departments of Defense and Justice and the National Security Council. At one point the FBI agents at Guantanamo were so concerned that they opened a "war crimes" file, but they were later ordered to close the file.[99] One agent reported this observation of a detainee when he was in Guantanamo: "the room was stifling hot, there was a strong smell of urine and feces, and there was a small pile of hair next to the detainee's head. The MPs on duty told the agent that the detainee had been there since the day before and that the MPs were told by his interrogators to leave him there and not bring him any food or water until the interrogators came back."[100] Mohammed al Qahtani was subjected to 160 days of isolation, with the lights on twenty-four hours a day.[101] During this period the DOJ-IG also reported that al-Qahtani was subject to the following techniques over the fifty days of his interrogation: stress positions, twenty-hour interrogations, naked in presence of female, sexual taunting, forced to dance with male, claims that his mother and sister were whores, forced physical training, and many others.[102]

As a result of the planning and use of these techniques in the summer of 2002, the FBI decided not to participate in joint interrogation of detainees.[103]

ICRC Report of 2004 on Iraq

The International Committee of the Red Cross (ICRC) visited fourteen U.S. detention sites in Iraq between March and November 2003 and objected to many cases of what were, in its judgment, abuse of detainees. It did not unilaterally publicize its findings because the agreed rules of its operation are that it works with governments to try to improve conditions rather than publicize abuses.[104] The ICRC issued a confidential report in February 2004, which has now been released.[105] The ICRC report catalogued a wide range of abuses and ill-treatment of detainees by U.S. and coalition forces. The main violations of the Geneva Conventions on treatment of those captured included: "Brutality against protected persons upon capture and initial custody, sometimes causing death or serious injury; absence of notification of arrest; physical or psychological coercion during interrogation; prolonged solitary confinement in cells devoid of daylight; excessive and disproportionate use of force.... "[106]

The report then specified methods of ill-treatment that were most frequently alleged, including: hooding to disorient and interfere with breathing, handcuffing with flexi-cuffs that damaged wrists, beatings with hard objects, threats against family members, pressing the face into the ground with boots, solitary confinement without clothes, acts of humiliation, etc."[107] At Abu Ghraib, ICRC members directly witnessed and documented "the practice of keeping persons deprived of their liberty completely naked in totally empty concrete cells and in total darkness, allegedly for several consecutive days."[108]

Perhaps most alarming in the ICRC Report is the statement: "Certain CF [Coalition Forces] military intelligence officers told the ICRC that in their estimate between 70% and 90% of the persons deprived of their liberty in Iraq had been arrested by mistake."[109] Even if the judgment of the military intelligence officers was vastly exaggerated, the implications are alarming. The routine brutal and dehumanizing treatment of prisoners was not limited to those of potential high military value, but many detainees routinely received such treatment, as evidenced by the terrible treatment that four Reuters employees suffered at the hands of U.S. soldiers.[110]

Parallel CIA Policy Track

The above accounts deal with torture and abuse by military authority, but the CIA had separate authorization to use "alternative" techniques to interrogate captives. The CIA legal authority and operational details are thus different from military operations, but the broader issues involved in torture are similar. This section will briefly analyze some of the issues related to the CIA use of black sites to interrogate suspected terrorists.

The CIA was given more leeway in the use of interrogation techniques than the military, and the justifications for the use of these techniques were made in several memoranda. The Bybee II memo of August 1, 2002, authorized ten techniques that the CIA had requested.[111] The techniques were:

1. the attention grasp
2. walling (pushing the individual into a specially constructed wall)
3. facial hold
4. facial slap
5. cramped confinement
6. wall standing (standing 4–5 feet from the wall, the individual leans forward so that his weight is supported by his fingertips)
7. stress positions
8. sleep deprivation
9. cramped confinement in a box with an insect (not used)
10. waterboard

On May 10, 2005, OLC Director Steven Bradbury issued a new memo to cover techniques the CIA had been using on high-value detainees.[112] It may have been written because the August 1, 2002, memo by Bybee had been withdrawn by the former OLC director, Jack Goldsmith. The memo begins with a statement that "torture is abhorrent both to American law and values and to international norms" and quotes President Bush as saying "torture is wrong no matter where it occurs, and the United States will continue to lead the fight to eliminate it everywhere."[113] The thrust of the memo was that 1) the techniques authorized do not constitute torture under U.S. law (section 2340 of title 18), and 2) the techniques are justified because they are seen as necessary to protect national security. The memo includes a detailed justification of thirteen techniques (with some overlap with the August 1, 2002, memo) and an argument why none of them violated the U.S. torture statute (section 2340 of title 18). The techniques included were (pp. 7–15):

1. dietary manipulation (liquid rather than solid food with caloric requirement)
2. nudity (to cause psychological discomfort, including presence of women)
3. attention grasp
4. walling
5. facial hold
6. facial slap (with fingers slightly spread)
7. abdominal slap
8. cramped confinement (for larger box, no more than eight hours at a time for a total of eighteen hours a day; for the smaller box, no more than two hours)
9. wall standing
10. stress positions (three types specified)
11. water dousing (ambient temperature of 64 degrees; water temperature of 41 degrees for twenty minutes; higher temperatures for longer periods)
12. sleep deprivation (maximum of 180 hours, hands shackled above head [two hour limit], and feet shackled; danger of edema, which is "not painful"[114]
13. waterboard (forty-second duration; two-hour limit; two sessions per twenty-four hours)

After describing each of the techniques and specifying limits on each, the memo (pp. 31–45) explains why each technique does not meet the standard for torture set in section 2340 of title 18, which says that to amount to torture, a technique must be "specifically intended to inflict severe physical or mental pain or suffering" (p. 17).

A second memo, also issued on May 10, 2005 (Bradbury II), authorized the use of the above techniques in combination with others.[115] The memo describes three levels of the interrogation process (pp. 4–6). The "initial conditions" are set when the person is "securely shackled and is deprived of sight and sound through the use of blindfolds, earmuffs, and hoods" in the flight to the interrogation location, and his head and face are shaved. The purpose of this phase is to imbue in the victim "dread" of "US custody." The second "transition to interrogation" phase includes bringing the detainee to "a baseline dependent state," in which he "has no control over basic human needs." Techniques for this phase include nudity, "sleep deprivation (with shackling and, at least at times, with use of a diaper)," and "dietary manipulation." Also used are the "insult slap," "water dousing or kneeling stress positions," the "abdominal slap," and "wall standing." The third and final phase is "coercive" and includes walling (with twenty to thirty impacts of the victim's head with the wall)[116] and stress positions combined with water dousing and insult slaps (p. 6). The culmination of the "coercive" phase is the use of the waterboard, which the memo says is limited to situations in which there is fear of an imminent attack and other methods have failed to convince the detainee to provide further information that the interrogators believe he possesses (p. 8).

ICRC Report of 2007 on "Black Sites"

This section will describe accounts of the application of the above techniques to fourteen individuals who were interviewed by the International Committee of the Red Cross after they had been transferred to Guantanamo from black sites in other countries. President Bush acknowledged the existence of the black sites in his statement of September 6, 2006, when he said that the sites were necessary to create "an environment where they [suspected terrorists] can be held secretly [and] questioned by experts" who would use "an alternative set of procedures" that "were designed to be safe, to comply with our laws, our Constitution, and our treaty obligations. The Department of Justice reviewed the authorized methods extensively and determined them to be lawful." He concluded that "The United States does not torture. It's against our laws, and it's against our values. I have not authorized it—and I will not authorize it."[117] The prisoners held at these sites were "high value," and CIA officials believed that they probably had information that might prevent future attacks on the United States.

During October 6 to 11 and from December 4 to 14, 2006, officials from the ICRC conducted interviews at Guantanamo with suspected terrorists who had been held and interrogated at the CIA black sites.[118] They wrote a report of what the accused terrorists told them about the conditions of their captivity and the abuse to which they had been subjected. The credibility of the prisoners was enhanced by the consistency of their accounts about certain techniques, even though they were all held separately and had no opportunity to communicate with each other or obtain information from the outside world.

In addition, not all of the detainees reported that they were subjected to all of the techniques. For example, only three detainees reported being waterboarded; if detainees were fabricating, it is likely that more than the three would have reported that they were waterboarded. (Before the ICRC report was made public the CIA confirmed that three detainees had been waterboarded.) The report stated: "The ICRC wishes to underscore that the consistency of the detailed allegations provided separately by each of the fourteen adds particular weight to the information provided below."[119] The table of contents provides some sense of the content of the report. The numbers in parentheses are the numbers of detainees who reported that that technique was used on them (these numbers are not in the TOC).

Introduction
1.	Main Elements of the CIA Detention Program
1.1	Arrest and Transfer
1.2	Continuous Solitary Confinement and Incommunicado Detention
1.3	Other Methods of Ill-treatment
1.3.1	Suffocation by Water (reported by three)
1.3.2	Prolonged Stress Standing (reported by ten)
1.3.3	Beatings by Use of a Collar (reported by six)
1.3.4	Beating and Kicking (reported by nine)
1.3.5	Confinement in a Box (reported by one)
1.3.6	Prolonged Nudity (reported by eleven)
1.3.7	Sleep Deprivation and Use of Loud Music (reported by eleven)
1.3.8	Exposure to Cold Temperature/Cold Water (reported by "most")
1.3.9	Prolonged Use of Handcuffs and Shackles (reported by "many")
1.3.10	Threats (reported by nine)
1.3.11	Forced Shaving (reported by two)
1.3.12	Deprivation/Restricted Provision of Solid Food (reported by eight)
1.4	Further Elements of the Detention Regime[120]

From the accounts that the prisoners gave to the ICRC, the interrogations were preceded by and interspaced with extremely uncomfortable treatment and violence. According to Abu Zubaydah, "I was taken out of my cell and one of the interrogators wrapped a towel around my neck, they then used it to swing me around and smash me repeatedly against the hard walls of the room. I was also repeatedly slapped in the face." "After the beating I was then placed in the small box. They placed a cloth or cover over the box to cut out all light and restrict my air supply. As it was not high enough even to sit upright, I had to crouch down. It was very difficult because of my wounds...." He also described waterboarding, during which a cloth was placed over his face and water poured over it, "I struggled against the straps, trying to breathe, but it was hopeless. I thought I was going to die. I lost control of my urine."[121]

Walid Bin Attash reported that he was forced to stand in his cell with his hands cuffed and held above his head (as were nine others, for various numbers of days). "I do not remember for exactly how many days I was kept standing, but I think it was about ten days.... During the standing I was made to wear a diaper. However, on some occasions the diaper was not replaced and so I had to urinate and defecate over myself. I was washed down with cold water everyday."[122]

Prolonged stress standing can have serious medical effects, far beyond temporary discomfort. An analysis of Communist interrogation techniques in 1956 reported that

> After 18 to 24 hours of continuous standing, there is an accumulation of fluid in the tissues of the legs. This dependent edema is produced by the extravasation of fluid from the blood vessels. The ankles and feet of the prisoner swell to twice their normal

circumference. The edema may rise up the legs as high as the middle of the thighs. The skin becomes tense and intensely painful. Large blisters develop, which break and exude watery serum.[123]

The prisoners also described being bombarded with extremely loud music or noise, having water thrown at them, being subjected to days of forced nudity, being kept in very cold cells, being slapped repeatedly, and being deprived of solid food and sleep. Khaled Shaik Mohammed said, "I was never threatened with death, in fact I was told that they would not allow me to die, but that I would be brought to the verge of death and back again."[124]

The interrogation of these prisoners was overseen by top CIA officials and indirectly by the National Security Council's Principals Committee. According to *ABC News* reports, "whether they would be slapped, pushed, deprived of sleep or subject to simulated drowning" was approved back in Washington. According to the reports, some of the instructions from Washington were so detailed that "some of the interrogation sessions were almost choreographed."[125]

As might be expected, not all of the forced confessions were true. Zubaydah said, "I gave a lot of false information in order to satisfy what I believed the interrogators wished to hear in order to make the ill-treatment stop.... I'm sure that the false information I was forced to invent ... wasted a lot of their time...."[126] Despite Bush administration claims that the use of harsh interrogation techniques saved lives and prevented attacks, the probable value of the interrogations involved useful information about the structure and operations of al Qaeda. Former CIA official John Kiriakou described the information that Abu Zubaydah gave the CIA.

What he was able to provide was information on the al-Qaeda leadership. For example, if bin Laden were to do X, who would be the person to undertake such and such an operation? "Oh, logically that would be Mr. Y." And we were able to use that information to kind of get an idea of how al-Qaeda operated, how it came about conceptualizing its operations, and how it went about tasking different cells with carrying out operations.... His value was, it allowed us to have somebody who we could pass ideas onto for his comments or analysis.[127]

As valuable as such intelligence is for dealing with terrorism, it is a far cry from a ticking time bomb situation.

It is likely that most of the persons held in CIA black sites were closely connected with al Qaeda or complicit in killing Americans. But one problem of using torture to try to gain information or force confessions is that once these tactics are used, it becomes much more difficult to convict guilty terrorists of crimes and put them in jail. Susan J. Crawford, who was the convening authority for military commissions at Guantanamo, felt compelled to dismiss the charges against Mohammed al-Qahtani because he had been tortured. It may be possible to reconstruct legal cases against some terrorists and carefully separate out all evidence obtained through torture, but that is a difficult task. Thus, aside from all other objections to using torture to gain intelligence, it is counterproductive to legally punishing persons guilty of war crimes.[128]

Summary of Techniques

From the preceding accounts of abuse and torture at Guantanamo, Bagram, Abu Ghraib, and CIA black sites, some of the techniques seem to have been derived from the memoranda issued by Secretary Rumsfeld on December 2, 2002, and April 16, 2003. An FBI inquiry of August 17, 2004, stated that of twenty-six summaries of mistreatment of detainees observed at Guantanamo, seventeen "were deemed to be appropriate DOD approved interrogation techniques."[129] Another memo from an FBI agent said "I know these techniques were approved at high levels w/in DoD and used on [redacted] and [redacted] ... the techniques employed against them in the interrogation process were, based on numerous inquiries I made, in addition to my personal review of the DOD interrogation plans, approved by the Deputy Secretary of Defense."[130]

Other techniques seem to be based on the SERE training for Guantanamo interrogators and in Iraq, which was based on Chinese techniques and the Biderman chart.[131] Even though the SERE techniques were not explicitly authorized in Rumsfeld's memos, SERE trainers were brought to both Guantanamo and Abu Ghraib to train interrogators in their use. This training constituted effective, authoritative policy, even if the techniques were not listed in a memo signed by the Secretary of Defense. Finally, some of the instances of torture were clearly crimes and cannot be connected with authorized techniques, but rather grew out of the atmosphere of complete control over persons who were categorized as the enemy and, through implications by President Bush and Vice President Cheney, partly responsible for the atrocities of 9/11. The CIA techniques were generally more harsh than the approved military techniques and were authorized in separate memoranda. They were based on the SERE techniques and included waterboarding, which most of the world considers to be torture.

It must be emphasized that, in contrast to the antiseptic language of legal and operational memoranda, the reality of prisoner abuse and torture is that it is very difficult to limit. As research and experiments have demonstrated, once a green light is given to a certain level of brutality, the psychology of the physical power and complete control over other persons in a penal or punitive context often leads to escalating violence. Thus the progression from the seemingly limited techniques of official policy to the brutality that occurred in these prisons was predictable. That is why careful training, strict discipline, and careful supervision is crucial in prison environments. When these factors are missing, as they were in at the U.S. interrogation facilities, instances of abuse and torture are likely to occur.

In the spring of 2006, the Army issued a revised version of its field manual FM 34–52 with a new field manual (2.22–3), *Human Intelligence Collector Operations* (September 2006). Its preface states: "In accordance with the Detainee Treatment Act of 2005, the only interrogation approaches and techniques that are authorized for use against any detainee, regardless of status or characterization, are those authorized and listed in this Field Manual." The new manual clarified the application of the Geneva Conventions: "Protected Persons: Include civilians entitled to protection under the

GC, including those we retain in the course of a conflict, no matter what the reason." Military lawyers were clearly relieved to be returning to interrogation practices in conformance with the Geneva Conventions. This return to traditional Army norms officially changed policy away from the Bush administration policies of 2001–2006. The administration maintained, however, that the CIA was not bound by the same standards as the military. On March 8, 2008, President Bush vetoed a bill that would have held the CIA to military standards for interrogation.

Waterboarding

During President Bush's second term, waterboarding came to symbolize the conflict between the Bush administration and those who thought that the United States should not engage in torture. Although waterboarding, or the "water cure," had been used for centuries, it became an iconic form of torture during the Spanish Inquisition.[132] During the Spanish American War, U.S. soldiers were prosecuted and convicted for waterboarding prisoners. After World War II, Japanese soldiers were prosecuted for war crimes, including waterboarding, and were sentenced to long jail terms at hard labor.[133] The issue of waterboarding was raised again when rumors surfaced that U.S. personnel had used the technique on suspected al Qaeda terrorists.

The rumors were reinforced after the vice president was interviewed in the White House by a reporter who asked: "Would you agree that a dunk in water [of a suspected terrorist] is a no-brainer if it can save lives?" Cheney replied: "It's a no-brainer for me ... We don't torture ... But the fact is, you can have a fairly robust interrogation program without torture, and we need to be able to do *that*. And thanks to the leadership of the President now, and the action of the Congress, we have that authority, and we are able to continue to [sic] Program." (emphasis added) Asked in another question about "dunking a terrorist in water," Cheney replied: "I do agree. And I think the terrorist threat, for example, with respect to our ability to interrogate high value detainees like Khalid Sheikh Mohammed, *that's* been a very important tool that we've had to be able to secure the nation." (emphasis added). The antecedent to the words "that" and "that's" in the vice president's statements was clearly "dunking a terrorist in water," indicating that the Bush administration did not consider waterboarding to be torture.[134] The administration was making semantic distinctions in what it considered to be the definition of torture, a line of reasoning that follows the arguments laid out in the Bybee memo of August 2002.

At the same time that the Bybee memo on torture was signed, a second memo, Bybee II, was also issued specifically to allow the CIA to use certain methods of interrogation on al Qaeda suspects. The Bybee II memo was secret, but in 2009, the Obama administration made it public.[135] The memo described waterboarding, in which a cloth is placed over the individual's mouth and nose, and water is poured over the cloth until the person cannot breathe. The Bybee II memo states that the "individual does not breathe any water into his lungs." The first Bradbury memo of May 10, 2005, however, indicated that "water may enter—and may accumulate in—the detainee's mouth and nasal cavity, preventing him from breathing. In addition ... the detainee as a countermeasure may swallow water, possibly in significant quantities (p. 13). [136] Also, "the detainee might aspirate some of the water" (p. 14). In the same memo, Footnote no. 51 (p. 41) refers to a "CIA IG (inspector general) Report" that says that "in some cases the waterboard was used with far greater frequency than initially indicated" and in a "different manner." It notes that the "waterboard technique ... was different from the technique described in the DoJ opinion and used in the SERE training." In fact, according to the Bradbury memo of May 30, 2005, Abu Zubaydah was waterboarded 83 times in August 2002, and Khalid Sheikh Mohammed was waterboarded 183 times in March 2003.[137]

Thus actual CIA application of the waterboard technique did not conform exactly to the precise language used in the legal memoranda.

The administration's claim that its practices did not amount to torture were reflected in the executive order issued by President Bush to comply with the Military Commissions Act of 2006. The executive order issued on July 20, 2007, said that MCA "reinforced" the president's authority "to interpret the meaning and application of the Geneva Conventions," including Common Article 3.[138] The order forbade the most egregious forms of torture, including actions covered in Title 18 sections 2441 and 2340, actions of violence that are "considered comparable to murder, torture, mutilation, and cruel or inhuman treatment" and "willful and outrageous acts of personal abuse *done for the purpose of* humiliating or degrading" persons (emphasis added). Using the reasoning of the August 1 Bybee memo, if acts done in the process of harsh interrogation, including waterboarding, were done for the purpose of extracting information, they would be presumably allowed.

The Bush administration continued to make its public argument that waterboarding did not amount to torture. White House spokesman Tony Fratto briefed reporters on administration policy on interrogation techniques and said that waterboarding might be used "under certain circumstances." He said that the Justice Department had "made a determination that its use under specific circumstances and with safeguards was lawful."[139] In congressional testimony in February 2008, the head of the Office of Legal Council (OLC), Steven Bradbury, explained the administration's rationalization that waterboarding did not amount to torture. An interrogation technique does not amount to torture if it is

> subject to strict safeguards, limitations and conditions, does not involve severe physical pain or severe physical suffering—and severe physical suffering, we said in our December 2004 Opinion, has to take account of both the intensity of the discomfort or distress involved, and the duration, and something can be quite distressing or uncomfortable, even frightening, [but] if it doesn't involve severe physical pain, and it doesn't last very long, it may not constitute severe physical suffering. That would be the analysis.[140]

Let us compare Bradbury's description of waterboarding with what experienced professionals and victims have said about it.

When a person is subjected to the water torture, he is strapped to a board with his hands and feet tied down. The board is then tipped so that his head is lower than his heart. The perpetrators then cover his nose and mouth with a cloth and begin to pour water on his upper lip. (In a variation, water is forced down the victim's throat.) At first, he can hold his breath and expel some of the water, but that is soon overcome and, unable to breathe, he begins to lose consciousness, unless the procedure is stopped before that.

Malcolm Nance was a master instructor and chief of training at the U.S. Navy Survival, Evasion, Resistance, and Escape (SERE) School in San Diego for the Navy SEALs. Nance personally supervised the waterboarding of "hundreds of people." He said that we live in an era in which many are "enthralled by vengeance-based fantasy television shows like *24*." Nance's training took him to the most notorious torture chambers of the world in Phnom Penh (in Cambodia), Dachau, Bergen-Belsen (in Germany), and Yad Vashem (in Jerusalem). In order to design a training program for U.S. personnel to resist torture, he read hundreds of classified accounts of torture as well as personal memoirs of prisoners throughout American history.

Nance concluded that "waterboarding is a torture technique. Period ... Waterboarding is not a simulation ... It does not simulate drowning, as the lungs are actually filling with water. There is no way to simulate that. The victim is drowning.... Usually the person goes into hysterics on the board.... When done right it is controlled death. Its lack of physical scarring allows the victim to recover and be threatened with its use again and again."[141] The personal experience is that of "slow-motion suffocation with enough time to contemplate the inevitability of blackout and expiration—usually the person goes into hysterics on the board. You can feel every drop. Every drop. You start to panic, and as you panic, you start gasping, and as you gasp, your gag reflex is overridden by water. And then you start to choke, and then you start to drown more."[142]

In 2008, journalist Christopher Hitchens agreed to have himself waterboarded in order to make an informed personal judgment about whether it was torture. Before he underwent the procedure, he had to have a medical check-up and sign a document to indemnify the administrators from legal consequences should he be injured during the process. The document stated that "waterboarding is a potentially dangerous activity in which the participant can receive *serious and permanent* (physical, emotional, and psychological) injuries and even death, including injuries and death due to the respiratory and neurological systems of the body" (emphasis added). This warning, written by the people who perform waterboarding professionally, does not make the process sound like the merely uncomfortable experience that Bradbury and other administration officials justified as not being torture.

Hitchens reported that "I fought down the first wave of water, and some of the second wave of nausea and terror but soon found that I was an abject prisoner of my gag reflex.... I would quite readily have agreed to supply any answer." Hitchens concluded that "if waterboarding does not constitute torture, then there is no such thing as torture."[143] Richard Mezo was waterboarded in survival training for Navy pilots and wrote, "The water streamed into my nose and then into my mouth when I gasped for breath. I couldn't stop it. All I could breathe was water, and it was terrifying." Even though his mind knew that he was in training and that his trainers would not let him die, "my body sensed and reacted to the danger it was in."[144]

The U.S. criminal code (section 2340(2)(c) of title 18) includes as torture "the threat of imminent death," and waterboarding must qualify as a very effective death threat. The victim is convinced that he is in the process of dying. Even if interrogators say that they will stop pouring the water when the victim is ready to talk, the victim's nervous system overcomes any rational thought, and his body reacts as if it were going to die. Thus, regardless of what the perpetrators say, the threat of death is very convincing physical reality to the person being waterboarded. Experiencing a near death must be as threatening to an individual as a mere verbal threat of death.

The Bybee II memo of August 1, 2002, acknowledged this when it stated: "We find that the use of the waterboard constitutes a threat of imminent death."[145] Nevertheless it concluded that waterboarding was not torture: "Although the waterboard constitutes a threat of imminent death, prolonged mental harm must nonetheless result to violate the statutory prohibition on infliction of severe mental pain or suffering." Steven Bradbury, in his first memo of May 10, 2005, discussing waterboarding, asserts that "There may be few more frightening experiences than feeling that one is unable to breathe." But, Bradbury concludes "however frightening the experience may be, OSM personnel have informed us that the waterboard technique is not physically painful."[146] Since waterboarding, in the judgment of Bradbury, "could not reasonably be considered specifically intended to cause severe physical or mental pain or suffering," it would not be torture under the torture statute.

John McCain, who had experienced real torture in North Vietnam, had no hesitation in stating that waterboarding is torture. "It is not a complicated procedure. It is torture."[147] In the Republican primary campaign of 2008 McCain asserted: "It's [waterboarding] in violation of the Geneva Convention. It's in violation of existing laws." He and Senator Lindsey Graham (R, SC) wrote a letter to Attorney General Mukasey, saying that it is "beyond dispute that waterboarding 'shocks the conscience.'"[148] The Judge Advocates Generals of the armed forces considered waterboarding to be torture and a violation of Common Article 3 of the Geneva Conventions.[149]

In December 2007, thirty retired generals and admirals signed a letter to the chairs of the Senate and House intelligence committees, urging the passage of Section 327 of the Conference Report on the Intelligence Authorization Act for Fiscal Year 2008, H.R. 2082. The act would have required the CIA to conform to the same standards of interrogation that the Armed Forces had to comply with after the field manual on interrogation (FM 2–22.3) was rewritten in 2006, which explicitly outlawed any violation of the Geneva Conventions. They argued that conformance with Geneva would help "maintain the integrity of the humane treatment standards on which our own troops rely." They concluded that the use of harsh techniques, such as waterboarding, "does immense damage to the reputation and moral authority of the United States essential to our efforts to combat terrorism. This is a defining issue for America."[150] The bill was passed by the House and Senate, and in 2008 President Bush vetoed it.

In 2008, CIA Director Michael Hayden admitted that the CIA had used waterboarding on three "high-value" detainees: Abu Zubaydah, Abd al-Rahim al-Nashiri, and Khalid Sheikh Mohammed (KSM). He argued in a congressional hearing that waterboarding was not illegal and that the option to use it should be available to the CIA.[151] He said that the technique "led to reliable information," but that he had stopped the CIA from using the practice in 2006.[152]

When President Obama took office, one of the first official actions was to order the CIA to comply with Common Article 3 of the Geneva Conventions and to use only those techniques specified in the Army Field Manual on Interrogations (2–22.3 2006).[153] Waterboarding is not allowed by the Army Field Manual.

Extraordinary Rendition

One of the problems that President Bush foresaw after 9/11 was that captured (suspected) terrorists might be able to resist interrogation practices that U.S. interrogators were allowed to use. In talking with Prince Bandar of Saudi Arabia two days after the 9/11 attacks, President Bush suggested a solution to the problem that foreshadowed the practice of extraordinary rendition. In talking about captured terrorists on September 13, 2001, he said to Prince Bandar, "if we get somebody and we can't get them to cooperate, we'll hand them over to you."[154]

The practice of rendition is common in international relations. Regular rendition occurs when a government delivers an individual to another government through a legal process pursuant to treaty agreements. The person is turned over to authorities in the receiving country for regular judicial proceedings and trial. In the United States it is established law that in order to render a person to a foreign government, the president needs authority granted by a treaty or law. In 1936 the Supreme Court declared that "there is no executive discretion to surrender [a person] to a foreign government, unless that discretion is granted by law."[155] In 1979 the Office of Legal Counsel of the Department of Justice took up the question of whether the United States could extradite the deposed Shah of Iran. It concluded that "the President cannot order any person extradited unless a treaty or statute authorizes him to."[156] Until the Bush administration, no president has claimed the unilateral authority, absent a treaty agreement, to render individuals to foreign countries.[157]

For most of U.S. history, renditions were routinely carried out according to law and for the purpose of handing over a fugitive to a foreign country so that the judicial process in that country could take action. In the late twentieth century, the United States also occasionally abducted persons for "renditions to justice," that is, to bring them to trial in the United States or another country, such as the capture of Antonio Noriega in Panama by U.S. forces in 1989.[158] FBI Director Louis Freeh said that in the 1990s the United States conducted thirteen successful renditions of international terrorists to U.S. courts. After 9/11, the scale and regularity of extraordinary renditions exploded. According to Cofer Black, head of counterterrorism for the CIA, while testifying in Congress: "All you need to know is that there was a 'before 9/11' and there was an 'after 9/11.' After 9/11, the gloves came off."[159]

Renditions designed not to bring the suspect into a judicial process but rather for purposes of interrogation became known as extraordinary renditions; that is, outside of a legal process. "Extraordinary rendition" occurs when a country, in this case, the United States, turns over an individual to non-judicial authorities in another country, usually with the expectation that the individual will be interrogated and maybe tortured in order to obtain intelligence information.[160]

The practice of extraordinary rendition developed in the United States in the 1980s and 1990s when the United States made an agreement with Egypt that the CIA would locate and abduct terrorists wanted by Egypt and return them to Egypt. Although this process was at the margins of legality, it was seen as legitimate because the suspected terrorists were wanted by Egypt and the United States was merely apprehending them for the Egyptian government. After 9/11, however, the practice was often used by the U.S. government to send terrorist suspects who were resistant to U.S. interrogation techniques to Egypt and other countries where they could be interrogated by harsher methods. Jane Mayer has termed this practice "outsourcing torture."[161] After 9/11, the Bush administration conducted what has been estimated as 100 to 150 extraordinary renditions to countries reported by the State Department to be frequent perpetrators of torture, including Syria, Saudi Arabia, Yemen, Morocco, Jordan, and Egypt.[162]

One problem with extraordinary rendition is that it is forbidden by Article 3 of the U.N. Convention Against Torture (CAT): "No State Party shall expel, return ("refouler") or extradite a person to another State where there are substantial grounds for believing that he would be in danger of being subjected to torture."[163] In implementing CAT, Congress in 1998 passed the Foreign Affairs Reform and Restructuring Act of 1998, and stated that it is the policy of the United States "not to expel, extradite, or otherwise effect the involuntary return of any person to a country in which there are substantial grounds for believing the person would be in danger of being subjected to torture, regardless of whether the person is physically present in the United States."[164]

Robert Baer, who worked on the Middle East for the CIA for twenty-one years before retiring, said that the Syrians had offered to work with the United States, and "at least until 11 September these offers were turned down. We generally avoided the Egyptians and the Syrians because they were so brutal." According to Baer, after 9/11 the United States rendered hundreds of prisoners to Middle East countries; he said it was the end of "our rule of law as we knew it in the West."[165]

Bush administration officials, when asked about extraordinary rendition of terrorist suspects to countries like Syria or Egypt, claimed that they received assurances that the prisoners would not be tortured. After U.S. extraordinary rendition flights had been exposed in the press, President Bush said in January 2005 that "torture is never acceptable, nor do we hand over people to *countries that do torture*."[166] Several months later, in April 2005, he had changed his wording: "We operate within the law, and we send people to countries where *they say they're not going* to torture the people" (emphasis added in both cases).[167] The change in wording seems to have been a significant revision of the claim of the administration.

Those countries to which the United States rendered suspected terrorists were primarily Egypt, Syria, Saudi Arabia, Jordan, Morocco, and Yemen; all of these states were identified by the State Department as using torture. In a 2003 report, the State Department said that in Egypt those interrogated were

stripped and blindfolded; suspended from a ceiling or door frame with feet just touching the floor; beaten with fists, whips, metal rods, or other objects; subjected to electrical shocks; and doused with cold water. Victims frequently reported being subjected to threats and forced to sign blank papers for use against the victim or the victim's family in the future should the victim complain of abuse. Some victims, including male and female detainees and children reported that they were sexually assaulted or threatened with rape themselves or of family members.[168]

Assurances by other countries that the rendered suspects would not be tortured were often not taken seriously by U.S. officials. Edward Walker, who was U.S. Ambassador to Egypt, told Stephen Grey, "I can't say to you with any candour (sic) that there was anything more than the verbal assurance, or even a written assurance. There was very little effort to follow up on that."[169] According to Michael Scheuer, who ran renditions for the CIA in the 1990s, "No one was kidding anyone here. We knew exactly what that kind of promise was worth."[170]

One case of extraordinary rendition that backfired was that of Ibn al-Sheikh al Libi. Al Libi was captured by Pakistani forces who turned him over to the CIA, who then rendered him to Egypt. While in Egypt he confessed to having worked with Iraqis to learn about chemical and biological weapons. But as it turned out, his confession was false as reported by the Defense Intelligence Agency (DIA) in the spring of 2002. Nevertheless, President Bush used his false confession in his October 7, 2002, war speech to the nation (for details and citations, see Chapter Four).[171] Thus President Bush used Libi's false confession (due to torture) to convince the U.S. public that Iraq was a threat to the United States and to justify the invasion of Iraq.[172]

In 2003, a CIA kidnapping team abducted a Muslim cleric known as Abu Omar and rendered him to Egypt, where he was tortured. At the Italian trial of the twenty-six CIA agents (in absentia) and Italian officials who helped them, Omar's wife said that when he returned from Egypt he was "wasted" and "skinny." "He was tied up like he was being crucified. He was beat up, especially around his ears. She testified that he was subjected to electroshocks to many body parts," including his genitals. Italian law enforcement authorities were upset at the CIA actions because they had been building a criminal case against Omar and would not be able to prosecute him because of the Egyptian torture.[173]

Another case of extraordinary rendition characterized "the wrong man" problem (which will be analyzed in Chapter Four). A Canadian citizen of Syrian origin, Maher Arar, was transferring planes at Kennedy International Airport in New York City in September 2002. U.S. officials were pursuing a Canadian official's mistaken report that Arar was a terrorist. Arar was tortured by the Syrians for ten months and forced to sign false confessions before he was released when it became apparent that it was a case of mistaken identity. The false confessions of these people illustrate the problem of obtaining truth through torture.

A committee of the New York Bar Association specified and documented ten examples of extraordinary rendition that resulted in torture.[174] Overall, the best estimates are that the United States rendered between one hundred and two hundred captives to other countries for purposes of interrogation.[175]

When Michael Hayden took direction of the CIA in 2006, he indicated that CIA policy had changed. He said that in order to render a person to another country, "we have to receive assurances—and we have to have confidence in the assurances—that this individual will be handled in a way that is consistent with international law.... We have to believe that it is less rather than more likely that the individual will be tortured."[176]

Conclusion

From the above U.S. government reports of detainee abuse, it is clear that many of the abusive practices and torture of detainees by U.S. personnel had their roots in formal policy choices made by Bush administration officials and in the operational decisions they made to implement those policies. Personnel choices consciously reinforced the policy choices. General Baccus left Guantanamo because he adhered closely to the Geneva rules. General Miller replaced Dunlavey because, despite his lack of intelligence experience, he was seen as someone who would get the job done. In Iraq, General Karpinski was then replaced by General Miller because he had demonstrated his willingness to be harsh on detainees at Guantanamo. At Abu Ghraib, Miller told soldiers to treat detainees "like dogs" and insisted that the military police assist military intelligence in order to "set the conditions" for interrogations.

Some of the interrogation techniques used by U.S. personnel came from the Army Field Manual 34–52 (1992) and were compatible with the Geneva Conventions. But when these techniques did not produce the "actionable intelligence" demanded by those at the top of the chain of command, Secretary of Defense Rumsfeld authorized a range of alternative techniques in December of 2002 and April of 2003. In addition, the Office of the Secretary of Defense requested information on SERE training and how those techniques, derived from Chinese and Russian techniques for extracting false confessions, could be used on detainees. SERE trainers subsequently visited Guantanamo personnel and Abu Ghraib interrogators to teach them how to "break" detainees.

Many of the instances of abuse and torture stemmed directly from the policies, instructions, and personnel decisions that came down the chain of command. The authorized methods of interrogation were harsh enough, but in the hands of young, inexperienced, undertrained, and stressed-out interrogators, those techniques were driven beyond even the brutality that was intended by policymakers. Beyond that, many of the actions of U.S. guards constituted criminal behavior and were not based in any policy directive, but were condoned by the permissive atmosphere and the failure of military leaders to end the abuse. The behavior of some U.S. personnel got so out of control that a good portion of the many deaths of detainees in U.S. custody were deemed homicides by military investigators. A permissive command climate, as documented in the military investigations, contributed to the abuse and torture.

As documented in this chapter, however, a significant number of career professionals in the government objected to the treatment of detainees at Guantanamo and Abu Ghraib. FBI agents recoiled at the harsh treatment of detainees, not only because it was not effective at eliciting intelligence but also because it was illegal and immoral. Civilian intelligence professionals working for DOD reported to their superiors the questionable actions of the young interrogators at Guantanamo. Military lawyers registered their judgments that abandoning the Geneva Conventions and U.S. law was harmful to the national security interests of the United States and the safety of our own troops. Alberto Mora and Anthony Taguba effectively ended their military careers by speaking truth to power. So it cannot be said that the Bush administration had no warnings about the dangerous direction in which their policies were leading. Finally, the top levels of the Bush administration, meeting in the White House itself, specifically authorized torture techniques to be used on selected detainees. President Bush said publicly that he was aware of the meetings and approved of their actions. There can be no credible argument that the Bush administration did not have a policy of torture that was ratified from the president down the chain of command to the enlisted personnel who perpetrated the torture.

CHAPTER 4

The Logic of Torture

Moral and Behavioral Issues

On the question of so-called 'torture,' we don't do torture, we never have. It's not something this administration subscribes to ... that program ... was authorized and that it was legal. And any suggestion to the contrary is just wrong.

— Vice President Cheney[1]

As has happened with every other nation that has tried to engage in a little bit of torture— only for the toughest cases, only when nothing else works—the abuse spread like wildfire, and every captured prisoner became the key to defusing a potential ticking time bomb. Our soldiers in Iraq confront real "ticking time bomb" situations every day, in the form of improvised explosive devices, and any degree of "flexibility" about torture at the top drops down the chain of command like a stone—the rare exception fast becoming the rule.

— Former Marine Commandant Charles Krulak and Marine General Joseph P. Hoar[2]

Accuracy in torture is exceedingly poor.... The Battle of Algiers is a textbook illustration. ... We find only two instances in which one could say torture generated true, critically timely information....

— Darius Rejali, author of *Torture and Democracy*[3]

In considering whether to use torture as a means of interrogation, two questions must be answered: is it morally justified, and does it work? If either of these questions is answered in the negative, torture is not an appropriate public policy. This section will first take up the logic of torture. That is, what justification could a modern, liberal democracy provide that would lead to a public policy of torture? The most common justification that has been proffered in contemporary America involves the "ticking time bomb" scenario, which will be examined in the first section of the chapter. But even if one were to conclude that torture was morally justified, the question remains: does it work? That is, will torture as a technique extract the essential intelligence that might be held by a prisoner?

Even if one concluded that torture is morally justified and sometimes effective, once begun, torture is very difficult to control and has corrosive effects on the society that condones it. These effects must be considered in making a decision about making torture public policy. Finally, in order for torture to be useful in gathering intelligence, the detainee must have the information sought; if he doesn't, torture will not help. The final section of the chapter will take up cases in the U.S. war on terror in which the person detained was not the person he was thought to be or was innocent of any wrongdoing: the "wrong man problem."

The Logic of Torture

Throughout history, governments have used torture for a number of purposes. Torture has been used to intimidate enemies. Public torture or well-known secret torture sends a message: if you resist us, this may happen to you. U.S. officials, in refusing to divulge interrogation techniques, ostensibly so that terrorists could not prepare to resist them, also send the message: if you are captured by Americans, terrible things could happen to you. So think twice about fighting the United States.

Torture can also be used as punishment for someone who has committed so terrible a crime that torture is deemed appropriate punishment. When detainees misbehaved in U.S. prison camps, they were sometimes restrained in painful positions, put in solitary confinement, or put in cold cells without clothes or blankets to keep themselves warm. In 2006, Abdul Hamid al-Ghizzawi (Detainee 654 at Guantanamo), who was turned over to the Americans in Afghanistan for a bounty and thought to be a terrorist, took some toilet paper with him to a shower; it was in his pocket, which was against the rules. For this infraction of the rules, he was put into an orange jumpsuit to indicate that he was a troublemaker, and sent to Camp Six for solitary confinement. His thermal shirt was taken away, and when his lawyer visited him, he was ill and shivering and had been in isolation for two months.[4] Such punishments might be considered torture or abuse, but the clear intent was to punish individuals for their behavior. (Of course, these same techniques were often used to "soften up" detainees before interrogation.)

Exacting revenge is also a common purpose of torture, and the atrocities of 9/11 certainly motivated some U.S. soldiers to treat detainees very harshly in the belief that the person had some connection with the terrorist attacks on the United States. Even in Iraq, which had nothing to do with 9/11 and was covered by the Geneva Conventions, soldiers were led to believe that they were acting in response to 9/11. In these circumstances, revenge might likely motivate some interrogators. Revenge for the deaths of their comrades killed by improvised explosive devices (IEDs) was also a common factor in the mistreatment of detainees in Iraq.

Officially, however, U.S. policy justified abuse of prisoners as a means to obtain intelligence that might help the United States stop another terrorist attack. The question is, was there any alternative way to obtain intelligence that did not involve the types of techniques authorized by U.S. leaders? Why use abuse that could amount to torture if other approaches to intelligence might accomplish the same goal? Why not take the time to use conventional means of intelligence? The most common answer in the U.S. debate over the use of torture has been the assertion that if time is short and many deaths will occur if certain information is not obtained, then torture is morally justified. This rationalization of torture will be examined next.

The Ticking Time Bomb Scenario

The most popular argument that torture may be necessary as a tactic is the "ticking time bomb" scenario. Blanket condemnations of torture are often countered with a hypothetical situation in which a captive knows where a time bomb has been hidden and refuses to divulge the information.[5] In such a case, the argument goes, torture would be necessary in order to save many innocent lives and thus be justified.

This seductive scenario was popularized in the television program 24, in which intrepid terror fighter Jack Bauer foiled weekly fictional attempts to kill Americans with deadly weapons. Frequently he was forced to resort to extreme measures (and the torture is often graphically depicted) to get the bad guy to cough up the answers to his questions, which leads to saving innocent lives in the nick of time. Bauer is always the patriotic hero and his brutal means were always necessary to save the day.[6] The secretary of Homeland Security, Michael Chertoff, lent the prestige of his office to the message of the TV program by visiting the actors when they were filming an episode in Washington, D.C.[7] The program was also a source of "creative" ideas for the interrogators at Guantanamo in the summer of 2002.

The American public may be convinced that such situations are often encountered by U.S. law enforcement, anti-terrorism, and military officials. But the reality is that rarely, if ever, do such situations occur in real life. Even the creator of the show, Bob Cochran, conceded: "Most terrorism experts will tell you that the 'ticking time bomb' situation never occurs in real life, or very rarely. But on this show it happens every week."[8] The show is so compelling that the dean of the U.S. Military Academy at West Point, Brigadier General Patrick Finnegan, went to see its creators in California to ask them to tone things down a bit. Military cadets were so enamored of the show that it was difficult to get them to accept the professional military doctrine on the rule of law and the laws of war. Finnegan said: "I'd like them to stop. They should do a show where torture backfires."[9]

One problem with the ticking time bomb scenario is that no one has presented an actual case of a bomb being deactivated as a result of torturing an individual who knew where it was.[10] If there was, there are many apologists for torture who would make a big deal out of the case. Of course, people have given up intelligence information under torture; but that is not part of the scenario. Outside the scenario, torture becomes just another means to acquire tactical intelligence (what might happen in the near future) or strategic intelligence (e.g., structure of the enemy chain of command). Justifying torture for such tactical or strategic purposes would be a much more difficult case to argue, and few proponents of torture try. The Bush administration did, however, list such information as part of the "success" of harsh interrogations.

The type of intelligence necessary to justify torture in a ticking bomb scenario is very difficult to come by; and if one had it, one would likely have enough information to thwart the bomb plot without using torture. To engage in torture without the certain knowledge of a bomb and the specific time frame before it goes off, one would have to torture based on the mere possibility that the captive might know the location of a possible bomb.

The ticking time bomb scenario is a hypothetical that is often used to distinguish between a Kantian, absolutist argument against torture and a utilitarian perspective, which weighs the costs and benefits of using torture. Once a person has conceded that it might be acceptable to torture one individual in order to save thousands, the proponents of torture say that torture is acceptable in principle, if the right circumstances exist; and those circumstances usually involve a ticking bomb scenario or planned attack. Charles Krauthammer argues that torture, though "terrible and degrading," is acceptable in principle in a ticking time bomb scenario (short fuse or long fuse, in his terms). He dismisses as naïve anyone who holds to a Kantian position of "no-torture absolutism" as indulging in "moral foolishness, tinged with moral vanity." Krauthammer illustrates the ticking time bomb scenario with a hypothetical terrorist who knows where a suicide bomber is about to strike or a car bomb to go off. Krauthammer would allow only professionals to conduct the torture, "specialized agents who are experts and experienced in interrogation."[11] They would have to obtain written permission to use torture, and would be subject to oversight. His position on the institutionalization of torture is similar to the argument by Alan Dershowitz that the use of torture in interrogation should be authorized by "torture warrants."[12] Dershowitz frames the scenario this way: "Is there anybody who wouldn't use torture to save the life of his child? And if you would, isn't it a bit selfish to say, 'It's okay to save my child's life, but it's not okay to save the life of 1,000 strangers?' That's the way people will think about it."[13] Dershowitz uses this unlikely hypothetical to justify an official policy, enacted in law, that would specify the conditions under which a torture warrant would be issued.

The ticking bomb scenario, however, becomes less seductive the more carefully the premises upon which such a scenario rests are examined.[14] *First,* there must be a planned attack. Intelligence officials must be aware of the planned attack and know that it will inevitably happen unless certain specific information about it is obtained quickly. If it is only *probable* that an attack *might* occur, it is much more difficult to justify torture in order to find out if there might be an attack planned. In the war on terror, U.S. officials did not know for certain that there was another planned attack. Expecting that another attack would probably occur some time in the future does not meet the ticking bomb scenario. Most military enemies will be planning for some attack at some time in the future.

Second, intelligence officials must have captured a person who certainly knows sufficient details about the planned attack. Merely capturing a member of the enemy forces is no guarantee that he has information about any specific attack. If one speculates that any high-level member of the enemy *might* have the information, it could lead to a lot of torture with no guarantee that torture would be fruitful. Terrorists may be clever enough to compartmentalize information so that few people know the details of possible future attacks.

Third, given the justification for torture presented in this scenario, torture must be the only way to obtain the information. As discussed below, it is not certain that torture is the most effective way to educe information. Many very experienced interrogators see torture as an ineffective and often counterproductive means of interrogation. In U.S. prosecution of terrorists, FBI nonviolent techniques have been effective in obtaining intelligence.

Fourth, the captive must provide accurate information. If the time frame is truly short enough to justify torture according to the ticking bomb scenario, the terrorist would only have to hold out for a relatively short period of time to ensure that the bomb would go off. Alternatively, the captured terrorist might creatively invent plausible locations for the bomb that would lead the captors on wild goose chases, and of course they would all have to be checked out in case one of them was accurate. Would it be morally justified to continue to torture the captive while a location was checked out? As recent social science analysis has shown, it is not possible to detect lies with any level of certainty.[15]

Although some terrorists may deceive in a purposeful way, some detainees will make up any answer just to get the pain to stop. Alternatively, the terrorist may have been purposefully provided with incorrect information in case he were to be captured.

Finally, if the correct information is obtained, there must be both the time and means to defuse the bomb. It is entirely possible that the design of the bomb could be so clever that any attempt to defuse it would cause it to explode.

If any one of these premises is absent, torture will not solve the problem. Thus even if one posits that torture could be justified in order to save innocent lives, as in the ticking bomb scenario, most torture scenarios are ruled out. The further a situation is removed from the ticking bomb scenario, the less compelling would be the justification of torture.

Another problem with the ticking time bomb scenario is that the scenario is used to make an argument that torture is justified at the "retail" level; that is, in an individual case in which torture would certainly reveal a clever plot that would be foiled by using torture to interrogate a villain. The problem is that this type of argument about one case is used then to justify torture at a "wholesale" level. That is, when faced with widespread instances of torture, apologists will bring up the ticking bomb scenario and imply that the cases of torture must be justified because they probably were used only in such extreme situations. In a speech on September 15, 2006, President Bush asserted that the results of harsh interrogation by U.S. personnel discovered "information about terrorist plans we couldn't get anywhere else; this program has saved innocent lives."[16] He was arguing that, in a general way, torture gave the United States useful intelligence. This is a far cry from the ticking time bomb scenario.

Even if one admits the hypothetical possibility of a genuine ticking time bomb situation, it does not follow that there should be a governmental policy that allows the use of torture in such situations. One might posit the possibility that a person might legitimately resort to torture in a case in which all of the criteria of the ticking time bomb scenario are met. Since torture is illegal in the United States, the torturer would be vulnerable to prosecution and punishment. But if the person is to be legally punished, a prosecutor must first charge the person, a trial must be held, and a jury (or judge) must convict the person and impose a sentence. If the defendant makes a compelling argument that torture was the only way to prevent the deaths of others, it is doubtful that he would be prosecuted, and if he were, it is doubtful that he would be convicted. A parallel would be murder: U.S. laws do not sanction murder. Yet there is a variety of circumstances under which killing a person might be justified or excused. But the law still forbids murder. Similarly, if torture remains against the law, a person in a genuine ticking time bomb situation could use the defense of necessity and most likely not be punished for his actions. Enshrining torture in the law would lead to a range of problems that are discussed below.

Practical Difficulties

Even if it were conceded that in a genuine ticking time bomb situation torture might be justified to obtain specific information that would almost certainly save innocent lives, most real-life situations do not conform to the ticking bomb scenario. In his justification of the abuse of detainees at Guantanamo and by the CIA, President Bush and other administration officials have often asserted that the interrogation results saved lives. This significantly loosens the criteria specified in the ticking time bomb scenario. If "saving lives" were to justify the use of torture, then torture would be justified in many, if not most, tactical military situations. After all, any captured enemy soldier *might* know when a future attack might occur or where an IED might be hidden. This justification would thus lead to routine torture of enemy captives in many military combat situations. That is why the Lieber Code and Geneva Conventions were created: to prevent torture from becoming acceptable, routine conduct during war.

This likely justification for the use of torture to extract tactical information is the reason that rules of warfare have developed over the centuries and why the United States is a party to the Geneva Conventions. The generally accepted rules of warfare thus forbid torture and provide for the humane treatment of enemy captives. Without these rules, all armed forces would be vulnerable to torture if captured by the enemy; therefore all sides have a stake in limiting the use of torture. Even if one side (e.g., al Qaeda) does not adhere to the rules of Geneva, the abandonment of the prohibitions of torture undermines the broader international agreements prohibiting torture. It is not difficult for any nation to label as terrorism any independence movement or threat to the ruling coalition. The abandonment of Geneva by President Bush has allowed China and Russia to use the terrorism label to justify putting down internal dissent. The United States, if it uses the threat of terrorism to justify torture, is thus left with little moral authority to condemn such practices in other countries.

The ticking bomb scenario clearly did not apply with respect to Abu Ghraib, since the detainees were Iraqis who did not have knowledge of future planned attacks on the United States by al Qaeda. Although some detainees were involved with the insurgency, many were ordinary criminals, and some were innocent civilians detained by mistake. What the U.S. interrogators seemed to want was tactical intelligence about the Iraqi insurgency, assuming that the detainees had such information and that it would help U.S. forces tactically suppress the insurgency and avoid casualties.

In addition to the above requisites of the ticking bomb justification for torture, there are very real practical difficulties. When one thinks of a desperate scenario involving danger to loved ones or even innocent strangers, one is likely to embrace any type of torture that will save the people in jeopardy. But the public debate about torture in the United States is not about what you or I would do in an extreme situation; it is about what is appropriate public policy.[17]

For it is not you or I who would be doing the torture; it would be some set of professional torturers. Presidents and generals do not torture; they delegate it to subordinates, usually those far below them in the hierarchy. One problem with this is that the people who do the torturing in a military situation are likely to be low-status people, perhaps who have been self-selected because they enjoy it. Such people might not have the requisite skill to do a good job. They might cause the victim to lose consciousness or even die before they learned of the supposed bomb. Given the time limits posited in the ticking bomb scenario, the torture would have to be effective quickly; if more time were available, more effective means of interrogation might work better, and torture would not be necessary. The implication here is that a country would have to train professional torturers in order to administer it effectively. This and other likely drawbacks to torture will be taken up later in the chapter.

Another realistic problem with the scenario is that such bombs are likely to be planted only by committed terrorists, and such people are likely to anticipate being tortured if caught. Thus a rational terrorist would likely minimize the time between setting the fuse and its explosion, even if it entails danger to himself. Indeed, the popularity of suicide bombers as a tactic of terrorism shows that the scenario of the ticking bomb is less likely to occur. The committed terrorist would probably be willing to endure torture and able to delay his confession for a least a while. In addition, he might use the ploy of giving incorrect locations to his captors, as described above.

Summing up the record of the use of torture to discover ongoing plots, Darius Rajali, who has written one of the most comprehensive books on modern torture methods, concludes that "accuracy in torture is exceedingly poor.... The Battle of Algiers is a textbook illustration ... we find only two instances in which one could say torture generated true, critically timely information.... "[18]

The Efficacy of Torture: Does It Work?

One of the key elements of the ticking time bomb scenario is the ability to get a person to divulge crucial information to save innocent lives. While there is a wide range of interrogation techniques, from seemingly friendly trickery to the most extreme infliction of pain, the results are mixed.[19] There is no doubt that torture can force people to talk in some cases; the question is whether they are telling the truth. The ability of professional interrogators to detect lies is very limited, especially with the type of inexperienced interrogators who worked at Guantanamo in 2002. Interrogation using torture is also specific to individual victims and interrogators; approaches that work with some people do not work with others.[20] Willie J. Rowell, an Army Criminal Investigation Division (C.I.D.) agent for thirty-six years, is dubious, "They'll tell you what you want to hear, truth or not truth."[21] The next two sections will examine the question of efficacy from the perspectives first of the military and then the CIA.

Military Experience

The Army Field Manual (FM 34–52, 1992) on interrogations stated: "Army interrogation experts view the use of force as an inferior technique that yields information of questionable quality. The primary concerns, in addition to the effect on information quality, are the adverse effect on future interrogations and the behavioral change on those being interrogated."[22] Several concrete examples illustrate the problems with taking confessions induced by torture at face value. When John McCain was in captivity in Hanoi, his torturers wanted him to divulge the names of others in his squadron. McCain gave them the names of the offensive line of the Green Bay Packers. There is no reason to believe that members of al Qaeda are not capable of the same sort of deception.[23]

According to Dan Coleman, a retired FBI agent who worked closely with the CIA for ten years on terrorism directed against the United States, the FBI approach to interrogation was to treat detainees civilly, develop a rapport with them, and induce them to talk about their activities. Coleman and other professional interrogators argue that this technique is more effective than torture, and importantly, it allows the evidence obtained to be used in trials to convict the detainees and their accomplices. CIA agents and inexperienced military interrogators at Guantanamo, however, were impatient with these lengthy tactics, and wanted to move quickly to harsh and coercive techniques.[24]

Three British detainees at Guantanamo (the "Tipton Three") said that they were tortured in order to force them to "confess" that they were in a video with Osama bin Laden in 2000. They denied that they were the persons in the film, but said that they confessed to stop the pain and ill treatment. Torturing prisoners to "confess" is even less defensible than revenge as a rationalization and is reminiscent of the worst of Soviet prisons and the Grand Inquisition. British intelligence later produced evidence that the accused men were in Britain at the time the video was made, and thus could not have been photographed with bin Laden.[25]

In December of 2006, a 374-page report of the Intelligence Science Board called into question the efficacy of torture in gaining accurate information. After an exhaustive review of the evidence and scientific literature, the Board concluded that there is little evidence that torture can produce truthful answers to questions and that torture might even inhibit gaining intelligence. In the words of Colonel Steven M. Kleinman, who was a member of the study team and had been one of the military's senior officers on intelligence and survival training, "The scientific community has never established that coercive interrogation methods are an effective means of obtaining reliable intelligence information."[26] One author, Robert Coulam, concluded that "there is little systematic knowledge available to tell us 'what works' in interrogation."[27] Another author, Randy Borum, wrote: "There is little or no research to indicate whether [coercive] techniques succeed.... [B]ut the preponderance of reports seems to weigh against their effectiveness.... Psychological theory ... and related research suggest that coercion or pressure can actually *increase* a source's resistance and determination not to comply." (emphasis in the original)[28]

Torture as a source of accurate information is problematic for a number of reasons. First, not all people respond to pain in similar ways. For some, merely the anticipation of torture will get them to confess to anything in order to avoid it. Truly committed enemies may be able to endure extreme pain without divulging information. And, as the Kubark Manual warns, "torture may intensify, rather than weaken, the resistance of the prisoner."[29] Also, pain is not scalable; it is not experienced in easily measurable or detectable units, so it is difficult to judge the intensity of pain in different people. There is also the reality that as a body becomes more damaged, it becomes desensitized to pain; so pain must be administered very carefully.[30] Unconsciousness will defeat the purpose of inflicting increasing levels of pain, and death of the victim precludes any chance of obtaining further information. Under time pressure, pain has to be maximized before the victim passes out or dies. As the CIA lawyer told the trainees at Guantanamo, "If the detainee dies, you're doing it wrong."[31]

Darius Regali argues that torture as a means of eliciting truthful information is most often not successful. He maintains that there are "three different sources of error that systematically and unavoidably corrupt information gathered through torture. These are deceptive, but actionable information given by uncooperative or innocent prisoners; the well-documented weakness of most interrogators for spotting deception; and mistaken, but high-confidence, information offered by cooperative prisoners after torture."[32] Don Dzagulones was an interrogator who was involved with the torture of individuals captured during the Vietnam War. When asked if the torture was successful in obtaining useful intelligence, he said:

> If it happened, I'm certainly not aware of it. Like prisoner X comes in, you beat the living snot out of him. He tells you about a Viet Cong ambush that is going to happen tomorrow, you relay this information to the infantry guys, and a counter-ambush and the goods guys win and the bad guys lose all because you tortured a prisoner. Never happened. Not to my knowledge.[33]

The U.S. experience using harsh interrogation methods in the war on terror has not been notably successful. For instance, according to a DOD report, Mohammed al Qahtani implicated thirty people whom he said were Osama Bin Laden's bodyguards. But according to the report, al Qahtani was subjected to sleep deprivation, sensory deprivation, sexual humiliation, intimidation by dogs, and interrogation for seven weeks for twenty hours a day.[34] Obviously, it is reasonable to infer that a person subjected to such prolonged and intense torture might say things that were not true in order to please his torturers or that he might attest to dubious assertions out of exhaustion or delirium. In May of 2008, the United States dropped charges against al-Qahtani (the so-called twentieth hijacker), probably because his statements were gained under extreme duress.

Matthew Alexander, a military officer who "conducted more than 300 investigations and supervised more than 1000" in Iraq, argues that the harsh abuse approach to interrogations is vastly inferior to the rapport-building approach he used to interrogate successfully a number of high-value captives. He testified that the abusive approach acts as a recruiter of terrorists and suicide bombers; it makes the United States look like hypocrites; and it makes it more likely that enemy fighters will fight to the death because they expect that they will be tortured if they are taken prisoner by Americans. He argued that even in a ticking time bomb situation, which he encountered in Iraq with suicide bombers, a relationship-building approach is superior and does not have to be time-consuming. Among other successes, his approach enabled him to turn a high-level detainee who led U.S. forces to capture Abu Masab al-Zarqawi.[35]

The CIA and Efficacy

In 2001, Ibn al-Shaykh al-Libi, who was thought to be a high-level al Qaeda operative, was captured in Afghanistan. An FBI agent, Jack Cloonan, began to interrogate him, and was making progress in gaining information on al Qaeda training camps in Afghanistan. The FBI said that al Libi did give them enough information to foil a plot to bomb the U.S. embassy in Yemen.[36] But CIA agents became impatient and rendered him to Egypt where he was severely tortured and confessed to training Iraqis in the use of poisons and gas to kill large numbers of people. But the Defense Intelligence Agency became suspicious of his story because al Libi could not specify the places he had met with the Iraqis, the names of the people he dealt with, or the types of weapons he discussed.[37] Consequently, in February of 2002, the DIA issued a report that al Libi's confession was suspect, and that he was probably telling his torturers what he thought they wanted to hear.[38] As noted in the previous chapter, despite this finding of the DIA, President Bush used al Libi's allegations in his war speech of October 7, 2002, when he said, "We've learned that Iraq has trained al Qaeda members in bomb-making and poisons and deadly gasses." In 2004, al Libi formally recanted his confession to the torturers. As al Libi told FBI agents, "They were killing me. I had to tell them something."[39]

In 2005 a Bush administration official asserted that enhanced interrogation techniques were authorized to be used only on "High-Value Detainees" who 1) are senior members of al-Qaeda, 2) know of an imminent threat against the United States or its allies, or who were involved in planning attacks, or assisted in planning attacks on the United States or its allies, and 3) "if released, constitute[s] a clear and continuing threat to the USA or its allies."[40] In addition, any planned use of enhanced techniques would have to be approved by the director of the Counterterrorist Center, and in 2005 it required the approval of the director of the CIA.[41]

One captive who American officials thought was a high-level member of al Qaeda, Abu Zubaydah, was interrogated by FBI agents who, using nonviolent techniques, got him to talk to them about his al Qaeda activities.[42] The FBI agent who first questioned Abu Zubaydah was Ali Soufan, a professional interrogator with many years of experience interrogating terrorists. In congressional testimony, Soufan described his initial sessions of interrogating Zubaydah as successful. Within an hour "we had gained important actionable intelligence."[43] Zubaydah told him about the role of KSM in 9/11, his place in al Qaeda leadership, and later about Jose Pedilla. CIA Director George Tenet was impressed with the intelligence until he found out that the FBI agent was the one eliciting the information. He then ordered the CIA personnel and their contract interrogators (despite the contractors' lack of any experience in interrogation) to take over, and they began to use "enhanced interrogation techniques." This led FBI Director Robert Mueller to declare that "we don't do that," and Soufan stopped participating in the interrogation. Zubaydah resisted through the escalation of the harsh techniques until he was waterboarded eighty-three times in August 2002. Soufan also elicited important tactical and strategic intelligence about al Qaeda from Abu Jandal, immediately after 9/11.

One of the possible reasons that the CIA insisted on questioning Zubaydah themselves was that President Bush had made much of his capture and implied that he would be a valuable source of information. When word got to Bush that Zubaydah was a lower-level member of al Qaeda who made travel arrangements rather than plotting terrorist attacks, he reportedly told Tenet: "I said he was important. You're not going to let me lose face on this, are you?"[44] Zubaydah was subjected to a range of extremely brutal treatments, including sleep deprivation, stress positions, death threats, isolation, and waterboarding.

In the summer of 2002, interrogators at the location of some of the questioning of Zubaydah believed that he had given up all of the information that he had, but officials at CIA headquarters insisted that he knew more and that the brutal interrogations continue. One intelligence officer recalled, "You get a ton of information, but headquarters says, 'there must be more.'" And so Zubaydah was subjected to eighty-three sessions of waterboarding during the month of August 2002. But no new information came out; the intelligence officer said, "He pleaded for his life, but he gave up no new information. He had no more information to give."[45]

In contrast to the harsh techniques, Soufan described what he called the FBI "Informed Interrogation Approach," which begins with learning everything available about the subject and leveraging that to convince him to disclose information. He explained that the approach is successful in building a rapport with the subject and then drawing out the information needed. He explained that first, the subject is fearful and surprised not to be abused; his only human contact is with the interrogator and he will try to extend that contact through talking. Second, the subject craves respect and continued contact with the interrogator. Third, the interrogator, by learning details about the subject's background, can convince the subject that he knows much of the information already (p. 2). Soufan noted that when he first asked his name, Zubaydah gave him an alias. Then Soufan said "how about if I call you Hani? That was the name his mother nicknamed him as a child. He looked at me in shock, said 'ok' and we started talking (p. 3)."[46]

Soufan concluded that the harsh approach to interrogating terrorists evokes un-reliable information, is too slow, violates our moral ideals, and is "too risky to allow someone to experiment with amateurish, Hollywood style interrogation methods that in reality, taints sources, risks outcome, ignores the end game, and diminishes our moral high ground in a battle that is impossible to win without first capturing the hearts and minds around the world."[47]

Of the total of ninety-four detainees that the CIA controlled, twenty-eight were subjected to enhanced interrogation, and only three to waterboarding (Rahim Al-Nashiri, Abu Zubaydah, and KSM).[48] The CIA said that waterboarding would be limited in its use to "two 'sessions' per day of up to two hours," a total of twelve minutes of water application per twenty-four hour period, and only "as many as five days during a thirty-day approval period."[49] Thus the stated limits on the use of the waterboard would limit the total number of days per month the technique could be applied on a person to ten times (two sessions for five days out of thirty). Neverthe-less, the CIA applied waterboarding to Abu Zubaydah "at least eighty-three times during August 2002," and 183 times to KSM during March 2003.

Two points might be made on the CIA use of waterboarding:

1) The stated limits on the use of waterboarding (admittedly the harshest of the techniques and constituting a threat of imminent death) were not observed by the CIA in its application. This calls into question whether the CIA complied with the limits specified on the other harsh interrogation techniques, and indeed, whether torture, once begun, can be controlled.

2) The number of times that waterboarding was applied to KSM (an average of 6 times per day in March 2003 for a total of 183 times) indicates that there is no obvious limit on what the interrogators think the detainee knows that they want to educe. As Darius Rejali points out, "The notion that one stops when one hears the right information presupposes that one knows the truth when one hears it."[50] How did the CIA interrogators know that there was still more information that KSM was refusing to divulge after 50 waterboarding sessions, 100 sessions, 150 sessions, or 183 sessions? Was all of this informa-tion of the ticking bomb variety?

The CIA claimed of the enhanced interrogations program: "The intelligence ac-quired from these interrogations has been a key reason why al-Qa'ida has failed to launch a spectacular attack in the West since 11 September 2001," and that "KSM and Abu Zubaydah have been pivotal sources because of their ability and willing-ness to provide their analysis and speculation about the capabilities, methodologies, and mindsets of terrorists."[51] According to Steven Bradbury's May 30, 2005, memo, enhanced interrogation led to the "discovery of a KSM plot, the 'Second Wave,' to use East Asian operatives to crash a hijacked airliner into a building in Los Angeles." In addition, Zubaydah gave information that led to the capture of Jose Padilla, who it was claimed planned to detonate a "dirty bomb" in the Washington, D.C., area.[52] The FBI agent who interrogated Zubaydah for two months before the CIA took over noted that "the harsh techniques were approved in the memo of August 2002. Mr. Padilla had been arrested that May."[53]

Despite the above claims of success, the inspector general of the CIA concluded that "it is difficult to determine conclusively whether interrogations have provided information critical to interdicting specific imminent attacks."[54] In order to justify torture with the ticking time bomb scenario, the torturer must know that the subject has specific information about a future plot. The released memos do not claim that the CIA knew of a plot to bomb a building in Los Angeles, though they said they learned of one through the enhanced interrogation of KSM. If true, this was very valuable intelligence and may have saved U.S. lives, but it was based upon torture "on speculation"; that is, Zubaydah was tortured in case he might know about future attacks.

If the CIA did not know of the existence of such a plot before interrogating KSM with harsh techniques, it was torturing him because of the possibility that he might know of a future plot. If one argues that it is justifiable to torture any enemy leader because he might know of a future attack, the scope for torture is broadened much more than the ticking time bomb scenario would allow. And it would be difficult to argue that any enemy of the United States should not torture any high-level U.S. officer who, for instance, might know about future air strikes (which might kill civilians as well as military personnel). Thus, even if it is admitted that the CIA did discover a plot through the torture of KSM, that one victory does not justify a policy of using torture on any high-level enemy captive—unless one thinks that such routine torture is always justified.

Most of the CIA claims for the success of harsh interrogations, however, were much less spectacular. The information had to do with more mundane, though undoubtedly important, intelligence. For instance, the Bradbury memo of May 30, 2005, says that the harsh interrogations "produced over 3,000 intelligence reports from" a few high-value detainees. "A substantial majority of this intelligence has come from detainees subjected to enhanced interrogation techniques." The CIA also argued that "[t]he program has been virtually indispensable to the task of deriving actionable intelligence from other forms of collection."[55] But arguing that this valuable intelligence, discovered through torture, justifies the use of torture opens the door for the use of torture as a regular source of intelligence.

In sum, even if one admits that a serious threat was discovered as a result of torture, most of the intelligence claimed as the result of harsh interrogations did not reach the level of importance that would justify torture under the ticking time bomb scenario. If one wants to justify torture in most cases of the CIA claims for success, one is required to justify torture as a routine method of intelligence collection whenever intelligence officials believe that there may be another attack on the United States.

These accounts show that in addition to any "imminent threat" that the CIA was trying to discover, they justified harsh interrogation techniques (including waterboarding) to gather admittedly useful intelligence about the general structure and function of al Qaeda. This type of intelligence is undoubtedly important, but does it justify torture?

The Social and Human Dynamics of Torture

In the wake of the publication of the Abu Ghraib photographs of abuse, many citizens wondered, "How could these outrageous acts have been committed by U.S. soldiers?" Part of the answer is that most human beings can be strongly influenced by their immediate social settings.

The essence of professional military forces is the channeling of violence in an effective and controlled manner. Military training must first overcome the socialized inhibitions against killing other humans; then it must limit killing to the designated enemy. The dynamics of violence are so volatile that strict discipline is essential in any military force. Discipline is necessary in order to get humans to risk their lives in the face of extreme danger and to coordinate forces in battle. But discipline is also necessary to limit the violence to mission accomplishment and not allow it to spill over to unnecessary brutality or violence to noncombatants. Thus discipline and honor have been the hallmarks of the best professional military organizations throughout history. In addition to the protection of noncombatant persons from violence, the system of limits extends to enemy forces that are captured. Despite the failure of many military organizations to live up to these ideals, the ideals constitute an important limit on the destructiveness of warfare and the need to control the most violent tendencies of humans under pressure.[56]

U.S. military training includes familiarity with the general limits of violence and specifically the provisions of the Geneva Accords with regard to prisoners. What then, went wrong at Abu Ghraib and other U.S. prison camps? How could U.S. soldiers commit the terrible acts that have been recorded in the photographs that have been spread throughout the world? Some general conclusions about the potential for inhuman behavior by ordinary individuals can be gleaned from some psychological experiments.

In trying to understand how the Holocaust could have occurred in Germany in the 1930s and 1940s, scholars have posited a number of explanations. But it has become clear that the actions necessary to exterminate Jews in large numbers were carried out in part by ordinary people (military and civilian) and not merely by Nazi party members or S.S. forces. One of the insights of Hannah Arendt, in what she describes as "the banality of evil," was that ordinary people, doing what they saw as their jobs and duties, were capable of contributing to heinous acts.[57] In *Unmasking Administrative Evil,* Guy Adams and Danny Balfour explore how public administrators can contribute to evil acts as they conscientiously perform their expected duties. Their argument is that large-scale evil is often masked; that is, the perpetrators believe that they are merely doing their assigned tasks conscientiously and do not believe they are doing anything wrong. But their acts can cumulatively result in evil outcomes, as in the Holocaust.[58]

In the 1960s, psychologist Stanley Milgram of Yale designed an experiment intended to show how Americans would not be as compliant as were Germans when asked to inflict pain on other human beings. The subject was told that the experiment was about the connection between electrical shock and memory. The subject was supposed to deliver a shock to a person (in reality, an actor) in the next room every time an incorrect response was given. The shocks were calibrated from 15 volts to 450 volts, and as the supposed voltage of the shocks was increased the actor expressed increased pain. If the subject hesitated to administer the next level of shock, the experimenter, with the help of a white lab coat and the voice of scientific authority, prompted the subject to apply the shock despite the screams of pain from the actor in the next room. Ninety-nine percent of the subjects were willing to administer the "strong" shock of 135 volts, and 62 percent were willing to go to the "XXX" categories of 435 and 450 volts.[59]

This classic experiment demonstrated that regular Americans, with their individualistic cultural values, were not as different from what Germans were thought (by Americans) to be, with their supposedly more authoritarian and conformist culture. One of the lessons of this experiment is that Americans would go much further than was predicted (by Milgram) along a path of inflicting pain on others when it appeared to be sanctioned by science and authority. In 2008 the Milgram experiment was replicated, and more than half the subjects were willing to go past the 150 (imaginary) volt level of electricity.[60]

Another classic experiment on the malleability of Americans' behavior was conducted at Stanford University in the 1970s. The purpose of the "Stanford Prison Experiment" was to examine how social forces, in this case the "total environment" of a closed "prison," would affect the behavior of normal Americans. Dr. Philip Zimbardo selected "normal, healthy, intelligent college students to enact the roles of either guards or prisoners in a realistically simulated prison setting (in the basement of a university building) where they were to live and work for several weeks."[61] The students were assigned to be either guards or prisoners in a completely random way, so there was no question of self-selection or experimental bias.

The "ground rules" were that the prisoners would be treated as prisoners but would not be subject to any inhumane treatment. But very quickly, the role-playing students adopted the worst aspects of the behavior of their roles. The "guards" became overbearing and punitive toward the "prisoners," and the prisoners became passive and resentful. The experiment had to be terminated after six days rather than running the planned two weeks because of the brutality of the guards and their mistreatment of the prisoners.

This experiment provides evidence that seemingly ordinary and normal people can exhibit extraordinarily inhuman behavior under the right conditions. In this case the conditions were only the "prison" environment. The guards knew the prisoners were guilty of nothing but being part of the experiment, which assigned them the role of prisoner. The experimenters concluded: "In less than a week, the experience of imprisonment undid (temporarily) a lifetime of learning; human values were suspended, self-concepts were challenged, and the ugliest, most base, pathological side of human nature surfaced. We were horrified because we saw some boys ("guards") treat other boys as if they were despicable animals, taking pleasure in cruelty."[62]

This experiment illustrates the ways in which innate or learned values and inhibitions can be overcome in extreme social situations. Zimbardo later reflected: "we were surprised that situational pressures could overcome most of these normal, healthy young men so quickly and so extremely.... At the start of this experiment, there were no differences between the two groups; less than a week later, there were no similarities between them."[63] In Guantanamo, Bagram, and Abu Ghraib, young soldiers found themselves in situations of high stress and felt themselves to be under considerable pressure—particularly life-threatening pressure in the combat zones. Given pressure from above for "actionable intelligence," the condoning of extreme behavior from their superiors, and social pressure from their peers, it is understandable how the interrogators and military police got carried away in the infliction of violence on their prisoners. Social pressure and danger certainly do not excuse extreme abuse and torture; military discipline is designed to avoid just such situations. But the conditions do help explain how it happened and illustrate the importance of discipline and leadership.

The power of role-playing was also illustrated during Army training exercises at Guantanamo Bay in 2003. Specialist Sean Baker, 37, of the 438th Military Police Company, was playing the role of an uncooperative detainee. Baker was beaten so harshly by four soldiers that he suffered traumatic brain injury. Finally when the soldiers realized that he could be an American, they stopped beating him.[64]

Given these two classic experiments, it should not surprise us that good, normal young men and women would be capable of inhuman behavior at Abu Ghraib. Their crass behavior may have been aggravated because they were guarding prisoners who were of a different racial/cultural background and who they may have believed were guilty of attacks on U.S. forces. This is why rules, procedures, and strict adherence to standard operating procedures are so important in military prisons.

How do the above analyses of the malleability of human nature give us insights into how the abuse and torture could occur? In trying to understand the behavior of U.S. soldiers in their excessive abuse and torture at Guantanamo, Bagram, and Abu Ghraib (in addition to other U.S. prison sites), it may be useful to take up the metaphor of the "few bad apples" at the bottom of the barrel. Instead of beginning with the few bad apples, it may be helpful (following Zimbardo's reasoning) to look at the whole barrel as a system. Shifting the perspective in this way does not excuse in any way the behavior of the torturers, but it may help us understand how it happened.[65]

People, in spite of their innate character and early socialization, can be strongly influenced by the situation in which they find themselves. This is what goes on in military socialization and training. Recruits are treated in ways that de-emphasize their individuality and stress that they are part of a group that is their team that is working for a much larger goal, the protection of the country. Just as important as the particular military skills they learn, such as maintaining weapons and learning how to use them, is the training they receive in acting as part of a larger unit, which includes discipline, hierarchy, and intense focus on mission accomplishment. Once effectively indoctrinated (or trained), they eventually learn to take initiative (the military does not want mindless automatons) within the context of the broader rules and limits set in the military system. The longer the training and the higher the rank, the more discretion is granted, with the expectation that the discretion will be used in militarily approved ways because of the commitment demonstrated by those who successfully worked their way up the hierarchy.

Chapter Two of this book emphasized the formal policies that legitimated harsh in-terrogations that led to torture. But the formal policies were systematically reinforced by informal means. The importance of informal policies is analyzed by Guy Adams and Danny Balfour in their book *Unmasking Administrative Evil*.[66] In analyzing the organizational dynamics of the administration of the Holocaust, they cite several studies that emphasize informal pressure and expectations. The Holocaust "was not so much a product of laws and commands as it was a matter of spirit, of shared com-prehension, of consonance and synchronization."[67] Direct orders were not necessary: "Instead, new signals and directions were given at the center, and with a ripple effect, these new signals set in motion waves that radiated outward ... These were not stupid or inept people; they could read the signals, perceive what was expected of them, and adjust their behavior accordingly ... It was their receptivity to such signals, and the speed with which they aligned themselves to the new policy, that allowed the Final Solution to emerge with so little internal friction and so little formal coordination."[68] The Abu Ghraib abuses in no way are comparable to the Holocaust; the point here is one of social dynamics.

In addition, the social atmosphere at Abu Ghraib at times appeared to be chaotic, with no firm rules about what was allowed and what was not. Command discipline was not apparent, and there was confusion about who had final authority; military policy, military intelligence, and CIA personnel all seemed to have some control, but no single authority had clear control of U.S. personnel and their behavior. This confusion and chaos can lead to what sociologists call a "state of anomie," in which an individual's moral compass ceases to be effective.[69]

Robert J. Lifton has written about doctors who participated in U.S. torture in the war on terror by assisting in the torture, assuring that victims did not die, or falsifying death certificates. He helps explain their behavior by their presence in "atrocity-producing situations" in which ordinary people can become socialized into participating in atrocities. In his study of doctors who participated in the Holocaust, he argues that "the great majority of these doctors were ordinary people who had killed no one before joining murderous Nazi institutions. They were corruptible and certainly responsible for what they did, but they became murderers mainly in atrocity-producing settings."[70]

So how did these factors play into the abuse, torture, and murder committed by U.S. soldiers (and others) in the war on terror? What was the role of the system of the military, the framework within which they were acting, and what was the role of leadership?

Governmental systems legitimate the use of power, and military systems legiti-mize the use of violence. Political theory has recognized over the centuries that governmental use of power can be constrained, but only with carefully constructed institutions (like elections or separation of powers) and cultural acceptance of those restraints. Military systems can constrain the use of violence by strict disci-pline, hierarchy, and responsible leadership. The greater the professionalism of the military (within a constitutional system), the more effective responsible discipline, hierarchy, and leadership can be. The U.S. military system has become highly professionalized; the drafting of civilians is no longer used, and only volunteers join the military. Nevertheless, military interrogators engaged in abuse and torture in the war on terror. What factors worked to break down the professionalism and discipline of the Army in the abuse cases?

The United States' reaction to the atrocities of 9/11 provided the broad setting for the abuse. U.S. government officials were fearful of a "second wave" of attacks on civilians by the al Qaeda terrorists. President Bush framed the U.S. response as a "war on terror." Previous instances of terrorism in the United States had been dealt with as criminal actions in which the perpetrators, when caught, were charged, tried, and punished. England has experience with terrorism by the IRA and al Qaeda, and it has dealt with terrorists as criminals rather than as enemy fighters in a war. In framing the U.S. response to 9/11 as a war on civilization by "evildoers" who wanted to destroy the United States, President Bush was able to emphasize the high stakes and need to destroy the enemy. The invasion of Iraq was also framed as part of the war on terror, and the Bush administration was effectively able to convince many Americans that Saddam Hussein was complicit in the 9/11 attacks. Administration officials continued to connect Saddam with 9/11 long after it was known that there was no operational connection between Saddam and al Qaeda.

In keeping with the framing of the fight with terrorists as a war, on November 13, 2001, President Bush identified the enemy as "illegal enemy combatants" rather than as soldiers on the other side in a war. Thus U.S. personnel did not have to treat those captured as potentially honorable enemy soldiers but rather as illegitimate terrorists who sought to kill civilians. The detainees at Guantanamo were characterized by high administration officials as the "worst of the worst" and "illegal enemy combatants." As terrorists, it was asserted, they were not entitled to treatment in accord with the Geneva Conventions, but could be exploited for any intelligence value they might have.

Philip Zimbardo observes, "We can assume that most people, most of the time, are moral creatures," but in the right situation we should also realize "the ease with which morality can be disengaged by the tactic of dehumanizing a potential victim."[71] Seeing detainees not as legitimate enemy fighters but as terrorists who killed civilians enabled U.S. personnel to treat them as evildoers who did not deserve to be treated humanely. The labels of "enemy combatant" or "PUCs" (persons under control) helped to dehumanize detainees and treat them as subhuman (just as the labels of "Krauts" or "Japs" or "gooks" were used in previous U.S. wars). Detainees were presumed to be guilty of attacking America. In addition, cultural differences were emphasized, and detainees were identified with negative images of Muslims, such as the stoning of women or the cutting off of hands as punishment for stealing, or as barbarians who would cut the heads of Americans off with a knife, as happened with reporter Daniel Pearl. General Miller's statement to guards at Abu Ghraib that you have to treat the prisoners like dogs also helped soldiers see their captives as less than human.[72]

Once the war on terror was framed as a war in defense of civilization itself, and the detainees were characterized as evil plotters against the United States, the removal of the usual constraints on the behavior of interrogators contributed to the acceptance of abuse and torture. The removal of the constraint of the Geneva Conventions was one of the most important decisions in the war on terror. The Geneva Conventions had been accepted throughout the civilized world as necessary constraints on the treatment of enemy prisoners captured in a war. Without them or something like them, the temptation to torture enemy captives for intelligence or revenge would often lead to unnecessary atrocities in the conduct of a war.

This does not mean that the Conventions were always observed, but the *principle* that torture and abuse were wrong was an important frame for the treatment of prisoners. The U.S. military had a tradition of treating enemy captives humanely from the time of George Washington, through Lincoln's Lieber Code, through the Geneva Conventions. The essence of Geneva rules was taught to every Army recruit and reinforced with periodic training. The Geneva Conventions were part of the professionalism of the U.S. Army; we would fight battles fiercely, but we would treat unarmed enemy captives humanely.

President Bush's suspension of the Geneva Conventions on February 7, 2002, against the advice of most military advisers, lifted an extremely important constraint on military behavior. (That the suspension was formally limited to al Qaeda was not a message that was received very effectively throughout the military.) U.S. soldiers and interrogators knew that they no longer had to honor the Geneva rules in which they had been trained. The Geneva rules were thrown out, but no other rules or constraints were put in their place (except for the Bybee I memo's prohibition of extreme torture).

In 2002, top administration and military officials exerted significant pressure down the chain of command for "actionable intelligence" that would help prevent a potential future attack by al Qaeda. When significant intelligence was not forth-coming from the interrogators at Guantanamo using the traditional interrogation techniques of the standard Army Field Manual on interrogations, which honored the Geneva Conventions, the response to the pressure was a search for additional techniques to put pressure on captives, with the assumption that they were complicit in 9/11 and thus had valuable information. This search resulted in Secretary Rumsfeld's memos of December 2, 2002, and April 16, 2003, that authorized a number of techniques that went beyond what Geneva allowed. These techniques were intended for use at Guantanamo, but soon they "migrated" and were legitimized in Afghanistan and Iraq.

This is where the role of training and leadership should have come into play. The military interrogators at Guantanamo were young, nineteen- and twenty-year-old men and women who had about six weeks of training. The much more experienced and professional interrogators of the FBI and the Criminal Investigative Division of DOD were at first skeptical and then horrified at the treatment some detainees received at the hands of the young soldiers. They voiced their concerns but were overridden by military leaders at Guantanamo, particularly General Geoffrey Miller. They took their concerns to the Pentagon, but were ignored by General Counsel Haynes and Secretary Rumsfeld.

The MPs at Abu Ghraib who committed the terrible acts that were photographed had even less training than the soldiers at Guantanamo. They were young, inexperienced, and untrained kids from National Guard units. The use of dogs, isolation, and SERE techniques were authorized, and when concerns were raised at the brutality perpetrated at Abu Ghraib and other prisons in Iraq, the chain of command ignored the warnings. The officers who were supposed to be leaders chose to ignore or suppress complaints about abuse and in effect condoned and encouraged the barbarity. In the Iraq context (where the Geneva Agreements *did* apply), the pressure for tactical intelligence that might save American lives, the desire for revenge for 9/11, the disdain for prisoners from another culture (who were to be treated as "dogs"), the constant danger, and frustration from the terrible conditions in which they were working led the soldiers to act out their frustrations by abusing and torturing detainees.

Controlling Torture

In addition to the problems discussed above, torture as public policy has two more negative consequences: once authorized, it is very difficult to control; and it has corrupting influences on the organizations that use it.

In order for a government to use torture effectively, it would have to be institutionalized. Amateurs and untrained personnel would not be effective at its administration, so training programs and professionals would have to be developed. The problem with legitimatizing torture is that torture is very difficult to control once it has become a legitimate tool of public policy. Once institutionalized, the professionals will want to use their skills and to hone them; thus they will push to expand the categories of cases that would justify torture. Similarly, the police or military people who badly need tactical intelligence will be likely to say, "What's the use of having these experts if we never get to use them?" Insofar as torture is seen as an effective interrogation technique, regular units will press to be able to use the same "tools" as the special units that are authorized to use torture.

As Alberto Mora observed, the use of force is subject to "force drift." If a little force is not effective, more force may do the trick; if some force is effective, more force will be more effective. As scholar Bob Brecher observes: "Torture, like power, appears to be habit-forming. The rationale of torture in an age of terror—averting imminent and massive harm to civilians by torturing the right source—easily slides to cover ever more remote sources and more hypothetical harms. It is difficult to torture just a little."[73]

To make this point, one need look no further than Abu Ghraib, where the desire for tactical intelligence led to the horrible acts of the MPs. It is also clear that the interrogators and guards at Guantanamo went much further than they were officially authorized to go. The Bush administration argued that the use of harsh techniques was carefully limited to a few very important cases, but Charles Krulak, former commandant of the Marine Corps, argued that, once allowed by policy, torture is difficult to restrain. In commenting on "a policy of official cruelty," he said:

As has happened with every other nation that has tried to engage in a little bit of torture—only for the toughest cases, only when nothing else works—the abuse spread like wildfire, and every captured prisoner became the key to defusing a potential ticking time bomb. Our soldiers in Iraq confront real "ticking time bomb" situations every day, in the form of improvised explosive devices, and any degree of "flexibility" about torture at the top drops down the chain of command like a stone—the rare exception fast becoming the rule.[74]

It is an illusion to expect that, once torture is authorized, it can easily be contained.

Torturers continually try to push the envelope, as Darius Rejali observes: "No matter how lax the rules governing torture are, a professional always insists that if he had greater power to arrest and cause pain, he would have gotten results sooner ... Clean, selective, professional torture is an illusion."[75] Rejali continues: "torture has not one slippery slope, but three. Torture increasingly takes in more suspects than those approved, leads to harsher methods than are authorized, and leads to greater bureaucratic fragmentation. Moreover, these slopes are slicker and sharper when people are seeking urgent information abut the future than when they are securing false confessions about crimes in the past."[76]

In addition to the tendency of torture to expand beyond the original intentions of public policy, it has a corrupting effect on governmental institutions. All governmental organizations tend to want more autonomy; it is natural for professionals to think that they know more about their jobs than do other people, even their superiors. Organizational units are very competitive, from the minor to the top levels of government, e.g., the Defense Department and the CIA. Each unit strives to prove that it is more effective in accomplishing the mission, especially if there is pressure from the top, e.g., from the vice president. Thus if one unit has a tool that gives it an advantage, other units will be jealous and want the same leeway. This seemed to happen when the CIA and the Department of Defense were arguing over which organization would have control over "high-value" suspects of terrorism. Each organization wanted to take credit for breakthroughs in the war on terror.

If the option to torture is given to certain units (e.g., military or CIA), the unit will develop an esprit de corps and feel that they are special because they are custodians of power that other units are not allowed to exercise. Other units will also perceive them as being able to flout the rules that all other units must obey. Members of those units develop a mystique about them, as did the OGA (Other Governmental Agencies, i.e., CIA) personnel in U.S. interrogation centers. They also had presumed authority; they often did not wear name tags or rank insignia, and they acted as if they had unquestioned authority. Soldiers believed them.

The Wrong Man Problem

The premise of the Bush administration's argument that "aggressive interrogation" was necessary was that the persons to be harshly interrogated had valuable information, the knowledge of which would prevent future attacks on civilians in the United States.[77] This justification for imprisonment and harsh interrogation breaks down if it is not certain that the victim is indeed a terrorist who possesses such knowledge. Thus the possibility of capturing the wrong person and subjecting him to torture to extract evidence presented a serious problem to the advocates of the Bush administration's detention policies. Unfortunately, there is abundant evidence that many prisoners held by U.S. forces or rendered to foreign countries for coercive interrogation were innocent bystanders or low-level functionaries. Such people would have no knowledge of any possible future attacks on the United States, and may have been swept up by U.S. allies and handed over to U.S. forces. Evidence of the capture and incarceration of innocent individuals accused of being enemy combatants reinforces the importance of habeas corpus procedures in order to balance the zeal of executive branch personnel who genuinely want to protect the security of the nation.

One indicator of the presence of individuals in Guantanamo who were not dangerous terrorists is that by October 2008, more than 500 detainees had been released, including 127 sent to Afghanistan, 90 sent to Saudi Arabia, and 59 to Pakistan.[78] If the Bush administration had firm evidence that these individuals had been involved with the attacks of 9/11, it is doubtful they would have been released.

General Evidence of Mistaken Imprisonment

Two professors of law at Seton Hall undertook an analysis of the more than five hundred detainees held at Guantanamo in 2005.[79] They based their evaluation exclusively on official U.S. government documents, and did not use any assertions of those who had been detained. In contrast to what Secretary Rumsfeld called "the worst of the worst," the Seton Hall Report found, among other things, that:

- "Only 5% of the detainees were captured by United States forces. 86% of the detainees were arrested by either Pakistan or the Northern Alliance and turned over to United States Custody."
- "Fifty-five percent (55%) of the detainees were not determined to have committed any hostile acts against the United States or its coalitional allies."
- "Only 8% of the detainees were characterized as al Qaeda fighters. Of the remaining detainees, 40% have no definitive connection with al Qaeda at all and 18% are (sic) have no definitive affiliation with either al Qaeda or the Taliban."[80]

They found further that 60 percent of the inmates were detained because they were "associated with" groups that are deemed to be "terrorist organizations." Only ten detainees were charged with a crime regarding the laws of war.[81]

A study by the West Point Combating Terrorism Center, using the same DOD data, agreed with the Seton Hall study that only 5 percent of the detainees were captured by U.S. forces, but characterized the detainees differently than the Seton Hall study did. The West Point study found that 73 percent of the detainees (based on unclassified records) could be classified as a "demonstrated threat" as an enemy combatant; 95 percent were a "potential threat"; 77 percent were associated with terrorist group members who posed a threat; and that six detainees (1.6 percent) posed no threat.[82]

One of the reasons that prisoners were of little intelligence value and may not have participated in hostilities toward the United States was the way in which they came to be prisoners of the United States. In Afghanistan, most U.S. soldiers did not know the language of their captives nor did they understand the nuances of violent tribal rivalries, thus they had to depend on Afghan locals to capture and interrogate suspected hostile forces. The Seton Hall report pointed out that the 95 percent of detainees who were not captured by American forces were rendered to U.S. troops during the time that large bounties were offered for the capture of members of the Taliban or al Qaeda. One Afghanistan leaflet said: "Get wealth and power beyond your dreams. Help the Anti-Taliban Forces rid Afghanistan of murderers and terrorists."[83] Another said that those who helped capture Taliban or al-Qaeda fighters would be rewarded with $4285.[84] Secretary Rumsfeld said that leaflets advertising these offers were "dropping like snowflakes in December in Chicago."[85] With incentives like these, it does not take too much imagination to understand the temptation these bounty offers presented to turn in personal or tribal enemies. But it is also true that some of the detainees were captured by Pakistani forces who were not motivated by bounties.

In Guantanamo, the reality was that not all of the prisoners held were in fact enemy belligerents or knew information that the United States could use to prevent future attacks, and a number were released from Guantanamo. Major General Michael Dunlevey, who was in charge of interrogations at Guantanamo, estimated that up to half of the prisoners did not possess any intelligence of value to the United States.[86] Some U.S. personnel in Afghanistan tried to alleviate the problem by drawing up a list of detainees who were innocent, not dangerous, or who had little intelligence value. Interviews with military intelligence officers in Afghanistan and Guantanamo Bay and reading of files by *Los Angeles Times* reporters in 2002 found that at least fifty-nine of the detainees had been judged by U.S. intelligence officers in Afghanistan to be of little or no intelligence value.[87]

Some of the captives were farmers, taxi drivers, workers, or persons who had been conscripted by the Taliban and were not fighting U.S. forces but were fighting for the Taliban against the Northern Alliance. In 2002, there were so many prisoners of little intelligence value that Major General Michael Dunlavey actually went to Afghanistan to "chew us out," in the words of one U.S. officer. Dunlavey complained that many of those sent to Guantanamo were "Mickey Mouse" types in terms of military or intelligence value.[88] Despite documenting these cases of low-value (for intelligence purposes) captives, the danger of making even one mistake was so high that all of the fifty-nine ended up being flown to Guantanamo. And once in Guantanamo, it was very difficult to get out, although many of the detainees were eventually released. Detainees were presumed to be guilty, had little opportunity to prove their innocence, and were denied the opportunity to present their cases to an independent judge through a writ of habeas corpus. U.S. officials in the Pentagon denied the presence of any detainees who should not have been in Guantanamo. "All are considered enemy combatants lawfully detained in accordance with the law of armed conflict," according to one Pentagon official.[89] The Pentagon analysis of CSRTs concluded that about three hundred detainees were members of or associated with al Qaeda or the Taliban. Among those, only nine were classified as al Qaeda fighters and twenty-three as Taliban fighters.[90]

Given this evidence that many detainees in Guantanamo did not fight directly against U.S. forces or possess any intelligence of value, it is possible that habeas corpus hearings might have helped the military distinguish detainees of little intelligence value from those who actively supported al Qaeda. In addition to the general evidence cited above about the aggregate of detainees, some accounts of individuals who were wrongly imprisoned present compelling evidence of the dire consequences that can result from mistakes of U.S. forces. The following sections will provide brief summaries of people captured in the war on terror who turned out not to be guilty of the crimes of which they were accused: Maher Arar, Khaled el-Masri, Huzaifa Parhat, and Jose Padilla.

In Iraq, judgments about Abu Ghraib indicated that significant portions of the inmates probably did not fall into the category of those who might possess important information central to protecting the United States from future attacks. The International Committee of the Red Cross (ICRC), after a visit to Abu Ghraib, stated: "Certain CF [Coalition Forces] military intelligence officers told the ICRC that in their estimate between 70 percent and 90 percent of the persons deprived of their liberty in Iraq had been arrested by mistake."[91]

One soldier who had served in Iraq gave this statement under oath: "It became obvious to me that the majority of our detainees were detained as the result of being in the wrong place at the wrong time, and were swept up by Coalition Forces as peripheral bystanders during raids. I think perhaps only one in ten security detainees were of any particular intelligence value."[92] Another Iraq veteran stated: "I would say that the DAB [Detainee Assessment Board] identified about 85 percent to 90 percent of detainees who were of either no intelligence value or were of value but innocent and therefore should not have remained in captivity."[93]

The Case of Maher Arar

Maher Arar was a computer programmer who was a Canadian citizen of Syrian origin. As he was transferring planes at Kennedy International Airport in New York City in September 2002, he was seized by the FBI and not given an opportunity to appeal his seizure to the courts because he was not a U.S. citizen. Arar repeatedly denied that he was connected with al Qaeda. After thirteen days of interrogations, U.S. authorities, convinced that he was lying, put him on a plane and took him to Jordan. He was then driven to Syria, where he was tortured over a ten-month period and forced to confess that he had trained in an al Qaeda camp in Afghanistan to fight the United States, which was not true. Arar said that he was kept in a small underground cell with no windows and beaten with heavy electrical cables, among other torments. [94] Before he was finally released, he was forced to sign and put his thumbprint on several documents that he was not allowed to read.[95]

When U.S. authorities finally realized that his designation as an "Islamic extremist" resulted from the fabrication and incompetence of a member of the Royal Canadian Mounted Police, he was released in October 2003 with no apology or admission of fault by the United States. Arar brought a lawsuit against the U.S. government for his false imprisonment and torture in Syria, but the Bush administration invoked the "state secrets privilege" to argue that the "intelligence, foreign policy and national security interests of the United States" would be jeopardized by a court hearing.[96] A lawyer representing Arar said that the government lawyers "are saying this case can't be tried, and the classified information on which they're basing this argument can't even be shared with the opposing lawyers. It's the height of arrogance—they think they can do anything they want in the name of the global war on terrorism."[97]

The Canadian government conducted an inquiry and officially apologized for Arar's ordeal, and the head of the Royal Canadian Mounted Police resigned.[98] The head of the commission, Justice Dennis R. O'Connor, said after the report was released: "I am able to say categorically that there is no evidence to indicate that Mr. Arar has committed any offense or that his activities constituted a threat to the security of Canada."[99] Three other men of Syrian origin were picked up during visits to Syria and imprisoned for several years (one for only one month). They were released without any charge or explanation.[100]

The Case of Khaled el-Masri

On December 31, 2003, Khaled el-Masri, who had been residing in Germany, was arrested when he was on vacation in Macedonia, interrogated for twenty-three days by Macedonian police, and then flown by the CIA to a prison in Afghanistan.[101] While there, he was imprisoned, shackled, beaten, tortured, and had drugs injected into him by U.S. personnel. Masri was mistaken for Khalid al-Masri, a suspected member of al Qaeda.[102] In May of 2004, National Security Adviser Condoleezza Rice, after learning that it was a case of mistaken identity, ordered that Masri be released. He was taken to Albania, dropped off, and told that he could return home to Germany. In January 2007, the German Government issued warrants for the arrest of twenty-five CIA personnel and one Air Force officer for kidnapping and inflicting bodily harm on Masri.[103]

When Masri sued the CIA, the district judge in Alexandria, Virginia, said that his case had to be dismissed because of the state secrets privilege, even though Masri had evidently been done a great injustice. On appeal to the Fourth Circuit, the Justice Department asserted that judges were bound to defer to executive branch claims that continuing with the case would reveal state secrets. The lawyer for the Bush administration said that CIA Director Porter Goss had filed a secret statement arguing that hearing the case would "have a cascading effect that will have devastating consequences" for U.S. national security. Masri's lawyer pointed out that President

Bush admitted on September 6, 2006, that the CIA established secret prisons in other nations ("black sites") and undertook rendition flights to them.[104]

Since judges routinely defer to executive branch claims that cases involving "state secrets" cannot be heard by judges, there is no way that the executive branch can be brought under any oversight in cases in which it invokes state secrets. The Bush administration argued that judges cannot be trusted to make responsible decisions about what information should be kept secret: "Even disclosures to judges carry risks," said Justice Department attorney Gregory Katsas.[105] Thus the Bush administration had a legal license to keep secret any case they thought might be embarrassing to the administration, since not much more than an assertion is sufficient to dismiss any case in which the executive claims the state secrets privilege.

Parhat and Uighur Case

Huzaifa Parhat was an ethnic Uighur who left China because the Uighurs were being subjected to "oppression and torture" by the Chinese government, which considered the Uighurs to be a separatist group that engages in terrorism.[106] He left China and went to Afghanistan in June 2001 in order to help fight against the Chinese government. After September 11, 2001, in order to escape U.S. bombing, he (with sixteen other unarmed Uighurs) fled to Pakistan, where he was given shelter but later turned over to Pakistani forces who turned him over to American forces for a bounty.[107] U.S. personnel sent him to Guantanamo in June 2002 (Internment Serial Number 320). After five years in Guantanamo, Parhat appealed to the U.S. Court of Appeals of the District of Columbia, arguing that the Combat Status Review Tribunal that designated him an "enemy combatant" did not have sufficient evidence to do so.

Parhat said that he wanted to fight against China but that he and his comrades were not hostile to the United States. U.S. authorities admitted that he was not a member of al Qaeda or the Taliban and that he did not participate in any hostilities toward U.S. forces or its allies.[108] The CSRT, nevertheless, found on December 6, 2004, that he was an enemy combatant because he was "apparent[ly]" "affiliated" with (though not a member of) a group (the East Turkistan Islamic Movement, ETIM) that was "associated" with Al Qaeda.[109] *After* Parhat was imprisoned, the Bush administration decided that the EITM was a terrorist organization.[110] The government provided no specific evidence that supported the accusations against Parhat, but used statements that were generic to more than one hundred inmates at Guantanamo. Neither did the government present evidence that ETIM was connected in any way with the 9/11 attacks on the United States. In 2003, an officer of the Criminal Investigation Task Force (CITF) reviewed Parhat's case and recommend that Parhat be released (p. 5), and the CSRT report itself said that Parhat was "an attractive candidate for release," though he should not be sent back to China, which was likely to treat him harshly.[111]

According to the Department of Defense regulations (pursuant to the Detainee Treatment Act of 2005) for the conduct of CSRTs, there must be a "preponderance of the evidence" that the person was an enemy combatant. The court decided that no evidence produced at the CSRT hearing demonstrated that Parhat was an enemy combatant. On June 20, 2008, the Court of Appeals ruled that, since there was insufficient evidence that Parhat was an enemy combatant, the government had either to conduct expeditiously another CSRT hearing in which evidence was produced to prove the government's case or to release Parhat. Subsequently, the government decided it would no longer try to prove that Parhat or his sixteen compatriots was an enemy combatant. It argued, nevertheless, that it would not release the Uighurs until they found another country that would give them refuge from the Chinese government, which considered them terrorists.[112]

On October 7, 2008, U.S. District Judge Ricardo M. Urbina ruled that the executive branch had to release Parhat and his fellow Uighurs because no proof was offered that they were enemy combatants or risks to U.S. security. The government had cleared the Uighurs for release, but argued that if sent back to China, they would be persecuted and that other nations would not accept them for fear of offending China. Since no other nation would accept the Uighurs, they would have to be released into the United States. The Justice Department argued, however, that only the president had the authority to decide to release the Uighurs into the United States and could not be compelled to do so by a federal court. The Justice Department, in effect, argued that the president has the authority to imprison whomever he designates as an enemy combatant indefinitely without charging or trying that person, and that even if a prisoner wins a habeas corpus ruling from a federal judge, the president can decide to continue to imprison the person.

Judge Urbina, however, decided that "because the Constitution prohibits indefinite detention without cause, the government's continued detention of the [detainees] is unlawful."[113] The next day, however, the Justice Department convinced the Federal Appeals Court to issue an "administrative stay" that blocked the government from releasing the Uighurs and give the Justice Department more time to prepare an appeal of Judge Urbina's decision. On February 18, 2009, the federal appeals court reversed Urbina's decision and ruled that only the president or Congress could make a decision to allow aliens into the United States. The issue was not the habeas corpus decision per se, but the judicial order to allow the Uighurs into the United States. According to the court, "We do know that there is insufficient evidence to classify them as enemy combatants ... But that hardly qualifies petitioners for admission."[114] "The question here is not whether petitioners should be released, but where," stated the court.[115] In May of 2009, the Uighur detainees were still in Guantanamo.

The Case of Jose Padilla: A Possible Right Man

In the case of Jose Padilla, the Bush administration argued that it could imprison a citizen of the United States indefinitely without charging him and without allowing the courts to consider an appeal for a writ of habeas corpus. Because of court decisions, the administration was not able to act as it wanted to, and Padilla was eventually granted a trial.

Jose Padilla, a citizen of the United States and former resident of Chicago, was seized by U.S. marshals as he was reentering the country in May of 2002. Attorney

General John Ashcroft announced that Padilla was conspiring with al Qaeda to detonate a "radioactive dirty bomb" in the United States and that he had been trained in Pakistan in terrorist techniques. He was first held as a material witness, but in June of 2002, President Bush designated him an "enemy combatant" and ordered that he be placed in military custody, where he was denied access to a lawyer.

Padilla appealed for a writ of habeas corpus, and a district court ruled that it had jurisdiction to hear the case. The Second Circuit Court of Appeals declared that "the President lacks inherent constitutional authority as Commander-in-Chief to detain American citizens on American soil outside a zone of combat."[116] Padilla could not be held by the military and had to be turned over to civilian authority. In the Supreme Court, the case was remanded on procedural grounds. Without reaching the merits of the case, the court ruled that Padilla had filed his petition in the wrong jurisdiction and had to seek a writ in South Carolina rather than New York.

In September of 2005, the Fourth Circuit Court of Appeals ruled on the Padilla case and held that the president did have the authority to detain indefinitely American citizens and the government did not have to file criminal charges against U.S. citizens designated as enemy combatants. Padilla appealed to the Supreme Court and argued that the government could not legally hold him indefinitely without charging him with a crime. When faced with a potential loss in the Supreme Court, the Bush administration decided to indict Padilla in criminal court.[117]

Padilla was indicted in November 2005 (after four years in captivity) on terrorism and conspiracy charges unrelated to his alleged dirty bomb plans. His lawyers requested a competency hearing, arguing that his treatment by the government had rendered him unable to defend himself. Previously, Padilla had said that he was seriously abused during his more than three years in custody, including being forced to stand in stress positions, threatened with execution, and given "truth serums."[118] Padilla's lawyers said that he was denied counsel for twenty-one months and kept in isolation and sensory deprivation in his small cell, in which the windows were blacked out. He had virtually no contact with other human beings other than his interrogators. His meals were passed to him through the slot in his cell door, and he slept on a steel plate after his foam mattress was taken from him. His lawyers say that he was subjected to threats of execution, assaults, stress positions, and hooding.[119]

Some insight about the way American citizens who are declared enemy combatants could be gleaned from a videotape of his visit to the military dentist in 2006. On May 21, 2006, several guards in riot gear came to Padilla's cell and opened a small door at the bottom of his cell door. Padilla put his feet through the slot and the guards shackled them. Then he put his hands through another opening in the door and his wrists were handcuffed and attached to a metal belt. Blackened goggles were placed over his eyes and sound-blocking headphones placed over his ears. He was then taken to the dentist by the guards who had dark-shaded plastic covering their eyes. There was no evidence that Padilla struggled or complained. Padilla was described to his lawyers by brig staff as "so docile and inactive that his behavior was like that of a 'piece of furniture.'"[120] A forensic psychologist who examined Padilla said that he was, "an anxiety-ridden, broken individual who is incapacitated by that anxiety."[121]

As a result of his treatment, his lawyers argued that his mental capacity was compromised and that he could not assist in his own defense. Although a government psychiatrist judged that Padilla could participate in his own defense, the director of forensic psychiatry at Creedmoor Psychiatric Center in Queens, New York, judged that "as a result of his experiences during his detention and interrogation, Mr. Padilla ... has impairments in reasoning ... complicated by the neuropsychiatric effects of prolonged isolation."[122]

The Pentagon denied any impropriety in Padilla's treatment. Lieutenant Colonel Todd Vician denied Padilla's claims about his treatment, and court papers show that the prosecutors "deny in the strongest terms" any accusations of torture; they say that he was treated humanely. The government prosecutors asked the judge to disallow any descriptions of Padilla's treatment during his trial for fear that they would "distract and inflame the jury."[123] Padilla, despite watching his lawyers defend him in court, did not fully trust them and thought that they might have been part of the government's prosecution team. This feeling is not irrational. Part of the practice of interrogation at times was to tell a victim that his lawyers were not to be trusted.

The Florida district court judge ruled that Padilla was competent enough to be tried in court. The prosecution argued that in 1998 he had left the United States, that he intended to commit terrorist acts abroad, and that he went to a camp in Afghanistan for training in terrorism. The jury convicted him of conspiracy to commit murder because he was in training in order to learn how to kill. The defense argued that the prosecution offered no evidence that he was connected to al Qaeda or that he planned to engage in any terrorist activities or return to the United States to do so.[124]

Padilla's situation was symptomatic of the problems raised by the Bush administration's approach to its treatment of terrorism suspects and specifically American citizens who have been declared enemy combatants. If detainees are tortured or interrogated by harsh means, it is difficult to get a court to convict them on charges, the evidence for which is obtained through coercive means. In addition, the government is often unwilling to take detainees to trial because the trial might include evidence of the treatment the detainees received while in custody. Administration lawyers said that revelations of interrogation techniques might reveal the methods and techniques of interrogation and thus let terrorists learn how to most effectively resist those techniques. Critics of the administration argued that the administration was worried that the public would be outraged at the treatment individuals received at the hands of U.S. personnel, including what most nations would consider torture.

The unwillingness of the government to present evidence against Padilla, its shifting legal ploys over the years, and its alleged harsh treatment of Padilla, which led to his questionable mental competence, combined to make it very difficult if not impossible ever to know whether Padilla was guilty of the crimes with which Attorney General John Ashcroft publicly accused him.

At the end of the Bush administration, Vice President Cheney said of the 245 prisoners left at Guantanamo "now what's left, that is the hardcore." That "hardcore" included the 17 Uighurs whom the military commissions authorities had declared were not a threat to the United States. It also included an inmate who was ordered released by Federal District Judge Richard J. Leon, who had been appointed by President George W. Bush. Mohammed El Gharani was accused by the government of belonging to an al Qaeda cell in 1998, the year in which he was eleven years old. Judge Leon concluded, "Putting aside the obvious and unanswered questions as to how a Saudi minor from a very poor family could have even become a member of a London-based cell, the government simply advances no corroborating evidence for these statements it believes to be reliable from a fellow detainee."[125] The Guantanamo military authority also released Haji Bismullah, an Afghan, who after six years in captivity convinced them that he had fought against the Taliban. Bismullah was an official in Helmand Province, which was headed by a pro-American government. A rival clan wanted one of their members to fill his government position, so they told the Americans that he had worked for the Taliban. He was released and flown back to Afghanistan.[126]

Despite the cases of documented imprisonment of suspected terrorists who were innocent of the crimes of which they were accused, there were genuine terrorists and fighters against the United States in Guantanamo. The problem of dealing with the guilty has been illustrated by some freed Guantanamo detainees who returned to the battlefield in Afghanistan to fight U.S. forces.[127] It is also possible that some who were held in Guantanamo were radicalized by their experience and determined to avenge the lost years of their lives by fighting against the United States. The challenge was to convict those who were guilty of crimes, a challenge complicated by the use of evidence obtained through torture or harsh interrogation.

Conclusion

Although torture has been renounced by most modern democracies, after 9/11 a number of scholars, lawyers, and others have argued that torture is acceptable in certain circumstances. The hypothetical circumstances usually involve some form of a ticking time bomb scenario. This chapter has argued that such scenarios are highly unlikely to happen, and no compelling instances of such a situation have been proffered by advocates of torture.

Even in the case of a genuine ticking time bomb scenario, the likelihood of success is uncertain, and the dangers of its use are multiple. The main problem is that the slope from the ticking bomb to routine torture for tactical purposes is very slippery, as is evident from the Abu Ghraib experience, the French experience in Algeria, and the Landau Commission Report in Israel.[128] Rather than creating a policy that justifies torture in certain circumstances, it would be better to trust that the necessity defense would convince a military tribunal (or judge or jury) that torture was in any specific case justified.

Genuine cases of the ticking time bomb scenario might arguably be used as an adequate defense for torture in isolated cases. But the consequences of formally adopting torture in official policy, even in narrowly defined circumstances, are simply too dangerous. Once torture is justified, it is difficult to distinguish the "ticking bomb" scenario from the pressing need for "actionable intelligence" in tactical situations. A parallel argument can be made about murder. The United States does not have laws that justify murder. Nevertheless, there are a number of circumstances in which killing another human being can be justified, and that judgment is made by the decision to prosecute and by decisions by judges and juries. There is no need for a law justifying murder or torture.

In addition, consensus among experts holds that torture is usually not an effective way to educe information. Torture is likely to get people to talk, but the accuracy of what they say is dubious, at best. The Bush administration, despite claims that the fruits of torture have saved lives, has presented no compelling instances in which torture led to a ticking bomb and saved the lives of civilians. If learning about the structure and operations of al Qaeda are accepted as justifying torture, then torture will have to be accepted as legitimate in virtually any tactical situation. This is why many military combat leaders have decried the abandonment of the Geneva Conventions and fought to bring back the rules of the Army Field Manual banning torture.

This chapter has also argued that, in certain social situations, normal people are willing to engage in behavior that ordinarily they would think of as reprehensible. The pressures from above for "actionable intelligence" and the terrible conditions at Abu Ghraib provide examples of the type of situations that encourage and allow torture. Once allowed in official policy, torture takes on a momentum of its own. Organizations will argue that they need to use the tactic, and its use will undermine and corrupt those who use it. The documented instances of innocent people whom the United States subjected to very harsh conditions of imprisonment or torture serve as object lessons that mistakes of identity or intelligence can lead to horrific miscarriages of justice.

Darius Rejali summarizes the drawbacks of torture as public policy: "In short, organized torture yields poor information, sweeps up many innocents, degrades organizational capabilities, and destroys interrogators. Limited time during battle or emergency intensifies all these problems.... Clean, selective, professional torture is an illusion."[129]

CHAPTER 5

Torture and the Law

We're a nation of law. We adhere to laws. We have laws on the books. You might look at those laws, and that might provide comfort for you.
—President George Bush, June 10, 2004[1]

[A]s the lawyer, I was not the decision maker. I was the adviser.
—Department of Defense General Counsel William J. Haynes[2]

What "the law forbids and what policy makers choose to do are entirely different things."
—OLC Lawyer John Yoo[3]

In order for the Bush administration to undertake the harsh interrogation of detainees that it thought was necessary, it had to deal with a series of legal obstacles. These included most importantly the Geneva Conventions, U.S. laws, and customary international law. It also had to set aside the Uniform Code of Military Justice and Army regulations. In doing so, the administration argued that the president's commander-in-chief authority allowed President Bush to ignore international law and rendered any law that might limit the president's authority regarding detainees unconstitutional. The administration felt it also had to keep its treatment of detainees shielded from judicial scrutiny. It thus argued that habeas corpus, the centuries-old Anglo-American right of suspects who claimed they were innocent to get a hearing before an independent judge, did not apply to suspects of terrorism.[4]

Chapter Two of this book argued that many of the legal memoranda of the Bush administration were in fact policy decisions, since the legal judgments determined what type of treatment of detainees was allowed. This chapter will examine the legal (as opposed to policy) dimensions of Bush administration decisions. The chapter will first take up the legal arguments used by the Bush administration to exempt itself from the Geneva Conventions, U.S. law, and customary international law. It will then examine the arguments it proffered to deny terrorist suspects any appeal to the courts via habeas corpus. It will then look at new laws passed by Congress and responses to administration policies by the Supreme Court that dealt with habeas corpus and harsh interrogation practices. The conclusion will summarize how changes in laws and judicial decisions have affected detainee and interrogation policies of the U.S. government.

Legal Requirements to Be Overcome

The Bush administration went to great lengths to insulate itself from possible accountability for the actions of its interrogators. It argued that the president was not bound by the Geneva Conventions, by U.S. law, or by customary international law. The third Geneva Convention forbids any torture or abuse of prisoners of war, and Common Article 3 prohibits the abuse of all persons under the control of military forces. Section (1) of the article requires that detained persons be treated "humanely," and it prohibits "violence to life and person, in particular murder of all kinds, mutilation, cruel treatment and torture," and "outrages upon personal dignity, in particular, humiliating and degrading treatment."[5] The United States War Crimes Act (18 U.S.C. Sec. 2441) defined war crimes as "a grave breach" of the Geneva Conventions, or conduct "which constitutes a violation of common Article 3" of the Geneva Conventions.[6] The U.S. Torture Statute (18 U.S.C. Sec. 2340) was passed to implement the U.N. Convention Against Torture, and it provided for criminal sanctions, including the death penalty, for perpetrators of torture.

In addition to the above general laws, military laws and regulations forbid torture and abuse. Article 93 of the Uniform Code of Military Justice covers cruelty and maltreatment; Article 128 covers assault; and Article 134 prohibits threatening a prisoner with death.[7] Army Regulation 190–8, paragraphs 1–5a states that "All persons captured, detained, interned or otherwise held in U.S. custody during the course of a conflict will be given humanitarian care and treatment." Paragraph 1–5b provides that "all prisoners will receive humane treatment ... Murder, torture ... and all cruel and degrading treatment are prohibited."[8] The Army Field Manual 34–52, "Intelligence Interrogations" (1992), required in paragraph 1–7 that "enemy Prisoners of War, captured insurgents, civilian internees, other captures, detained, or retained personnel, foreign deserters or other personnel of intelligence interest are protected by the Geneva Conventions." Paragraph 1–8 says that "Geneva Conventions and U.S. policy expressly prohibit acts of violence or intimidation, including physical or mental torture, threats, insults, or exposure to inhumane treatment as a means of aid to interrogations ... Such illegal acts are not authorized and will not be condoned by the U.S. Army. Acts in violation of these prohibitions are criminal acts punishable under the Uniform Code of Military Justice."[9]

This section will first explain the constraints the United States agreed to when it signed and ratified the Geneva Conventions. It will then explain how the Bush administration went about suspending the Geneva Conventions with respect to the Taliban and al Qaeda. Next, U.S. laws as well as international law on torture will be examined. The Bush administration legal arguments for exempting itself from obeying the laws were dubious at best.

Legal efforts to shield the Bush administration from liability for its interrogation practices began immediately after 9/11 and continued throughout the Bush administration. In order to use the harsh interrogation methods that President Bush thought would be necessary in the war on terror, it would be necessary to get around the above mentioned laws and regulations. Since most of these laws and regulations were based on the Geneva Conventions, the first step was to make sure that the Geneva Conventions would not get in the way of interrogations of prisoners. After that, policy decisions could be made that allowed harsh interrogation practices. John Yoo in the Office of Legal Counsel of the Justice Department and David Addington in the vice president's office prepared legal memoranda that construed the law so as to exempt the president from Constitutional law, criminal law, international law, and customary international law.

These legal efforts would not have been necessary if President Bush had intended to comply with the normally accepted requirements of the Constitution, criminal law, and international law.[10] In effect, the intense efforts to construct legal justifications for harsh interrogations, combined with the secrecy with which they were developed and carried out, signaled the intentions of the administration. These legal documents foreshadowed the actions the administration was going to take with regard to the treatment of prisoners and the interrogation of suspected terrorists and other detainees. Chapter Two described the way in which policies surrounding the Geneva Conventions were formulated; the following section will present a legal analysis of those policies.

Suspending the Geneva Conventions

The four Geneva Conventions of 1949 were designed to protect individuals who are captured or at the mercy of enemy forces during times of war. The articles assume that fighting in a war is not illegal. Different parts of the Conventions cover different classes of those who fall under the control of the armed forces of a nation during times of war. Geneva Convention I covers the sick and wounded on land. Convention II covers those shipwrecked at sea. Convention III covers those who are prisoners of war, and Convention IV covers civilians. The protections of Article III for POWs are available to those who are lawful belligerents in warfare, and they are given the highest level of protection. Geneva Convention III provides that prisoners must be treated humanely, and that if interrogated, they cannot be forced to reveal information beyond their name, rank, date of birth, and serial number.[11] The Convention does not forbid interrogation, but it limits the methods that can be used to those that are humane.[12] The Conventions apply to those countries that have signed the treaty. This includes the United States, Iraq, and arguably Afghanistan.

In order to qualify as a prisoner of war, an individual must be a soldier of a state that has signed the treaty and must (among other things): belong to an organized group that is a party to the conflict and that is commanded by a responsible person; they must wear a "distinctive sign" identifying them as a combatant; and they must carry arms openly.[13] If there is some doubt as to whether a detainee is entitled to status as a prisoner of war, Geneva Convention III, Article 5 requires that the person is to be treated with POW status until a properly constituted tribunal has determined the person's status. The person is entitled to some procedural rights in order to act in his own self-defense. The United States recognized as prisoners of war those captured by U.S. forces in the Korean, Vietnam, and first Gulf Wars.

Even if the Convention III, Article 5 tribunal determines that the person is not a covered belligerent and thus not a POW who is entitled to the full protections of Geneva III, the person may be covered by Geneva Convention IV, which applies to civilians. Article 4 of this Convention applies to: "those who, at a given moment and in any manner whatsoever, find themselves, in case of a conflict or occupation, in the hands of a Party to the conflict.... " Article 27 of Convention IV provides that these persons are entitled to: "respect for their persons," to be "humanely treated," and to be protected "against all acts of violence or threats thereof and against insults and public curiosity." Many of the prisoners at Abu Ghraib fell into the category of civilians detained by an occupying power.

Each of the four Geneva Conventions has several common articles that are identical. Common Article 3 prohibits certain practices in the treatment of those persons under the control of military forces. Section (1) of the article requires that detained persons be treated "humanely," and it prohibits "violence to life and person, in particular murder of all kinds, mutilation, cruel treatment and torture," and "outrages upon personal dignity, in particular, humiliating and degrading treatment." Thus all captives of the United States were entitled to the protections of Common Article III. Alberto Gonzales wrote an in article in the *New York Times* in 2004 that Iraq had signed the Geneva Conventions and that the United States was bound by them in the war in Iraq.[14] That the Geneva Conventions were blatantly violated at Abu Ghraib attests to the tendency for torture sanctioned for one purpose to be used for different purposes.

United States Army Regulations (AR 190–8), in accord with the Geneva Conventions, provided for treatment of enemy prisoners of war and state that "all persons taken into custody by U.S. forces will be provided with the protections of the GPW until some other legal status is determined by competent authority." The regulation prohibits "inhumane treatment," specifically "murder, torture, corporal punishment ... sensory deprivation ... and all cruel and degrading treatment."[15] The United States has had a long record of officially requiring humane treatment of prisoners taken in wartime, from the early years of the Republic, to the Lieber Code of the Civil War, to World War II, Korea, and Vietnam.

The fact that the United States officially adhered to the principle of treating POWs humanely throughout its history up to the Bush administration does not mean that U.S. troops never committed atrocities or that torture never occurred. During wartime it is impossible to eliminate all acts of barbarism. The difference is that it was official U.S. policy throughout all previous U.S. wars that prisoners be treated humanely, even if the spirit of the law was not always honored. In past U.S. wars, soldiers who tortured and mistreated enemy captives did so in spite of official policy; after 9/11 they acted in conformance with Bush administration policy.[16]

On the face of it, President Bush arguably acted against his duties and oath of office, as set out in the Constitution. Article VI of the Constitution declares that "This Constitution, and the Laws of the United States which shall be made in Pursuance thereof; and all Treaties made, or which shall be made, under the Authority of the United States, shall be the supreme Law of the Land.... " Article II of the Constitution declares that the president "shall take Care that the Laws be faithfully executed." Thus, although presidents have some leeway in interpreting treaties, President Bush acted in a way incompatible with his constitutional authority in unilaterally suspending the Geneva Agreements.[17] The Supreme Court's *Hamdan* decision rejected the arguments of the administration and ruled that the United States was bound by Common Article 3 of the Geneva Conventions.[18]

U.S. War Crimes Act and the Federal Torture Statute

After 9/11, one of the main concerns of the Bush administration was that U.S. soldiers could be prosecuted under the U.S. War Crimes Act (18 U.S.C. Sec. 2441). The law provides that "whoever, whether inside or outside the United States, commits a war crime ... shall be fined under this title or imprisoned for life or any term of years, or both, and if death results to the victim, shall also be subject to the penalty of death." The law defined a war crime as "a grave breach" of the Geneva Conventions, or conduct "which constitutes a violation of common Article 3" of the Geneva Conventions.[19]

In 1994 the United States passed legislation to implement the UN Convention Against Torture (discussed below) by passing the torture act (18 U.S.C. Sec. 2340), which provides for criminal sanctions, including the death penalty, for perpetrators of torture. Section 2340 states: "Whoever outside the United States commits or attempts to commit torture shall be" punished, including if, "the alleged offender is present in the United States, irrespective of the nationality of the victim or alleged offender." The law defines torture as "an act committed by a person acting under the color of law specifically intended to inflict severe physical or mental pain or suffering (other than pain or suffering incidental to lawful sanctions) upon another person within his custody or physical control." The law covered only torture outside the United States because acts of torture within the United States were forbidden by other statutes.[20]

In January of 2002, Alberto Gonzales argued that the suspension of the Geneva Conventions would preclude prosecution of U.S. personnel and that the suspension "substantially reduces the threat of domestic criminal prosecution under the War Crimes Act (18 U.S.C. Sec. 2441) ... A determination that the GPW [Geneva prisoner of war convention] is not applicable to the Taliban would mean that Section 2441 would not apply to actions taken with respect to the Taliban."[21] This argument by Gonzales indicated that the administration expected that the actions that it would authorize in treating detainees would likely be liable to criminal prosecution under the U.S. War Crimes Act unless some legal protection was provided. That legal protection, they calculated, was the suspension of the Geneva Conventions by President Bush.

Customary International Law

Lawyers for the administration asserted that the president is not bound by international law and that he is not bound by treaties (which Article VI of the Constitution establishes as "the supreme Law of the Land").[22] Nevertheless, several international laws arguably bind the United States. The treatment of prisoners is constrained by the United Nations Convention Against Torture and Other Cruel, Inhuman or Degrading Treatment or Punishment.[23] The Convention Against Torture (CAT) defines torture as "any act by which severe pain or suffering, whether physical or mental, is intentionally inflicted on a person for such purposes as obtaining from him or a third person information or a confession."[24] The U.N. Torture Convention provides that "no exceptional circumstances whatsoever, whether a state of war or a threat of war, internal political instability or any other public emergency, may be invoked as a justification of torture."[25]

With respect to prisoners, customary international law may bind the United States, regardless of whether the Geneva Conventions are considered to apply or not. According to the U.S. Army Field Manual of the Law of Land Warfare, "unwritten or customary law is firmly established by the custom of nations and well defined by recognized authorities on international law ... The unwritten or customary law of war is binding upon all nations."[26]

Sources of customary international law include: Protocol I, article 75 of the Geneva Conventions, Common Article 3 of the Geneva Conventions, and the UN Convention Against Torture. Protocol I, article 75 of the Geneva Conventions, signed in 1977 but not ratified by the United States, is considered to be part of customary international law. Protocol I provides that some acts "shall remain prohibited at any time and in any place whatsoever, whether committed by civilian or by military agents." These acts include (among others): "murder," "torture of all kinds," and "outrages upon personal dignity, in particular humiliating and degrading treatment."[27]

Common Article 3 is also considered part of customary international law. It provides that in conflicts "not of an international character" its provisions "shall be bound to apply as a minimum" to "[p]ersons taking no active part in the hostilities." "International" in this context means wars between sovereign nations, in contrast to other types of conflicts such as the one between the United States and al Qaeda.[28] In *Hamdan,* Justice Stevens wrote that the principles articulated in Article 75 are "indisputably part of the customary international law."[29] The *Law of War Handbook* of the Department of the Army states that Common Article 3 "serves as a minimum yardstick of protection in *all* conflicts, not just internal armed conflicts" (emphasis added).[30] Even the Office of Legal Counsel, when it revised the Bybee memo of 2002, admitted that the United States might be bound by customary international law.[31]

The Bybee ("Torture") Memo

After purporting to establish that suspending the Geneva Conventions would insulate U.S. personnel from prosecution, the administration sought to protect U.S. personnel from prosecution by defining torture very narrowly, so that U.S. personnel had leeway to engage in a wide range of harsh practices that would not legally be defined as torture. In making this argument, the administration used the definition of torture contained in U.S. law (18 U.S.C. Sec. 2340). Assistant Attorney General Jay S. Bybee, head of the Office of Legal Counsel, signed a legal memorandum (hereinafter Bybee memo I) dealing with what would constitute torture under Title 18, Sections 2340 and 2340A of the U.S. code.[32]

Many of the policy implications of the Bybee memo were analyzed in Chapter Two; this section will review briefly some of the major legal arguments of the memo. The memo addresses the U.S. law that implements the UN Convention Against Torture (18 U.S.C. Sec. 2340). The act defines torture as "an act committed by a person acting under the color of law specifically intended to inflict severe physical or mental pain or suffering." The memo parses the word severe and argues that it means physical pain "equivalent in intensity to the pain accompanying serious physical injury, such as organ failure, impairment of bodily function, or even death." It consequently concludes that "certain acts may be cruel, inhuman, or degrading, but still not produce pain and suffering of the requisite intensity to fall within Section 2340A's proscription against torture." [33] Thus the Bush administration was free to use "a wide range of . . . techniques that will not rise to the level of torture." This opened the door to many of the interrogation techniques described in Chapter Four. As argued there, many of these techniques amounted to torture in the eyes of much of the world.

The memo also argues that any U.S. person accused of torture who was acting pursuant to the orders of the commander in chief could defend against the charge by arguing, among other things, "the right to self-defense," since "the nation itself is under attack."[34] This overly broad defense of torture could be used in virtually any military or combat situation. The memo argues further that even if a person is guilty of breaking the law, the law itself would be unconstitutional insofar as it tries to limit the discretion of the president acting as commander-in-chief of the armed forces. "Any effort to apply Section 2340A in a manner that interferes with the President's direction of such core war matters as the detention and interrogation of enemy combatants thus would be unconstitutional."[35]

Despite Article I, Section 8 of the Constitution, which provides that Congress shall have the power "To make Rules for the Government and Regulation of the land and naval Forces," the Bush administration denied that the president could be bound by public law with respect to torture.[36] According to John Yoo, Congress cannot "tie the President's hands in regard to torture as an interrogation technique . . . It's the core of the Commander-in-Chief function. They can't prevent the President from ordering torture."[37] According to this argument, Congress cannot regulate presidential actions when he is acting as commander in chief, and any law, such as the torture law, "must be construed as not applying to interrogations undertaken pursuant to his Commander-in-Chief authority."[38] This reasoning leads to the conclusion that Congress cannot pass a (constitutional) law that forbids torture by any member of the executive branch, as long as the president claims that he is ordering the torture under his commander-in-chief authority.

The Article II, Section 3 provision of the Constitution that the president "shall take care that the Laws be faithfully executed," would thus be negated by the commander-in-chief clause, as would the Article I, Section 8 provision that Congress has the authority to "make Rules concerning Captures on Land and Water."[39] The administration argued that the president, when acting as commander in chief, is above the law because no statute can impinge on the president's authority with respect to the interrogation of enemy combatants. The further implication is that the commander-in-chief clause can override the "take care" clause or the authority of Congress to "make rules concerning captures." That is, the president is above the law.

After Jack Goldsmith was appointed by President Bush to head of the Office of Legal Counsel in October of 2003, he concluded that the legal arguments in the Bybee memo were seriously flawed, and "in effect gave interrogators a blank check." He characterized the reasoning of the memo as "legally flawed, tendentious in substance and tone, and overbroad and thus largely unnecessary."[40] He decided that the Bybee memo was so flawed that he had to withdraw the opinion. This extraordinary action was particularly sensitive because the memo "had been vetted in the highest circles of government."[41] "Highest circles" in this context must mean Vice President Cheney and President Bush, thus tying the very narrow definition of torture directly to President Bush. The task of withdrawing and replacing the memo fell to OLC lawyer Daniel Levin; after six months of work, the replacement memo was issued on December 30, 2004, several weeks before the Senate hearings on the nomination of Alberto Gonzales to be Attorney General.[42]

The Levin memo began with a ringing denunciation of torture: "Torture is abhorrent both to American law and values and to international norms. This universal repudiation of torture is reflected in our criminal law ... international agreements ... and the longstanding policy of the United States repeatedly and recently reaffirmed by the President."[43] The White House, however, insisted that Levin include a footnote undermining much of the substance of the memo.[44] In footnote 8, Levin stated: "While we have identified various disagreements with the August 2002 Memorandum, we have reviewed this Office's prior opinions addressing the issues involving treatment of detainees and do not believe that any of their conclusions would be different under the standards set forth in this memorandum." Goldsmith concluded that "in other words, no approved interrogation technique would be affected by this more careful and nuanced analysis."[45]

John Yoo, who claimed to have written (at least part of) the "Bybee memo," condemned the Levin memo as "second guess[ing]" his work with "the benefit of 20/20 hindsight." He also concluded that "the differences in the opinions were for appearances' sake. In the real world of interrogation policy nothing had changed. The new opinion just reread the statute to deliberately blur the interpretation of torture as a short-term political maneuver in response to public criticism."[46] Thus the White House, despite the memo's rhetoric condemning torture, prevented the memo from having any legal effect on interrogation practices. Whatever was legal under the reasoning of the Bybee memo was considered by the administration to be legal after the Bybee memo was withdrawn. The "Bybee II" memo of August 1, 2002 (discussed in Chapter Three), was based on the legal and constitutional reasoning of the Bybee I memo, but its focus was on the specific techniques that the CIA would be allowed to use in its interrogations.

John D. Hutson, judge advocate general for the Navy from 1997 to 2000, said of the legal memoranda prepared to defend President Bush's interpretation of the law: "The

January, 2002 memo from Judge Gonzales ... is a short-sighted, narrow minded, and overly legalistic analysis. It's too clever by half, and frankly, just plain wrong. Wrong legally, morally, practically, and diplomatically ... The Bybee and Yoo memoranda are chilling. They read as though they were written in another country, one that does not honor the Rule of Law or advocate on behalf of human rights. They contain an air of desperation."[47]

After Gonzales became attorney general in 2005, he replaced OLC Director Daniel Levin (author of the memo retracting the Bybee memo) with Stephen G. Bradbury. Before he was nominated by President Bush in the summer of 2005, Bradbury wrote two new secret memoranda approving the use of aggressive interrogation techniques. Before Congress passed the McCain amendment that would forbid "cruel, inhuman and degrading" treatment, Bradbury issued a memorandum on May 10 that declared that none of the interrogation techniques currently being used would violate that standard, thus providing a preemptive legal judgment that current interrogation practices would not violate the (yet to be passed) Detainee Treatment Act.[48] U.S. interrogation practices would thus not have to change when the DTA was passed. Deputy Attorney General James Comey objected to the memo, but he was overruled by Gonzales, and he left the administration in the summer of 2005.[49] The same day, Bradbury issued another memo that approved the use of a number of techniques in combination with others.[50]

The Bybee I memo was concerned with the definition of torture, and concluded that the harsh techniques authorized did not violate U.S. law. After that memo was withdrawn, the memo of May 10, 2005, by OLC Director Steven Bradbury, argued that by the definition of torture in Section 2340 of Title 18 of the U.S. code, the harsh techniques of the CIA did not constitute torture. The memo used similar reasoning to the Bybee I memo in parsing the words of the statute.

Congress Acts

Congressional reaction to news about the harsh interrogation techniques used by the Bush administration in the war on terror was mixed. In 2005 it passed the Detainee Treatment Act in order to constrain the administration's treatment of detainees by forbidding the use of cruel techniques of interrogations. But it limited the force of that DTA by passing the Military Commissions Act, which allowed the president to reinterpret Common Article 3 of the Geneva Conventions. Thus the Bush administration could use techniques considered by much of the world as "cruel, inhuman, and degrading" by a presidential assertion that they were not proscribed by Common Article 3. This section will analyze the passage of those laws and their effects.

The McCain Amendment: The Detainee Treatment Act of 2005

Senator John McCain (R-AZ) endured five years as a prisoner of war in Vietnam and suffered severe torture. Thus his publicly expressed outrage at reports of torture perpetrated by U.S. soldiers and civilians at Guantanamo, Abu Ghraib, and in Afghanistan carried a large measure of legitimacy.[51] McCain introduced an amendment to the Department of Defense Appropriations Act for 2006 that would ban torture by U.S. personnel, regardless of geographic location. Section 1003 of the Detainee Treatment Act of 2005 provides that "no individual in the custody or under the physical control of the United States Government, regardless of nationality or physical location, shall be subject to cruel, inhuman, or degrading treatment or punishment."[52] Section 1002 of the act also mandated that military personnel were bound by the Army Field Manual in conducting interrogations.

President Bush threatened to veto the bill if it was passed, and Vice President Cheney led administration efforts in Congress to defeat the bill.[53] Cheney first tried to get the bill dropped entirely, then to exempt the CIA from its provisions. Their efforts, however, were unavailing, and the measure was passed with veto-proof majorities in both houses, 90 to 9 in the Senate, and 308 to 122 in the House. In a compromise, McCain refused to change his wording, but he did agree to add provisions that would allow civilian U.S. personnel to use the same type of legal defense that is accorded to uniformed military personnel.[54] After the McCain Amendment passed, the Army revised its field manual on interrogations and returned to its traditional policy of treating all prisoners according to the rules of the Geneva Conventions. In 2008, Congress passed a bill that would have required the CIA to limit its interrogation methods to those approved by the Army Field Manual. President Bush, however, vetoed the bill on March 8, 2008. The administration was thus able to preserve its policy that the CIA would be able to continue to use harsh interrogation methods, though those techniques were not made public.[55]

In a signing statement after signing the DTA bill into law, President Bush used language that called into question whether he considered himself or the executive branch bound by the law. A signing statement is a statement by the president when a bill is signed indicating how the president interprets the bill. When President Bush signed the bill, he issued a signing statement that declared: "The executive branch shall construe Title X in Division A of the Act, relating to detainees, in a manner consistent with the constitutional authority of the President to supervise the unitary executive branch and as Commander in Chief and consistent with the constitutional limitations on the judicial power."[56] Previous memoranda of the Bush administration interpreted executive power in expansive ways that argued that the president is not subject to the law when acting in his commander-in-chief capacity.[57] So it is a reasonable conclusion that President Bush did not consider himself bound by this law.

President Bush's memorandum excluding al Qaeda from the Geneva Accords declared that detainees would be treated humanely "to the extent appropriate and consistent with military necessity."[58] This presidential directive led to (or allowed) the abuses that occurred at Guantanamo, Bagram, and Abu Ghraib. Thus if the reservation expressed by President Bush in his signing statement to the McCain amendment is interpreted in a similar fashion, the administration may have created a loophole that allowed harsh interrogation techniques that were deemed by the executive to be a "military necessity."[59]

Passing the Military Commissions Act of 2006

In order to overcome the roadblock that the Supreme Court threw in the way of administration policy with its *Hamdan* decision, President Bush sought legislation that would authorize the creation of military commissions and spell out limits on the rights of detainees. *Hamdan* had called into question whether harsh interrogation techniques were legal and in accord with Common Article 3 of the Geneva Conventions. The Military Commission Act would allow the president to interpret Common Article 3, and the president issued an executive order that specified which interrogation techniques the CIA would be allowed to use.

President Bush argued that the types of harsh interrogation methods that he termed "the program" used by the CIA to interrogate detainees were essential to the war on terror. He threatened that he would shut down "the program" of harsh interrogations unless Congress passed a law authorizing them. "The professionals will not step up unless there's clarity in the law. So Congress has got a decision to make: Do you want the program to go forward or not? I strongly recommend that this program go forward in order for us to be able to protect America."[60] He said that the administration's proposal would provide "intelligence professionals with the tools they need."[61] The allowed interrogation techniques were not specified in the law, but were said to include prolonged sleep deprivation, stress positions, and extremely loud noises, though administration sources said that "waterboarding" would not be used in the future.[62] Members of Congress, including John McCain, also said that waterboarding was not allowed by the Military Commissions Act.[63] Waterboarding was not allowed under the revised rules of interrogation for the Armed Forces. In John McCain's words: "It [waterboarding] is not a complicated procedure. It is torture."[64] The public statements of Vice President Cheney, however, seemed to indicate that the administration still considered waterboarding a legitimate interrogation practice (see Chapter Four).

There was not unanimity in the Bush administration over the use of harsh interrogation techniques. In June of 2005 Gordon England, the acting deputy secretary of defense, and Philip Zelikow, counselor to the State Department, wrote a nine-page memo urging the administration to adhere to the minimum standards of treatment of detainees required by the Geneva Conventions.[65] On September 13, 2006, former Secretary of State Colin Powell wrote a public letter to Senator McCain urging him to oppose the provisions of the MCA that allowed the president to interpret Common Article 3 to allow harsh interrogation practices. Powell said that "the world is beginning to doubt the moral basis of our fight against terrorism," and "it would put our own troops at risk."[66] It is very unusual for a former Secretary of State to publicly argue against a bill that the president who appointed him is advocating.

Forty retired generals and high-level DOD officials wrote a letter to Senators Warner and Levin urging them to resist the proposed MCA language intended to "redefine Common Article 3 of the Geneva Conventions." They said that the United States has abided by CA3 "in every conflict since the Conventions were adopted … even to enemies that systematically violated the Conventions themselves.… If degradation, humiliation, physical and mental brutalization of prisoners is decriminalized

... we will forfeit all credible objections should such barbaric practices be inflicted upon American prisoners."[67] Former Chairman of the Joint Chiefs of Staff Hugh Shelton, in a letter to John McCain, said that approving those sections of the MCA reinterpreting Common Article 3 would be an "egregious mistake" that would send a "terrible signal" to other nations, and that it would invite "reciprocal action" by other nations.[68] The consensus of so many distinguished general officers of the armed forces as well as civilian officials and diplomats that passing the MCA would abrogate our obligations under Common Article 3 and undermine protections for U.S. troops is striking.

Nevertheless, after several weeks of contentious debate between the two political parties, the Bush administration was successful in having its version of the bill passed. The MCA was passed by both houses of Congress, and President Bush signed the Military Commissions Act of 2006 (PL 109–366) into law on October 17, 2006. It provided a lawful way for the president to establish military commissions. The MCA forbids the use of testimony obtained through "torture," and it explicitly outlawed the more extreme forms of torture. But it also opened the door for the administration to continue the harsh interrogation methods that it argued did not amount to torture by providing that the president could issue an executive order that interprets U.S. obligations under Common Article 3 of the Geneva Conventions.

Formerly, 18 U.S.C. Sec. 2441 defined as a war crime any "grave breach" of the Geneva Conventions. In order to allow the Bush administration to get around compliance with Common Article 3 of the Conventions, the MCA repealed references to the Geneva Conventions and replaced them with a list of egregious actions and any action that would "amount to cruel, inhuman, or degrading treatment prohibited by section 1003 of the Detainee Treatment Act of 2005" (Sec. 948r). Left out of the MCA was "outrageous and humiliating" treatment that was prohibited in Common Article 3 (which forbade "Violence to life and person, in particular murder of all kinds, mutilation, cruel treatment and torture" and "outrages upon personal dignity, in particular humiliating and degrading treatment").[69] According to the MCA, "outrageous and humiliating" treatment would not constitute a war crime. Under the administration's interpretation the new law would forbid only techniques that "shock the conscience."[70]

The MCA satisfied President Bush that "the program" of "enhanced" interrogations could legally continue. The allowable techniques were not specified in the law but left to interpretation by President Bush in his executive order, and the law required the president to issue an executive order that interpreted U.S. obligations under Common Article 3 of the Geneva Conventions. The techniques that the administration had been using that probably violated Common Article 3 of the Geneva Conventions included techniques such as painful stress positions, sensory deprivation, sleep deprivation, and extremely loud music. These techniques could amount to torture, depending on the intensity and duration of their use. Proponents of the act in Congress said that "waterboarding" was outlawed. But the terms of the law were not explicit on these techniques, and Vice President Cheney implied that waterboarding would still be used.

The administration worked hard in order to get the top military lawyers of the Judge Advocate General corps to state that they did not oppose the Military Commissions Act. The lawyers thought that the definition of allowable interrogation techniques under the Act were broader than those allowed under Common Article 3 of the Geneva Conventions. After several hours of persuasion by the Pentagon General Counsel, William J. Haynes II, the lawyers agreed to sign a letter that stated: "We do not object ... " to several sections of the act.[71]

The executive order (No. 13304) mandated by the MCA and issued by President Bush on July 20, 2007, said that MCA "reinforced" the president's authority "to interpret the meaning and application of the Geneva Conventions," including Common Article 3.[72] The order excluded the most egregious forms of torture, including actions covered in Title 18 sections 2441 and 2340, actions of violence that are "considered comparable to murder, torture, mutilation, and cruel or inhuman treatment," and "willful and outrageous acts of personal abuse *done for the purpose of* humiliating or degrading" persons (emphasis added). Using the reasoning of the Bybee I memo, if the acts of personal abuse were done for the purpose of extracting information rather than humiliating a person, they would be presumably allowed by the executive order.

According to the executive order, the interrogation practices are to be used with (A) an alien detainee who is determined to be "a member" or supporter of al Qaeda or "associated organizations," and (B) "likely to be in possession of information that: could assist in detecting ... attacks within the United States ... or [upon] other personnel, citizens, or facilities, or against allies or other countries cooperating in the War on terror ... or their armed forces or other personnel, citizens, or facilities," *or who* "could assist in locating the senior leadership of al Qaeda, the Taliban, or associated forces." This formulation is quite broad. The person does not have to be suspected of acting against the United States or being a member of al Qaeda, but merely to be suspected of supporting an "associated organization" and "likely" to have information that might help mitigate a terrorist attack in a "cooperating country" in the war on terror. It called for the "professional operation of the program," with "appropriate training for interrogators." Thus harsh interrogation, which most of the countries of the world might consider torture, was to be entrusted to CIA personnel specially trained in these techniques.

The executive order allowed the CIA to continue the harsh interrogation methods, excluding only those techniques covered in the exceptions listed above, though the specific techniques allowable were not listed in the executive order and were kept secret by the administration. The MCA and executive order amounted to congressional authorization of an unspecified range of techniques that members of Congress presumably did not know about. Thus the Bush administration convinced Congress to pass a law about interrogation techniques that did not specify which interrogation techniques would be allowed. Under these conditions, it would be difficult for members of Congress to make an informed decision. The Justice Department prepared a legal opinion certifying that the techniques were within President Bush's discretion in interpreting Common Article 3 of Geneva.[73]

Critics of the MCA and the president's executive order argued that they seemed to allow many of the methods that many would consider torture, including painful stress positions, sleep deprivation, ear-splitting music, and waterboarding. They argued that these techniques are cruel treatment and thus outlawed by Common Article 3 regardless of the administration's interpretation of the MCA and Common Article 3.[74] Former Commandant of the Marine Corps P.X. Kelley and national security law scholar Robert F. Turner condemned the president's interpretation of the MCA and observed that it was not in accord with Common Article 3 of Geneva. They argued that World War II and the war in Vietnam did not lead the United States to "compromise our honor or abandon our commitment to the rule of law" and that the war on terror should not cause the United States to do so. They concluded:

> Our troops deserve those protections, and we betray their interests when we gratuitously "interpret" key provisions of the conventions in a manner likely to undermine their effectiveness. Policymakers should also keep in mind that violations of Common Article 3 are "war crimes" for which everyone involved—*potentially up to and including the president of the United States*—may be tried in any of the other 193 countries that are parties to the conventions (emphasis added).[75]

British judge Sir Andrew Collins observed about a U.S. report on Guantanamo: "America's idea of what is torture is not the same as ours and does not appear to coincide with that of most civilized nations."[76]

The Supreme Court Acts

One of the challenges stemming from 9/11 concerned how to deal with suspected terrorists or members of al Qaeda. When U.S. forces captured terrorists, they had to be imprisoned in a location controlled by the United States and easily accessible to U.S. officials. The U.S. naval base at Guantanamo Bay, Cuba, seemed to be an ideal location. The base had been leased from Cuba for an indefinite time period and was under complete U.S. military control. The Bush administration was concerned that if the prisoners were held on the mainland of the United States, they would have access to the federal court system and be able to raise legal objections to their incarceration. Since Guantanamo was not technically U.S. territory, the executive branch thought it was exempt from appeals for a writ of habeas corpus to federal courts.

The purpose of the "Great Writ" of habeas corpus over the centuries has been to allow a person imprisoned by the executive to argue before an independent authority (a judge) that he was unjustly incarcerated. This centuries-old protection requires that an independent judge concur with the executive's reasons for depriving a person of liberty or that he be set free. If a judge grants a writ of habeas corpus, the executive must explain the grounds for concluding that the person has in fact broken a law and thus has been justly put in jail. If the judge is convinced that the executive has a reasonable case that the law has been broken, the executive will be allowed to keep the person in jail and take him to trial. But if the judge is convinced that the executive does not have reasonable grounds for imprisoning the person, the person must be set free.

This principle was stated in Magna Carta, which provided that "no free man shall be seized or imprisoned, or stripped of his rights or possessions, or outlawed or exiled, or deprived of his standing in any other way, nor will we [the king] proceed with force against him, or send others to do so, except by the lawful judgment of his equals or by the law of the land."[77] Thus if a person were imprisoned without a lawful reason or due process, a judge could command that he be set free. The framers of the Constitution valued the privilege of habeas corpus so highly that they embedded it in Article I of the Constitution, even before the Bill of Rights was considered. Article I, Section 9 provides that the writ can be suspended only in "Cases of Rebellion or Invasion." That it is in Article I implies that the suspension was meant to be exercised by Congress rather than the president.

Many in the United States questioned why we should grant rights to terrorists. Why should they be able to enjoy the advantages of our judicial system? Justice Scalia articulated the sentiment: "War is war, and it has never been the case that when you capture a combatant you have to give them a jury trial in your civil courts. Give me a break."[78] Although no one was suggesting that people picked up on a battlefield be tried in civil courts in front of juries, Scalia spoke for many Americans. But the whole point of habeas corpus is to determine *whether* the captive is, in fact, a terrorist and thus justly held by the executive.

The writ serves as a check on executive power, and it also may detect errors that the executive may have made in the capture and imprisonment of suspects. The section on the "wrong man" in the previous chapter demonstrates conclusively that, even in the judgment of U.S. military authorities, many of the detainees held in Guantanamo were not guilty of terrorism or of opposing U.S. forces. But many of these individuals had suffered harsh treatment and lost years of their lives before the government admitted that it had made mistakes and released the detainees. Habeas corpus hearings might have saved the health as well as years of the lives of innocent detainees.

The scope of the Bush administration's claims to authority to detain persons it suspected of connections to terrorism is illustrated by a hypothetical question federal judge Joyce Hens Green asked a Justice Department prosecutor who argued that the U.S. military could hold persons indefinitely at Guantanamo Bay. She asked him if "a little old lady in Switzerland" could be imprisoned indefinitely if she had contributed money to an orphanage in Afghanistan but the money was diverted to al Qaeda. The Justice Department lawyers answered that "she could," because "someone's intention is clearly not a factor that would disable detention" and that such detainees "have no constitutional rights enforceable in this court."[79]

It should be reiterated that a writ of habeas corpus does not mean that prisoners will be set free. It merely means that the executive must present reasonable evidence to a judge that the person has been imprisoned according to law and that there is sufficient evidence that the person committed a crime to keep him in jail until his trial.

By choosing Guantanamo to house the prisoners suspected of terrorism, the administration thought it could avoid habeas corpus appeals from prisoners. In a series of cases, however, the Supreme Court decided against the administration's interpretation of the law. In *Rasul* and *Hamdi* it decided that both non-citizens and citizens held in U.S. prisons were legally entitled to submit habeas corpus petitions to U.S. courts. In *Hamdan* it then decided that the military commissions designed by the administration were not legally constituted. Finally, in *Boumediene* it ruled that detainees in Guantanamo had a constitutional right to have their habeas appeals heard in federal court. This section will summarize these decisions and their impact on Bush administration policies.

Rasul v. Bush

In 2003, sixteen Guantanamo detainees appealed for writs of habeas corpus and argued that they were not guilty of terrorism but were innocent civilians who had been turned over to U.S. troops by bounty hunters.[80] Two lower courts agreed with the administration that they did not have jurisdiction to hear the pleas because *Johnson v. Eisentrager* established that foreign nationals captured outside the United States could not appeal to U.S. courts.[81] In *Eisentrager,* the Supreme Court decided that German soldiers who had been seized by U.S. forces in China after World War II for continuing to fight after Germany had surrendered could be tried by military commission and did not have the right to appeal to civilian courts for writs of habeas corpus. In order for U.S. courts to have jurisdiction, alien appellants had to be present in the sovereign territory of the United States. Thus the courts could not interfere with the military decision to try the Germans by military commission.[82]

When the appellants appealed to the Supreme Court to hear the case, the government argued that "aliens detained by the military abroad [only have rights] determined by the executive and the military, and not the courts."[83] The government relied on *Eisentrager,* in which Justice Jackson wrote: "We are cited to no instance where a court, in this or any other country where the writ is known, has issued it on behalf of an alien enemy who, at no relevant time and in no stage of his captivity, has been held within its territorial jurisdiction."[84] In a dissent, Justice Black, joined by Douglas and Burton, dissented and argued "that we went on to deny the requested writ, as in the Quirin case, in no way detracts from the clear holding that habeas corpus jurisdiction is available even to belligerent aliens convicted by a military tribunal for an offense committed in actual acts of warfare ... The Court is fashioning wholly indefensible doctrine if it permits the executive branch, by deciding where its prisoners will be tried and imprisoned, to deprive all federal courts of their power to protect against a federal executive's illegal incarcerations."[85]

In June 2004 however, the Supreme Court, in *Rasul v. Bush,*[86] overturned the two lower court decisions and ruled that federal courts did have jurisdiction to hear habeas corpus cases from detainees in Guantanamo. The court based its decision on the status of Guantanamo. Even though Guantanamo was on the island of Cuba, "by the express terms of its agreements with Cuba, the United States exercises 'complete jurisdiction and control' over the Guantanamo Bay Naval Base, and may continue to exercise such control permanently if it so chooses."[87] That the detainees were not

U.S. citizens did not matter; they were persons being held in a location over which the United States exercised complete control. The court distinguished Eisentrager by noting that the WWII *Eisentrager* appellants had already been tried and convicted of crimes. In contrast, the Guantanamo detainees claimed they were innocent and "have never been afforded access to any tribunal, much less charged with and convicted of wrongdoing."[88] The appellants had been held for more than two years without any charges having been made against them and were no longer in a combat zone. The court therefore decided that "aliens held at the base, no less than American citizens, are entitled to invoke the federal courts' authority."[89] The court noted that it was not deciding on a constitutional right of the appellants but rather on the statutory grounds of the habeas jurisdiction of the courts.[90]

Hamdi v. Rumsfeld

Yaser Esam Hamdi traveled from Saudi Arabia to Afghanistan in the summer of 2001 and was later captured on a battlefield by the Northern Alliance, turned over to U.S. forces, and sent to Guantanamo. When it was discovered that he had been born in the United States and was thus an American citizen (though having left at age three), he was moved from Guantanamo, put in a Navy brig in South Carolina, and held in solitary confinement. Hamdi appealed for a writ of habeas corpus, and the federal district judge ordered that Hamdi be given access to a lawyer. The Fourth Circuit Court of Appeals, however, overruled the district court and decided that Hamdi could be held in the United States without access to a lawyer and that the government did not have to charge him with a crime. Later, the full Fourth Circuit, sitting *en banc*, decided that special deference was owed to the president in making decisions about imprisoning enemy combatants and that Hamdi was not entitled to a writ of habeas corpus.

When the decision was appealed to the Supreme Court, Solicitor General Theodore Olson argued that the court did not have jurisdiction: "courts have an extremely narrow role in reviewing the adequacy of the government's return on a habeas action, such as this, challenging the quintessentially military judgment to detain an individual as an enemy combatant in a time of war."[91] The Supreme Court, however, ruled that although Congress had authorized the war against al Qaeda and the military could detain enemy combatants to prevent them from returning to the battlefield, "indefinite detention for the purpose of interrogation is not authorized."[92] Justice O'Conner wrote for a plurality of the Court and noted that the government claimed that "the Executive possesses plenary authority to detain pursuant to Article II of the Constitution." The opinion did not address that issue but reasoned that Congress had authorized the executive to engage U.S. forces in the war and that "detention to prevent a combatant's return to the battlefield is a fundamental incident of waging war."[93] Thus holding prisoners to prevent them from returning to the battlefield was reasonable. But the "indefinite" detention for the purpose of interrogation that, given the nature of the war on terrorism, might very well last for the rest of Hamdi's life, was not authorized by Congress.

In deciding against the Bush administration's contention that it could hold U.S. citizens indefinitely without charging them, Justice O'Conner said:

> the most elemental of liberty interests [is] the interest in being free from physical detention by one's own government [without due process of law] ... history and common sense teach us that an unchecked system of detention carries the potential to become a means for oppression and abuse of others who do not present that sort of threat. . . . We reaffirm today the fundamental nature of a citizen's right to be free from involuntary confinement by his own government without due process of law.[94]

She argued that "we must preserve our commitment at home to the principles for which we fight abroad" and that a citizen "must receive notice of the factual basis for his classification and a fair opportunity to rebut the Government's factual assertions before a neutral decisionmaker." This requirement of due process does not apply to "initial captures on the battle field," but "is due only when the determination is made to *continue* to hold those who have been seized."[95]

In a rebuke to the Bush administration's argument that the courts do not have jurisdiction over cases concerning detainees, Justice O'Conner declared: "we necessarily reject the Government's assertion that separation of powers principles mandate a heavily circumscribed role for the courts in such circumstances. . . . We have long since made clear that a state of war is not a blank check for the President when it comes to the rights of the Nation's citizens ... unless Congress acts to suspend it, the Great Writ of habeas corpus allows the Judicial Branch to play a necessary role in maintaining this delicate balance of governance, serving as an important judicial check on the Executive's discretion in the realm of detentions."[96] After holding that Hamdi had the right to argue his case before an independent judge, the case was remanded to the court of appeals for further proceedings.

In a strongly worded dissent, Justice Scalia, one of the most conservative justices, who often sided with the executive, wrote a defense of the writ of habeas corpus and its role in protecting individual liberty. Joined by Justice Stevens, Scalia began his argument by arguing that habeas corpus has been fundamental to Anglo-American jurisprudence. "The very core of liberty secured by our Anglo-Saxon system of separated powers has been freedom from indefinite imprisonment at the will of the Executive." He went on to argue that due process rights "deemed necessary before depriving a person of life, liberty, or property ... have historically been vindicated by the writ of habeas corpus. In England before the founding, the writ developed into a tool for challenging executive confinement."

In this case, Scalia saw a clear challenge to what he saw as one of the fundamental rights protected by the Constitution. He noted that some people concede that *inter arma silent leges* (during war the laws are silent), but "that view has no place in the interpretation and application of a Constitution designed precisely to confront war and, in a manner that accords with democratic principles, to accommodate it." Scalia concluded: "It follows from what I have said that Hamdi is entitled to a habeas decree requiring his release unless (1) criminal proceedings are promptly brought, or (2) Congress has suspended the writ of habeas corpus." Hamdi was subsequently sent to Saudi Arabia with the provision that he renounce his U.S. citizenship.[97] The key to Scalia's seeming reversal of his vote in *Rasul* against a habeas right for detainees was that Hamdi was a U.S. citizen detained on U.S. soil, whereas Rasul was an alien imprisoned in Guantanamo, which Scalia argued did not fall under U.S. sovereignty. The consequence of these two decisions was that detainees in Guantanamo had the legal right to a habeas corpus appeal.

Hamdan v. Rumsfeld

Related to the habeas corpus debate was the question of due process of law. Habeas corpus is considered fundamental to the constitutional due process to which an individual is entitled before the government can keep the person in prison. The Bush administration had set up military commissions pursuant to the president's Military Order of November 13, 2001, but the military commissions' procedures were challenged by one of the detainees, Salim Hamdan.

When the administration was preparing President Bush's Military Order of November 13, 2001, they felt that normal trials would afford too many legal protections to terrorists, and were "not practicable" (Sec. 1(f)), so the order required that military commissions be established entirely within the executive branch to try them.[98] In the order, President Bush declared that any non-citizen "whom I determine" (Sec. 2(a)) was a terrorist or abetted one could be "detained at an appropriate place" by the secretary of defense and tried by military tribunals created by the secretary of defense.[99] When Judge Advocate General lawyers found out about the order, some were upset and believed that the procedures for courts martial should have been used.[100] The order also declared that no court would have jurisdiction to hear any appeal of a decision or for a writ of habeas corpus (Sec. 2(a)). Any evidence would be admitted that would "have probative value to a reasonable person" (Sec. 7(2)). Evidence obtained through torture might be considered reasonable to a presiding officer.

It may be reasonable to use lawfully established military commissions to try enemy belligerents. However, the procedures set out in DOD Military Commission Order No. 1 (March 21, 2002) contained a number of problems.[101] They provided no independent authority, other than the president's decision, to establish military tribunals. Military commissions that have been established by previous presidents were created pursuant to acts of Congress, which has the constitutional authority to "define and punish ... Offenses against the Law of Nations" (Article I, Section 8, Clause 10). Neither did the commissions provide for any review outside the executive branch. That is, the person would be indicted by a subordinate of the president based on evidence provided by subordinates of the president; the defendant would be tried by subordinates of the president; the defendant would be sentenced by subordinates of the president; and the only appeal would be to the president.

In passing the Detainee Treatment Act (DTA) of 2005,[102] Congress banned the torture of detainees by U.S. forces anywhere in the world. But in addition, the Bush administration was able to append a restriction barring habeas corpus relief to any

Guantanamo detainee. The act said that "no court, justice, or judge shall have jurisdiction to hear or consider ... an application for a writ of habeas corpus filed by or on behalf of an alien detained by the Department of Defense at Guantanamo Bay, Cuba; or any other action against the United States or its agents relating to any aspect of the detention, transfer, treatment, trial, or conditions of confinement of an alien who is or was detained by the United States."[103]

The act required the Defense Department to set up what were called Combatant Status Review Tribunals (CSRTs) to determine whether each detainee was properly classified as an enemy combatant and whether he was entitled to POW status. The set of procedures in the CSRT was expected to substitute for the writ of habeas corpus in that they allowed the detainee to argue that he was not an enemy combatant. The law allowed only limited appeals to the D.C. Circuit contesting whether the procedures of the CSRT hearings were followed or concerning the constitutionality of the act itself (Section 1005). Thus, as with the military commissions, the whole set of procedures was conducted by the executive branch by executive branch personnel, and the only substantive appeal (e.g., on the merits of the argument or the facts) was to executive branch personnel.

Hamdan was a Yemeni national who was captured in Afghanistan in November 2001 and turned over to U.S. forces. He was transported to Guantanamo, where he was charged with conspiracy to aid al Qaeda (as Osama bin Laden's driver) and was going to be tried by a military commission established by President Bush. Hamdan filed a habeas corpus petition, arguing that he was entitled to be tried under the requirements of Common Article 3 of the Third Geneva Convention. The district court granted Hamdan's petition for habeas corpus, but the Court of Appeals for the D.C. Circuit reversed the district court. When the Supreme Court heard the appeal, the Bush administration argued that the Detainee Treatment Act, discussed above, denied jurisdiction to any U.S. court.

Justice Stevens, who wrote for the court, ruled that the DTA stripped courts of jurisdiction only for future appeals, not for those already pending when the law was signed, which Hamdan's was.[104] The court concluded that the military commissions and procedures established by President Bush were not authorized by the Constitution or any U.S. law (not the Authorization to use Military Force, the Detainee Treatment Act, or the Uniform Code of Military Justice). The UCMJ restricts the use of military commissions to those that comply with the provisions of the UCMJ and common law of war. Thus the president had to comply with existing U.S. laws. In making his argument, Stevens quoted Chief Justice Chase in *Ex parte Milligan*: "Congress cannot direct the conduct of campaigns, nor can the President, or any commander under him, without the sanction of Congress, institute tribunals for the trial and punishment of offences, either of soldiers or civilians, unless in cases of a controlling necessity." That necessity did not exist in the *Hamdan* case, Stevens argued, "so the procedural rights of courts martial must apply, the commission's procedures are illegal."[105] He concluded that the "the military commission convened to try Hamdan lacked authority to proceed because its structure and procedures violate both the UCMJ and the Geneva Conventions."[106]

With respect to elements of a fair trial, the procedures created by the Defense Department by Military Commission Order No. 1 had a number of defects.[107] For instance:

the detainee, though presumed innocent, had the burden of proof to show that the allegations of the government are incorrect (Sec. 5(b));
the detainee is limited in ability to gather and present his own evidence (Sec. 6(D)(5) and (9))
coerced testimony can be used against the detainee (Sec. 6(D)(1));
civilian defense counsel may be denied access to evidence (6(b)(3)).[108]

In addition, the accused could be excluded from being present or being told of the evidence used against him. Importantly, there was no provision for the decisions of the commissions to be appealed outside of the executive branch; the president would hear the final appeals, not a federal court.

The commissions thus violated the Geneva Convention Common Article 3, which provides that detainees, "as a minimum," are entitled to be tried "by a regularly constituted court affording all the judicial guarantees … recognized as an indispensable by civilized peoples."[109] Stevens noted that the U.S. Army *Law of War Handbook* says Common Article 3 "serves as a minimum yardstick of protection in all conflicts, not just internal armed conflicts."[110] The military commissions lacked the judicial guarantees to the accused of being informed of charges, having the opportunity to rebut them, and to be represented by counsel.

The court did not say that Hamdan could not be detained for the duration of the hostilities, but if the government wanted to try him for a crime, it had to use regularly constituted courts that comply with minimal requirements of procedural due process to do so. The court finally concluded: "Even assuming that Hamdan is a dangerous individual who would cause great harm or death to innocent civilians given the opportunity, the Executive nevertheless must comply with the prevailing rule of law in undertaking to try him and subject him to criminal punishment."[111]

The claim of President Bush that he had the constitutional authority to imprison terrorist suspects indefinitely without the due process of charging them and trying them in a regularly constituted court was repudiated by the *Hamdan* ruling. As a result of the Supreme Court ruling in *Hamdan,* the administration convinced Congress to pass the Military Commissions Act, which denied habeas corpus to all Guantanamo inmates.

Boumediene v. Bush

In order to overcome the roadblock that the Supreme Court decisions threw in the way of the administration's policy on military commissions, President Bush sought legislation that would authorize the creation of military commissions and spell out limits on the rights of detainees. In seeking this legislation, the administration wanted congressional authority to create military commissions, Combatant Status Review Tribunals (to determine if a detainee qualified as a prisoner of war or was an illegal combatant), and the leeway to use harsh interrogation procedures that would not be subject to prosecution under U.S. law.

After several weeks of contentious debate between the two political parties, S. 3930 was passed by both houses of Congress, and President Bush signed the Military Commissions Act of 2006 (PL 109–366) into law. It gave the Bush administration most of what it wanted in order to enable it to deal with detainees in ways that had been invalidated by the *Hamdan* ruling. Most directly, the law authorized the president to establish military commissions to try alien detainees believed to be terrorists or unlawful enemy combatants. The law defined "enemy combatant" as "a person who has engaged in hostilities or who has purposefully and materially supported hostilities against the United States or its co-belligerents," or "a person who ... has been determined to be an unlawful enemy combatant by a Combatant Status Review Tribunal" established by the president or secretary of defense (Sec. 948(a)). These provisions seem to allow for the possibility that U.S. citizens, if declared so by the president, could be treated as enemy combatants.

The MCA provided that any appeals of the decisions of the commissions could concern only questions of law—e.g., whether the law is constitutional or in conflict with other laws—and not of fact. The act also amended the DTA's limits on jurisdiction by stripping courts of the right to hear any habeas corpus appeals of any alien in U.S. custody who had been declared an enemy combatant.[112] In addition, no court could consider any other challenge concerning "any aspect of the detention, transfer, treatment, trial, or conditions of confinement of an alien who is or was detained by the United States" (MCA Sec. 7). Thus it appeared that aliens could be held indefinitely without any access to the courts to challenge their status or treatment. The act also declared that the president could interpret the Geneva Conventions and that the military commissions set up by the act were in accord with Common Article 3 of Geneva and thus regularly constituted courts.[113]

The court-stripping provisions of the act regarding habeas corpus were quickly challenged in court, and were upheld by the District of Columbia Court of Appeals in *Boumediene v. Bush*[114] in February 2007. The appeal challenged the court-stripping provisions of both the Detainee Treatment Act of 2005 and the Military Commissions Act of 2006. By a 2–1 majority, the court ruled that the language and congressional intent of the laws were clear and that U.S. courts did not have jurisdiction to hear habeas corpus appeals from aliens held at Guantanamo and that aliens held outside the United States had no constitutional rights.

The habeas-related Supreme Court rulings in *Rasul* and *Hamdan* were based on statutory interpretation and did not reach the constitutional question of whether the two laws amounted to a suspension of habeas corpus. The Constitution allows the suspension only in cases of "Rebellion or Invasion" (Art. I, Sec. 9), and then only by Congress. In *Boumediene v. Bush*, however, the Court of Appeals ruled that the alien inmates of Guantanamo did not have a constitutional right to habeas and thus the suspension clause was not violated by the MCA. The decision involved a constitutional ruling, and the Supreme Court was faced with the question of affirming or denying the decision of the appeals court.

In the fall of 2007, the Supreme Court heard the case and in the spring of 2008, in a 5–4 decision, it decided that the court-stripping provisions of the Detainee Treatment Act and the Military Commissions Act were unconstitutional and thus Boumediene (and other detainees) did have a constitutional right to habeas corpus. The court argued that "the habeas privilege was one of the few safeguards of liberty specified in a Constitution that, at the outset, had no Bill of Rights" and that the privilege "was designed to protect against cyclical abuses of the writ by the Executive and Legislative Branches."[115] The court noted that the United States has had "complete and uninterrupted control of Guantanamo for over 100 years," and that signing a lease with Cuba in 1903 did not change the fact of de facto U.S. sovereignty. Despite the government's argument that the lease meant that Guantanamo was outside the United States and thus U.S. prisoners were not covered by the Constitution, the Court stated that "the Nation's basic charter cannot be contracted away like this," nor can Congress and the president "switch the Constitution on or off at will" (Slip Opinion, p. 5).

The court ruled that the CSRT procedures did not operate as an adequate substitute for habeas corpus because detainees did not have sufficient opportunity to rebut the charge that they were enemy combatants, that they did not have a right to counsel, that they might not have access to the full charges against them, and that hearsay could be used to convict them. Furthermore, since the war on terror "may last a generation or more," the consequences of error on the part of the government were significant (Slip Opinion, p. 7).

The argument that aliens have a constitutional right to a habeas corpus hearing does not imply that they cannot be imprisoned by the military. It merely means that they can challenge the grounds of their imprisonment through a writ of habeas corpus and attempt to persuade a federal judge that the military was mistaken about the basis for their incarceration.[116] It is by no means certain that federal courts would agree with the arguments of detainees, but a hearing in court on the issue might disclose evidence about the conditions of their confinement. Thus in addition to their defense of the CSRTs, the Bush administration did not want any public disclosure of the methods of interrogation to which the detainees at Guantanamo were subjected, arguing that to do so would disclose sensitive intelligence techniques to the enemy. If terrorists knew about the techniques used by U.S. personnel in interrogations, they would be able to train to resist them. Critics of the administration, however, argued that the reasons for the administration not wanting to allow public evidence about detainee treatment was that they did not want their harsh interrogation methods to be made public. Former detainees and public accounts had already disclosed most, if not all, of the techniques that the interrogators used.

Military Officers Resign in Protest

The purpose of the Combat Status Review Tribunals (CSRTs) was to provide detainees with a hearing in which they could challenge the military's contention that they were enemy combatants. The CSRT process was intended to provide an adequate substitute for a habeas corpus hearing by an independent judge. Judge Judith Rogers of the District of Columbia Circuit, in a dissent in the *Boumediene* case, argued that the CSRTs were inadequate because the burden of proof was on the detainee rather than the government, classified evidence could be held secret from the detainee, the judges of the case were in the chain of command of the executive and thus not independent, and detainees were be denied the benefit of counsel.[117] Her judgment was vindicated when the Supreme Court ruled that detainees had a constitutional right to appeal to the judiciary for writs of habeas corpus.

Questions about the impartiality of the CSRTs and the military commissions were raised by two men who participated in their administration as military officers at Guantanamo. Lieutenant Colonel Stephen E. Abraham was an Army Reserve intelligence officer who was assigned to active duty (from 9/11/04 to 3/9/05) to the Office for the Administrative Review of the Detention of Enemy Combatants. He was assigned to gather information about detainees for the central computer depository. This evidence would be used in their CSRT hearings to determine whether or not they would be classified as enemy combatants.

In a statement to the Supreme Court in relation to a case on habeas corpus for Guantanamo detainees, Abraham criticized the process of information-gathering and CSRT decisions. He said that the information used by CSRTs that established that detainees were enemy combatants was fragmentary, generic, outdated, and often not specific to the individuals in question or the circumstances of their capture. "The classified information was stripped down, watered down, removed of context, incomplete and missing essential information . . . What purported to be specific statements of fact lacked even the most fundamental earmarks of objectively credible evidence."[118] In addition, the detainees often had no means of disputing the general evidence provided or questioning statements from other detainees that might have been obtained under duress.

Abraham reported that members of CSRTs felt pressure to decide cases quickly and to determine that detainees were in fact enemy combatants. "The prevailing attitude was 'if they're in Guantanamo, they're there for a reason' . . . Anything that resulted in a 'not enemy combatant' would just send ripples through the entire process. The interpretation is, 'you got the wrong result. Do it again.'"[119] When Abraham himself was assigned to a CSRT, he and two other officers found that there was "no factual basis" for determining the detainee to be an enemy combatant. After their determination, they were ordered to reopen the hearing, but with no further evidence presented, they reaffirmed their first determination that the detainee was not an enemy combatant. Abraham was not assigned to another CSRT panel.[120] All detainees had CSRT hearings, and of 558 cases, 38 were determined not to be enemy combatants.[121]

On October 4, 2007, Morris D. Davis, a career Air Force officer and the chief prosecutor for the military commissions, resigned from his position "because I felt that the system had become deeply politicized and that I could no longer do my job effectively or responsibly."[122] Davis explained that the secretary of defense had replaced a career military officer as "convening authority" with a civilian, Bush administration political appointee. The convening authority oversaw the military commissions process, but rather than acting as a neutral supervisor of the process, the new appointee aligned itself with the prosecution, thus compromising the fairness of the process. In addition, the chief prosecutor (Davis) was placed in the direct chain of command under the DOD general counsel, William Haynes, who had been active in implementing the harsh interrogation policies of the Bush administration. Davis argued that if the tribunals were to be truly impartial military commissions "and not merely a political smoke screen," control of them should be given to professional military officers: "It is time for the political appointees who created this quagmire to let go."[123]

Davis said that he had ruled out any evidence gained through waterboarding, but the legal advisor to the military commissions, Brigadier General Thomas Hartmann, refused to rule out evidence obtained through waterboarding. "Unfortunately, I was overruled on the question, and I resigned my position to call attention to the issue— efforts that were hampered by my being placed under a gag rule and ordered not to testify at a Senate hearing."[124] Hartman also said he was informed by the Pentagon that a military medal for his service at Guantanamo was denied to him because he did "not serve honorably."[125]

These were serious declarations made by officers who participated in the Guantanamo CSRT and commissions process in general, and in specific cases. Abraham, a lawyer, spent twenty-five years in the Army Reserve and was a political conservative; Davis was a career Air Force officer. These statements, based on personal experience, severely undercut any claim that the procedures of the CSRTs or commissions provided adequate, objective hearings about the status or guilt of Guantanamo detainees.

After formal military commissions were convened to prosecute detainees for war crimes, legal problems continued to exist, and concern about them led to the removal of one of the officers charged with administering the commissions. In September 2008, the Department of Defense removed Brigadier General Thomas W. Hartmann from his position as legal adviser to the Convening Authority of the military commissions. Several military judges ruled that Hartmann, though he was supposed to play a neutral role, had tried to convince prosecutors to move their case to trial more quickly and to use evidence that was gained through coercion. Lawyers of the defendants argued that Hartmann's behavior had compromised the cases of the persons they were defending. Thus even after several years of litigation and decisions about the procedures of CSRTs and military commissions, there were serious doubts about the neutrality of the processes.[126]

In late September 2008, Army Lieutenant Colonel Darrel Vandeveld, who was a prosecutor in a case against Mohammed Jawad, resigned from his position because he said that his office had failed to furnish potentially exculpatory evidence to the defense. In a statement made on September 24, 2008, Vandeveld wrote: "I am highly concerned, to the point that I believe I can no longer serve as a prosecutor at the Commissions, about the slipshod, uncertain 'procedure' for affording defense counsel discovery." Jawad was charged with throwing a grenade into a jeep in Kabul in 2002. His defense counsel said that he was sixteen or seventeen years old at that time and that others may have led him to participate in the attack. The chief prosecutor, Army

Colonel Lawrence Morris, said, "We are the most scrupulous organization you can imagine in terms of disclosure to the defense."[127]

On February 7, 2008, Secretary of Defense Robert Gates appointed Susan J. Crawford to be the "convening authority" to oversee the military commissions at Guantanamo. Crawford was a longtime Republican, having been General Counsel of the Army during the Reagan administration and appointed by President George H.W. Bush to be Inspector General of the Department of Defense in 1989. Bush also appointed her to be a judge on the Court of Appeals for the Armed Forces, where she served from 1991 to 2006.

As convening authority of the military commissions, she decided to dismiss war crimes charges against Mohammed al-Qahtani in May of 2008. She later recounted her reasoning:

> We tortured al-Qahtani. His treatment met the legal definition of torture. And that's why I did not refer the case [for prosecution]. The techniques they used were all authorized, but the manner in which they applied them was overly aggressive and too persistent.... You think of torture, you think of some horrendous physical act done to an individual. This was not any one particular act; this was just a combination of things that had a medical impact on him, that hurt his health. It was abusive and uncalled for. And coercive. Clearly coercive. It was that medical impact that pushed me over the edge. For 160 days his only contact was with the interrogators. Forty-eight of 54 consecutive days of 18–20 hour interrogations. Standing naked in front of a female agent. Subject to strip searches and insults to his mother and sister.[128]

She concluded that in the early days after 9/11 there was a lot of pressure on U.S. officials to learn about any possible future attacks. "I sympathize with the intelligence gatherers in those days after 9/11, not knowing what was coming next and trying to gain information to keep us safe. But there still has to be a line that we should not cross. And unfortunately what this has done, I think, has tainted everything going forward."[129]

Conclusion

The preemptive approach of the Bush administration to its legal defense of harsh interrogation and torture was revealing. They began to lay the groundwork for defense against charges of torture shortly after 9/11. John Yoo's memo of September 25, 2001, argued that the president's decisions about how to deal with any terrorist threat could not be constrained by law or treaty. "These decisions, under our Constitution, are for the President alone to make."[130] The Military Order of November 13, 2001, allowed no appeals by any prisoners to the judiciary. The memo to President Bush of January 25, 2002, signed by Alberto Gonzales, explicitly stated that suspending the Geneva Conventions would "substantially reduce[s] the threat of domestic criminal prosecution under the War Crimes Act."[131] The Bybee memo of August 1, 2002, parsed the legal definition of torture so as to include as torture only the most heinous acts, such as rape, mutilation, and abuse to the point of death, leaving leeway for a broad range of cruel, inhuman, and demeaning actions that could be used against suspects of terror.

Congressional action in response to the administration's interrogation policies was mixed. The Detainee Treatment Act outlawed "cruel, inhuman, or degrading treatment or punishment," but it limited access to habeas corpus and judicial oversight of administrative actions. The Military Commissions Act stripped the courts of habeas corpus jurisdiction and gave legal sanction to the military commission procedures that the president had sought. It also allowed the president to reinterpret Common Article 3 of the Geneva Conventions so as to allow the CIA to continue using harsh interrogation techniques, such as waterboarding and stress positions, that most of the world considers to be torture.

The Supreme Court, often with a narrow majority of five to four, set back some of the claims of the Bush administration. It ruled that U.S. citizens (*Hamdi*) and alien detainees (*Rasul*) were entitled to habeas corpus hearings. It also invalidated the military commissions, though the administration quickly convinced Congress to pass the MCA, allowing the president to create them. In *Boumediene* it made an important ruling that detainees in Guantanamo had a constitutional right to habeas corpus.

Allowing detainees to appeal for writs of habeas corpus does not mean that any enemy prisoner can get immediate access to the U.S. court system. Granting habeas relief is at the discretion of judges, and most often, administrative appeals have to be exhausted before a habeas writ is granted. A large part of the reason that the Supreme Court was willing to take such strong stands on habeas corpus and force the Bush administration to allow detainees to appeal for habeas relief was that detainees had been held in Guantanamo for years, and the Bush administration argued that it could incarcerate individuals indefinitely without trying them or giving them an opportunity to argue that they were innocent. Extreme claims by the administration led to a sweeping decision by the Supreme Court.

The strategy of the administration was to delay continually the implementation of Supreme Court decisions with legal arguments and appeals. For instance, after the Parhat decision that he was not an enemy combatant, the D.C. District Court ordered him and his fellow Uighurs released. But the Justice Department succeeded in blocking the release and argued that, regardless of the habeas corpus decision, only the president could decide whether to release detainees into the United States. This argument was in accord with the administration's expansive claims to executive power. The problem was that the administration could not find another country to receive the Uighurs and its refusal to release them into the United States meant that they could continue to be held in prison indefinitely, despite the habeas corpus order by the court.

Thus the extraordinary assertions of executive power by President Bush were only partially challenged by the other two branches. Many of its claims would remain as "loaded weapons" that any future president might use to justify further claims of executive power.[132]

CHAPTER 6

Command Responsibility

Torture is systematic in Iraq, and the most senior officials in the regime are involved.
—Donald Rumsfeld at a press conference held on December 3, 2002, the day after he signed the memo authorizing the use of harsh techniques on Guantanamo detainees[1]

We did not torture anyone.... The president instructed us that nothing we would do would be outside of our obligations, legal obligations, under the Convention Against Torture .... I didn't authorize anything. I conveyed the authorization of the administration to the agency ... by definition, if it was authorized by the president, it did not violate our obligations under the Conventions Against Torture.
—Condoleezza Rice[2]

America's idea of what is torture is not the same as ours and does not appear to coincide with that of most civilized nations.
—British judge Sir Andrew Collins[3]

The argument of this book has been that President Bush used his power as president very effectively in pursuing a policy direction that would allow U.S. personnel to use harsh interrogation methods to obtain intelligence in the war on terror. His aides marshaled legal arguments to support his position, despite serious objections from Secretary of State Colin Powell and professional military lawyers in the Judge Advocate General Corps, among others. Vice President Cheney was the driving force behind interrogation policy in the Bush administration and framed the issues for President Bush's consideration. Nevertheless, President Bush was responsible for the policies of his administration, and he publicly defended "the program" of an "alternative set of procedures" to interrogate prisoners who were suspected of terrorism.

President Bush's intentions were relayed down through the chain of command: from Defense Secretary Rumsfeld; to theater, field, and base commanders; to officers in charge of interrogations; to the noncommissioned officers and enlisted personnel who carried out most of the harsh interrogations. His policy directions were also carried out by CIA personnel who often had control of the highest ranking al Qaeda prisoners. The use of extremely harsh methods of interrogation came, however, at a high cost to the United States. President Bush's justifications for harsh interrogations have been challenged by a range of legal opinions, including criticisms by some of his own appointees. His policies and leadership contributed to the terrible excesses of abuse and torture publicized in the photographs of Abu Ghraib and documented by multiple military and non-governmental investigations.

This final chapter will begin with an argument that the impetus for increasingly harsh interrogations did not bubble up from interrogators at the bottom of the chain of command, but rather began at the top. Not all of the crimes that were committed by U.S. personnel were intended by President Bush. But the directions and pressure that led to abuses in interrogating detainees emanated from the top, and the excesses that followed were partially the result of the lifting of restraints that began with the suspension of the Geneva Conventions by President Bush. The chapter will then take up the concept of command responsibility as it has developed in the United States and apply the doctrine to the Bush administration.

Many officials warned their superiors about the consequences of the administration's interrogation policies, but these warnings did not lead Bush administration appointees to take serious steps to end the behavior. The abuse did end in the military after the Detainee Treatment Act was passed and the *Hamdan* decision was made by the Supreme Court. With these changes in governmental policy, the Army returned to honoring Common Article 3 of the Geneva Conventions and revised its field manual on interrogations. President Bush, however, insisted that the CIA continue to be authorized to use harsh interrogation techniques. Finally, the consequences of this episode in U.S. history for the United States will be examined. The chapter will conclude that if the United States is to return to its former status of defender of liberty and beacon of justice in the world, it must confront its abuse of detainees in the war on terror, admit its mistakes, and ensure that they will never happen again.

Bad Apples at the Bottom or Leadership from the Top?

A consistent theme of the Bush administration was that instances of torture and abuse were isolated and committed by a few sadistic individuals at the bottom of the military hierarchy. It was further implied that requests for harsh methods of interrogation originated from interrogators at Guantanamo who passed their ideas up the chain of command. These claims are undermined by the actions of the top levels of the Bush administration in the White House, the Department of Defense, and the Justice Department.

In addition to official memoranda and executive directives, leadership was also provided in public statements by high-level public officials, especially those at the top of the chain of command. Even if low-level perpetrators of torture do not directly hear the statements of their superiors, the impact of authoritative public statements is far-reaching. High-level officials in the administration and the military take seriously the statements as expressions of policy direction and pass down the chain of command the attitudes of governmental leaders. In the war on terror, statements by President Bush, Vice President Cheney, and Secretary of Defense Rumsfeld were effective in conveying the administration's point of view about detainees and the type of treatment they were expected to receive.

President Bush, in talking about the detainees at Guantanamo in July of 2003, declared: "The only thing I know for certain is that these are bad people."[4] Vice President Cheney said: "They [Guantanamo detainees] are very dangerous. They are devoted to killing millions of Americans, innocent Americans, if they can, and they are perfectly prepared to die in the effort."[5] On January 27, 2002, Secretary of Defense Donald Rumsfeld said just before he left for Guantanamo: "These are among the most dangerous, best trained vicious killers on the face of the earth."[6] Statements such as these set the tone for subsequent policy directives and personnel decisions that led to the torture of detainees.

In addition to statements by the Bush administration leadership, changes in policy set the conditions under which torture took place. The argument here is that formal changes from previous policy made a difference; memoranda were read and acted upon by civilian and military leaders, public statements by the president and other administration officials were heard, and pressure from above for "actionable intelligence" was taken seriously. These actions, taken together, constituted Bush administration policy with respect to the treatment of detainees.

Several key changes in the operation and organization of U.S. forces with respect to U.S. prisoners were made that allowed the abuses at Guantanamo, Bagram Air Force Base, and Abu Ghraib to occur. According to the Schlesinger Report, special techniques of interrogation were developed for use at Guantanamo, these techniques and procedures were then transferred to Afghanistan, and the techniques and personnel were transferred from Guantanamo and Afghanistan to Abu Ghraib.[7]

Members of the Bush administration argued that the impetus for using "enhanced" interrogation techniques came from interrogators at Guantanamo and their commander, General Dunlavey, in 2002. But as explained in Chapter Two, the direction of influence was much more of a two-way street, and pressure for intelligence originated at the top of the hierarchy. The path to abusive interrogations began with President Bush's military order of November 13, 2001, and the way was paved by his suspension of the Geneva Conventions on February 7, 2002. Rumsfeld appointed General Dunlavey to command Guantanamo with orders to extract intelligence more aggressively.

In the summer of 2002, inquiries about the use of SERE techniques originated in Defense Counsel Haynes's office, and training in the techniques by SERE trainers and CIA personnel were conducted in the fall of 2002. The Bybee memos of August 2002 (the "Golden Shield") laid the legal groundwork for justifying abusive techniques and the immunization of interrogation personnel from future prosecution. Top lawyers from the administration visited Guantanamo in the fall of 2002, demonstrating the purported legality of the techniques in use and the direct interest of President Bush and Secretary Rumsfeld.

Personal visits to Abu Ghraib impressed upon intelligence personnel the importance that the top levels of the administration placed on actionable intelligence. For instance, the visit of a "senior member of the National Security Council staff" to Abu Ghraib in November 2003 sent a strong signal that intelligence in Iraq was valued at the highest levels of the U.S. government.[8] Army Lieutenant Colonel Steven Jordan, head of the Joint Interrogation and Detention Center at Abu Ghraib, said that he felt pressure from senior officials to produce more actionable intelligence, particularly from the visit of Fran Townsend, deputy assistant to President Bush and one of the top aides to Condoleezza Rice on the NSC staff.[9]

Finally, and most authoritatively, meetings of the principals of the National Security Council explicitly authorized specific techniques to be used on detainees at Guantanamo. When asked about the techniques used on Khalid Sheikh Mohammed, which included waterboarding, Vice President Cheney said: "I was aware of the program certainly, and involved in helping get the process cleared."[10] In light of these facts, any argument that the initiation of the use of abusive techniques originated at the bottom of the hierarchy cannot be sustained.

Command Responsibility

The concept of command responsibility in the United States can be traced back to the Massachusetts Provisional Congress, which in 1775 adopted a statement of the responsibility of its military officers.

> Every Officer commanding ... shall keep good order, and to the utmost of his power, redress all such abuses or disorder which may be committed by any Officer or a Soldier under his command; if upon complaint made to him of Officer or Soldiers beating or otherwise ill-treating any persons ... the said commander, who shall refuse or admit to see Justice done this offender ... shall ... be punished, as ordered by General Court-Martial, in such manner as if he himself had committed the crimes or disorders complained of.[11]

During the war in the Philippines, President Theodore Roosevelt, referring to the court martial of a U.S. general, declared: "the very fact that warfare is of such a character as to afford infinite provocation for the commission of acts of cruelty by junior officers and enlisted men, must make the officers in high and responsible positions peculiarly careful in their bearing and conduct so as to keep a moral check over the acts of an improper character by their subordinates."[12]

In modern times, the principles of command responsibility have been set out most authoritatively in the International Military Tribunal at Nuremberg and the Military Tribunal of the Far East. The Nuremberg Tribunals established that a claim that one was carrying out orders does not constitute a defense for war crimes. Subordinates are obliged to obey only lawful orders. In addition, the Nuremberg trials established that a general in command of an occupied territory was responsible for preventing war crimes in his area of responsibility regardless of whether he had tactical command of the forces in the immediate area of the crimes.[13]

In the war with Japan in the Far East, General Tomoyuki Yamashita had overall command of Japanese forces in the Philippines, and in 1944 his troops killed thousands of innocent civilians and held prisoners of war who were starved and ill-treated.

The charge against him was that he "failed to discharge his duty as commandeer to control the operations of members of his command, permitting them to commit brutal atrocities and other high crimes against the people of the United States and its allies."[14] In his defense, Yamashita argued that at the time he did not have direct control over his subordinates, that he had lost communication with them, and that they had disobeyed his orders to leave Manilla. He argued further that he had not ordered the atrocities to be committed, that he had not tolerated them, and that he did not even know that they were going on.

Yamashita was nevertheless convicted on the grounds that awareness of the atrocities was common knowledge, that he tacitly permitted them to be committed, and that he did not take punitive action against those under his command who committed the crimes. The sentence was reviewed by a board headed by General MacArthur which concluded that the "conclusion is inevitable that the accused knew about [the crimes] and either gave his tacit approval to them or at least failed to do anything to prevent them or to punish their perpetrators."[15] Yamashita appealed the decision to the U.S. Supreme Court, but his appeal was rejected. In writing for the court, Justice Stone stated the crux of the matter:

> The question is then whether the law of war imposes on an army commander a duty to take such appropriate measures as are within his power to control the troops under his command for the prevention of specified acts which are violations of a law of war and which are likely to attend the occupation of hostile territory by an uncontrolled soldiery, and whether he may be charged with personal responsibility for his failure to take such measure when violations result.[16]

Stone argued that the purpose of the law of war is "to protect civilian populations and prisoners of war from brutality" and that this purpose "would largely be defeated if the commander of an invading army could with impunity neglect to take reasonable measures for their protection."[17] Stone concluded that, as commander in the Philippines, Yamashita had an "affirmative duty to take such measures as were within his power and appropriate in the circumstances to protect prisoners of war and the civilian population."[18]

The mistreatment and torture of detainees in the war on terror certainly does not compare with the vast atrocities committed by some in the military forces of Germany and Japan during World War II. The principles developed in response to the atrocities with American leadership do, however, provide guidance about how to judge the actions of superior leaders when their subordinates commit war crimes or merely allow abuse to occur. The doctrine of command responsibility has developed into a set of three principles that the doctrine embraces:

1. There must be a superior–subordinate relationship.
2. The superior must have known or had reason to know that the subordinate was about to commit a crime or had committed a crime.
3. The superior failed to take necessary and reasonable measures to prevent the crime or to punish the perpetrator. [19]

The doctrine of command responsibility was further developed in the trials of commanders of military units in the wars of the 1990s in the former Yugoslavia. In the prosecution of Sefer Halilovic for not preventing his troops from killing thirty-three Bosnian Croat civilians in Grabovica on September 8–9, 1993, the court elaborated on the doctrine. The court specified that the superior/subordinate relationship does not have to be "direct or immediate in nature" but can be remote as long as the element of control of subordinates is present. The superior does not have to have "actual knowledge" of crimes having been committed, but general information that "would put him on notice of the risk of" criminal acts would be sufficient. [20]

The principles of command responsibility have been widely accepted by the U.S. Army and by customary international law. The U.S. Army Field Manual 27–10, Section 501, lays out the criteria:

> In some cases, military commanders may be responsible for war crimes committed by subordinate members of the armed forces, or other persons subject to their control. Thus, for instance, when troops commit massacres and atrocities against the civilian population of occupied territory or against prisoners of war, the responsibility may rest not only with the actual perpetrators but also with the commander. Such a responsibility arises directly when the acts in question have been committed in pursuance of an order of the commander concerned. The commander is also responsible if he has actual knowledge, *or should have knowledge,* through reports received by him or through other means, that troops or other persons subject to his control are about to commit or *have committed a war crime and he fails to take the necessary and reasonable steps to insure compliance with the law of war or to punish violations thereof* (emphasis added). [21]

The U.S. Army Field Manual on the Law of Land Warfare states that: "The commander is also responsible if he has actual knowledge, or should have knowledge ... that troops or other persons subject to his control are about to commit or have committed a war crime and he fails to take the necessary and reasonable steps to insure compliance with the law of war or to punish violators."[22]

The above elements of the doctrine of command responsibility may be relevant to understanding the extent to which persons in the chain of command of U.S. forces or their advisors were responsible for preventing or punishing the abuse or torture of detainees during the U.S. war on terror. Ironically, the Military Commissions Act of 2006, section 950q, provides that:

> a person is punishable as a principal under this chapter who ... commits an offense punishable by this chapter, or aids, abets, counsels, commands, or procures its commission [or] is a superior commander who, with regard to acts punishable under this chapter, knew, had reason to know, or should have known, that a subordinate was about to commit such acts or had done so and who *failed to take the necessary and reasonable measures to prevent such acts or to punish the perpetrators thereof* (emphasis added). [23]

This formulation of command responsibility written into U.S. law in 2006 brings into sharp focus the actions of the top levels of the chain of command during the Bush administration.

Command Responsibility and U.S. Policy

The first criterion of command responsibility is a command–subordinate relationship. The military personnel at Guantanamo, Bagram Air Force Base, and Abu Ghraib all fall within the chain of command that extends up from their immediate commanders to the Secretary of Defense and to President Bush. Each of the persons is bound to follow the legal orders of their superiors. In addition to those directly in the chain of command, others, such as lawyers, had effective influence on detainee treatment policy. Perhaps most importantly, Vice President Cheney exercised effective control over much of detainee policy. He and his aide, David Addington, formulated crucial policies and enforced them in the executive branch. Addington's decisions played key roles in excluding Powell and Rice from deliberations concerning the military commissions order that authorized the designation of enemy combatants and denied any review by the courts. Cheney, Addington, and Gonzales were central to President Bush's decision to suspend the Geneva Conventions. Addington, Gonzales, and Haynes visited Guantanamo to encourage aggressive interrogations in order to obtain intelligence. Haynes was key to Rumsfeld's decision to authorize specific interrogation techniques in December 2002 and April 2003.

It could be argued that President Bush and his aides should have known that the consequences of their actions might involve harsh interrogation techniques that were tantamount to torture. But it is not necessary to establish that these government officials should have known the likely consequences of their initial decisions, because the highest officials did, in fact, know about and, indeed, participated in making decisions about the specific techniques used on at least some of the detainees. The specific techniques that were to be used, for example, on Abu Zubaydah and Khalid Sheikh Mohammed were the explicit subject of meetings of the NSC principles chaired by Rice and attended by Cheney, Powell, Tenet, Rumsfeld, and Ashcroft. President Bush publicly acknowledged that he knew of and approved of their meetings. Thus there can be no doubt that the very top levels of the administration had explicit knowledge and participated in decisions about the techniques, including waterboarding, that were to be used on detainees in order to force them to confess to crimes or reveal intelligence information.

Most of the official investigations of abuse and torture were framed so as not to address the issue of command responsibility or the possible culpability of senior officers. Their ambits were carefully circumscribed to those directly involved in the abuse of detainees. Several of the reports, however, did address leadership issues, though somewhat obliquely. Lieutenant General Anthony R. Jones was instructed not to investigate the possible involvement of personnel higher in the chain of command than the 205th Military Intelligence Brigade.[24] Jones, however, argued that "the events at Abu Ghraib cannot be understood in a vacuum." The causes of the abuse ranged from inadequate resources, to confusion about allowable interrogation techniques, to conflicting "policy memoranda," to "leadership failure."[25] Jones concluded that "leadership failure, at the brigade level and below, clearly was a factor in not sooner discovering and taking actions to prevent" the abuses.[26] General Fay, in his report on the behavior of intelligence personnel at Abu Ghraib, argued that the abuses resulted from "systemic problems" and "intense pressure felt by the personnel on the ground to produce actionable intelligence from detainees."[27]

The investigation and report that came closest to addressing command responsibility was that of James Schlesinger, which was commissioned by Secretary Rumsfeld. Schlesinger argued that the pressure from above to obtain intelligence played an important role in encouraging the abuse of detainees. "It is clear that pressure for additional intelligence and the more aggressive methods sanctioned by the Secretary of Defense memorandum resulted in stronger interrogation techniques. They did contribute to a belief that stronger interrogation methods were needed and appropriate in the treatment of detainees."[28] Military leaders in Iraq "conveyed a sense of tacit approval of abusive behaviors toward prisoners."[29]

Schlesinger found that Lieutenant General Sanchez, "reasoning from the President's memorandum of February 7, 2002," believed that the presence of "unlawful combatants" justified more aggressive interrogation techniques.[30] Sanchez subsequently changed his guidance, and the Schlesinger Report stated that "the existence of confusing and inconsistent interrogation technique policies contributed to the belief that additional interrogation techniques were condoned."[31]

Thus President Bush's decision to suspend the Geneva Conventions, though explicitly not applied to Iraq, nevertheless had far-reaching effects and was interpreted to encourage the harsh treatment of detainees. The Schlesinger Report also specifically mentioned the direct interest of the White House, indicated by the visit of a senior NSC staffer to Abu Ghraib in November 2003 (the time period when many of the abuses were taking place).[32] The Schlesinger Report concluded that "it is clear that pressure for additional intelligence and the more aggressive methods sanctioned by the Secretary of Defense memorandum resulted in stronger interrogation techniques."[33]

Warnings Disregarded

The doctrine of command responsibility requires that if superiors become aware of abuse or potential abuse, they must take steps to end it. Yet from the very beginning of the establishment of interrogation policy, members of the administration as well as civilian and military career professionals warned of the probable consequences of administration decisions. And when the policies were implemented, incidents of abuse and torture were reported, but largely ignored by Bush administration leaders. After abuse, mistreatment, and torture were conducted by low-level enlisted personnel, many instances were reported to various levels in the chain of command. If such behavior was *not* the policy of the administration, then one would expect that when administration officials became aware that abuse was occurring, they would have changed policies and put a stop to it. But this did not happen; administration officials were warned many times about the potential for abuse and abuse that was actually occurring, but they refused to take actions to stop it.

This section will first cite warnings about the probable consequences of administration policies, warnings that were ignored or suppressed by Bush administration officials. It will then describe accounts of actual abuse and torture reported to the chain of command; the administration did not take actions to stop the abuse. It will then show that, even after the abuses at Abu Ghraib were made public, the administration resisted any change in policy that would have reduced the "flexibility" of U.S. interrogators by outlawing cruel, inhuman, and degrading techniques. If the Bush administration did not intend for the harsh interrogation techniques to be used, they would have listened to the warnings and taken action to stop them. That they did not demonstrates that abusive interrogations were the implicit policy of the Bush administration and that the actions of administration leaders fell under the doctrine of command responsibility.

Warnings About Future Consequences of Detainee Policy

When military lawyers were allowed to read (but not copy) the draft of President Bush's Military Order of November 13, 2001, they objected that it did not accord with U.S. legal obligations under the Geneva Conventions, and their last-minute efforts to change it were not successful. When John Yoo wrote a memo arguing that the Geneva Conventions should not apply to the Taliban or al Qaeda, State Department Counsel William Taft wrote a memo arguing that the Geneva rules could be followed by the United States without compromising national security. Nevertheless, Alberto Gonzales recommended that President Bush abandon Geneva, despite Colin Powell's warning that the Geneva Conventions were intended to cover situations such as the war on terror.

On April 15, 2002, Amnesty International sent a memorandum to President Bush and Secretary Rumsfeld about terrible conditions in Guantanamo and the killing and poor treatment of detainees in Afghanistan.[34] When a draft of Rumsfeld's December 2, 2002, memo was seen by military lawyers in November, lawyers from the Air Force, Marine Corps, and the Army as well as the top legal adviser to the DOD Criminal Task Force at Guantanamo wrote pointed memos (quoted in Chapter Two) arguing that the recommendations to authorize exceptional interrogation techniques were ill-advised. In addition to warnings about the potential moral, legal, and policy problems with interrogation policy, there had been a number of warnings (explained in Chapter Three) that the people who had been transferred to Guantanamo were not all guilty of supporting terrorism and that there were many who had no information of any intelligence value.

In the summer of 2003, Jack Goldsmith was appointed to be director of the Office of Legal Counsel. After he had examined the Bybee I memo of August 2, 2002, he decided that the legal reasoning was so flawed that he had to withdraw the memo. He was opposed adamantly by David Addington and the vice president, but he nevertheless insisted and had it rewritten so that it did not provide the "golden shield" that the interrogators had considered the original version (see details in Chapter Two). His warnings, however, did not deter the administration from its policy of harsh interrogation techniques.

Warnings About Actual Abuse

In the summer of 2002, a senior CIA analyst went to Guantanamo and interviewed a random sample of about twenty-four detainees in their own languages, which he spoke. He concluded that about a third of detainees were not connected to terrorism, and that he thought the United States was committing war crimes by holding these people and treating them harshly. National Security Adviser Rice's counsel, John Bellinger, brought the report to a meeting in Alberto Gonzales's office in the White House, but David Addington insisted that the president had decided that all detainees at Guantanamo were enemy combatants, and that the decision could not be questioned. He saw it as an issue of presidential power.[35] The report was also rejected when it was delivered to the Pentagon. In the late fall of 2002, Spike Bowman of the FBI made three calls to professional colleagues in the Office of Secretary of Defense to express concern about the harsh techniques being used at Guantanamo. His concerns were politely noted, but no changes in policy followed.[36]

After Secretary Rumsfeld approved the December 2, 2002, memo authorizing expanded interrogation techniques, civilian members of DOD expressed alarm and concern. Dave Brant, head of the DOD Criminal Investigation Task Force; Mark Fallon, his deputy; and Mike Gelles, its chief psychologist, were so upset at the conduct of interrogations at Guantanamo that Brant and Gelles went to see Alberto Mora, general counsel of the Navy. Mora courageously confronted Haynes several times and finally convinced Haynes to get Rumsfeld to rescind his December 2 order. But Rumsfeld appointed a working group to examine interrogation policies that was led by a hardline appointee, and the group was ordered to use John Yoo's analysis as its basis. When the working group was deliberating over its recommendations to Rumsfeld, judge advocates of the Air Force, Army, and Marine Corps as well as Alberto Mora wrote serious objections to the direction the report was taking. The final report, however, was issued on April 4, 2003, without their knowledge, and it recommended a range of techniques to which they had objected.

Shortly after the Iraq War began, in March of 2003, the International Committee of the Red Cross began to send observers to U.S. prison sites in Iraq, and over the next six months made twenty-nine inspections of fourteen sites. It issued reports that were communicated to U.S. commanders about the poor conditions and abuse in U.S. detention centers. In July 2003, it reported fifty allegations of abuse of detainees, including stress positions, prolonged exposure to sun, isolation in dark cells, and strikes with fists and rifle butts.[37]

Early in the war, Paul Bremer and Colin Powell each raised issues about the treatment of detainees with Cheney, Rice, and Rumsfeld.[38] Amnesty International also raised the issue of treatment of detainees in May 2003. There were also numerous articles in the popular press in late 2003 and early 2004 reporting on the treatment of detainees.[39]

None of these warnings led the administration to change the fundamentals of its interrogation policies.

In addition to the objections to Bush administration policies, a number of individuals stepped forward to report abuses of detainees that they had witnessed or of which they had direct knowledge. Most importantly, on January 13, 2004, Army Specialist Joseph M. Darby disclosed to his superiors the CD containing the infamous photographs taken at Abu Ghraib. This led President Bush to denounce the abuses recorded in the photographs, and to the appointment of a number of DOD investigations cited in Chapter Three. These investigations led to changes in military policy intended to reduce the incidence of abuse. It did not, however, lead to serious actions that would have eliminated the continued use of abusive techniques or the denial of their use by the CIA.

Reports of Abuse After Publication of the Abu Ghraib Photos

When photographs of the abuse and torture at Abu Ghraib were made public in the spring of 2004, expressions of outrage poured out from throughout the world as well as in the United States. President Bush expressed his own disgust at the incidents portrayed in the photographs and said that these were isolated incidents that did not reflect American values or administration policy. The argument of the administration was that these were a few bad apples who broke the law and that the perpetrators would be punished. There can be no argument that the revelation of the photographs and worldwide public outrage did not constitute a blatant warning to the administration that torture and abuse were in fact taking place. A number of internal, executive branch investigations were undertaken, and the military services took remedial actions intended to stop the abuse and torture.

One warning from a professional military perspective came in the form of an editorial of the *Army Times*, which is not published by the government, but which reflects views of many career Army professionals. A hard-hitting editorial took the administration to task for its policies. It argued that responsibility

> extends all the way up the chain of command to the highest reaches of the military hierarchy and its civilian leadership.... The entire affair is a failure of leadership from start to finish. From the moment they are captured, prisoners are hooded, shackled and isolated. The message to the troops: Anything goes.... This was not just a failure of leadership at the local command level. This was a failure that ran straight to the top. Accountability here is essential—even if that means relieving top leaders from duty in a time of war.

The editorial concluded that, "the damage done to the U.S. military and the nation as a whole by the horrifying photographs of U.S. soldiers abusing Iraqi detainees at the notorious prison is incalculable."[40] The difficulty with its recommendation of "relieving top leaders from duty" was that the highest officials in the chain of command were complicit in the policies that led to the abuses.

In September 2005, Captain Ian Fishback, a West Point graduate who served in both Afghanistan and Iraq, wrote a public letter to Senator John McCain to complain about the lack of responsiveness of his superiors to his reports of abuse of detainees. He wrote after the frustration of trying for seventeen months (since about January 2004) to obtain guidance on how prisoners should have been handled.

> While I served in the Global War on Terror, the actions and statements of my leadership led me to believe that United States policy did not require application of the Geneva Conventions in Afghanistan or Iraq. On 7 May 2004, Secretary of Defense Rumsfeld's testimony that the United States followed the Geneva Conventions in Iraq and the "spirit" of the Geneva Conventions in Afghanistan prompted me to begin an approach for clarification. For 17 months, I tried to determine what specific standards governed the treatment of detainees by consulting my chain of command through battalion commander, multiple JAG lawyers....[41]

He said that the inability of U.S. troops to get clear and consistent guidance from their leaders about the correct treatment of prisoners led to "a wide range of abuses including death threats, beatings, broken bones, murder, exposure to elements, extreme forced physical exertion, hostage-taking, stripping, sleep deprivation and degrading treatment" that he and his troops witnessed in both Afghanistan and Iraq.[42] He argued that "prisoner abuse was systemic in the Army."[43]

He and two other soldiers from the 82nd Airborne Division reported that military intelligence personnel told them to soften up detainees before interrogation. According to one sergeant, "They wanted intel. As long as no PUCs [persons under control] came up dead, it happened. We kept it to broken arms and legs."[44] Fishback said that his commanders conveyed the idea that the United States was not bound by the Geneva Conventions, about which he had been trained, and that he did not have to report incidents of prisoner abuse. When he approached his immediate superiors, he was told to "remember the honor of the unit is at stake," and not to make public his experience.[45] Significantly, Captain Fishback's resort to going public with his concerns came a year and a half *after* the Abu Ghraib photos appeared. When Matthew Alexander served as an interrogator in Iraq in 2006, he found that U.S. Army personnel were still using the "deeply flawed, ineffective and un-American way" of conducting interrogations. They were using the "Guantanamo Bay model" of using fear and control.[46]

Even after these warnings, the Bush administration continued to resist restrictions on its harsh interrogation policies. Several policy decisions in the spring and summer of 2005 demonstrate that the administration continued to protect its harsh interrogation policies from those in the administration who objected.

After Alberto Gonzales was confirmed as the Attorney General in February 2005, Steven Bradbury was designated as acting director of OLC, and he drafted two memos that authorized the CIA to use combinations of several techniques at the same time. These included stress positions, sleep deprivation, waterboarding, slapping, and extremes of temperature.[47] James Comey, the deputy attorney general, refused to go along with the policies authorized in the memo because he thought they could easily amount to torture. His judgment was: "It's wrong and you shouldn't do it."[48] Attorney General Gonzales appeared to agree with Comey's arguments, but nevertheless, in a meeting of the Principals Committee, Vice President Cheney, supported by Secretary of State Rice, insisted that the techniques were legal and that Bradbury's draft memos be approved and issued. The memos may have been written to preemptively assure the (purported) legality of such techniques even if the McCain Amendment was passed later that year. (It was passed in the fall of 2005. See Chapter Three for analyses of the memos.)

In June 2005, officials in the Pentagon, as well as military lawyers, felt uneasy about the legality (and the worldwide appearance) of U.S. interrogation policies, and decided to broach a change in policy. Three high-level officials decided to try to persuade President Bush to shut down the CIA interrogation program. In order to do so, they thought that if they could get Secretaries Rumsfeld and Rice to agree, they could get past the vice president. Philip Zelikow had been executive director of the 9/11 Commission and was counselor to Secretary of State Rice. John Bellinger was counsel to Secretary Rice. Matthew Waxman was assistant secretary of defense for detainee issues and formerly a clerk to Justice David Souter. Gordan England was deputy secretary of defense and had been secretary of the navy and president of Lockheed Martin.[49] They met (without Bellinger) in June of 2005 to work out a strategy. They argued that the secret CIA programs would eventually be exposed and that the United States should return to international standards of treatment of detainees, and they proposed closing Guantanamo and the secret CIA prisons abroad. They wrote, "We are not doing this for them [the detainees], we are doing this for us. There is a risk that some intelligence may be lost. As in prior wars, this risk should be accepted as necessary to maintain the integrity of our common-found values."[50]

Secretary Rice seemed to be sympathetic to the proposal, but Secretary Rumsfeld was angry that it had been sent to Rice without his clearance. Rice showed it to national security adviser Hadley, who called a principals meeting to discuss the proposals. Rumsfeld, however, insisted that the draft not be considered in the discussions, and no positive recommendation for changing interrogation policies was issued from the meeting. President Bush did learn of the proposals and thus was aware that the senior members of his administration, including the deputy secretary of defense, strongly advised that his detainee policies be changed and that the proposals had some support from his secretary of state. He decided against any change in his administration's policies.[51]

In the fall of 2005, President Bush had threatened to veto the Detainee Treatment Act authored by John McCain, demonstrating that he did not want his administration to be hindered by a requirement that forbade "cruel, inhuman, or degrading treatment or punishment" (see Chapter 5 for details). When he saw that his veto would probably be overridden, he signed the bill but issued a signing statement indicating that he did not consider himself bound by the law.

In late 2005, Deputy Secretary of Defense Gordon England made another attempt to change administration policy. He chaired a meeting in the Pentagon to consider making it mandatory for the military to treat all prisoners in accord with Common Article 3 of the Geneva Conventions. This would forbid cruel, inhumane, and degrading treatment and outrages on the personal dignity of detainees. The civilian secretaries of each of the services were present as well as the top military officers in each service and their lawyers. Of course, the Geneva Conventions, including CA 3, had been the supreme law of the land (Constitution, Article VI) since they were ratified by the United States in 1955. Each of the military leaders of the services argued in favor of the principle, but William Haynes and Undersecretary of Defense for Intelligence Stephen Cambone argued that it would limit the "flexibility" of the United States. Thus the proposal was not adopted as policy.[52] (In 2006 the *Hamdan* decision of the Supreme Court ruled that the United States *was* bound by the Geneva Conventions, and thus Common Article 3 did apply to U.S. treatment of detainees.)

Immediately after the Supreme Court *Hamdan* decision, the Department of Defense issued an order that restored Common Article 3 of the Geneva Conventions as U.S. policy. The order was signed by Deputy Secretary of Defense Gordon England, rather than Donald Rumsfeld.[53] In September 2006, the Army issued a revised Field Manual, *Human Intelligence Collector Operations,* which reinstalled the Geneva Convention requirements, including Common Article 3, to official Army policy. The previous Field Manual (FM 34–52, 1992) had been overridden by Bush administration policies on interrogation.[54] In the fall of 2007 Congress passed a bill that would have required the CIA to conform to the same rules on interrogation as the military. But on March 8, 2008, President Bush vetoed the bill, and Congress did not have the votes to override his veto.[55]

From these consistent and continued refusals of the Bush administration to change its interrogation policies, it can be concluded that President Bush intended them to continue. The Detainee Treatment Act of 2005 did compel the Department of Defense to return to the pre-2001 policies of conforming to the Geneva Conventions. Of course, many military officers had been arguing since 2001 that the United States should comply with the Geneva Conventions. Even after the military returned to a policy of compliance with Geneva, President Bush continued to insist that the CIA be allowed to use harsh interrogation techniques. He used his authority from the Military Commissions Act to interpret Common Article 3 of the Geneva Conventions in a way inconsistent with the interpretation of other signatories to the Agreements.

The Chain of Command

President Bush used his power as president very effectively in pursuing a policy direction that would allow U.S. personnel to use harsh interrogation methods to obtain intelligence in the war on terror. His aides marshaled legal arguments to support his position, despite serious objections from Secretary of State Colin Powell, some general officers in the military, and professional military lawyers in the Judge Advocate General Corps. His leadership on the interrogation issues was reinforced by Vice President Cheney and his staff down through the chain of command.

The following individuals acted at various places in the chain of authority in making or implementing policies that led to abuse and torture. Each made authoritative decisions that affected the way detainees in the war on terror would be perceived and treated. This list is illustrative rather than exhaustive; there is no attempt to be comprehensive. The actions of these officials contributed to the abuse and torture of detainees.

- President Bush's military order of November 13, 2001, created the status of "enemy combatant" that placed persons so designated outside of the protections of the Geneva Conventions and outside the U.S. court system.
- President Bush decided that the Geneva Conventions did not apply to al Qaeda.
- Vice President Cheney said that the CIA asked him "what they could and couldn't do ... to explain what they wanted to do. And I supported it."[56]
- Secretary Rumsfeld appointed General Dunlavey to head military intelligence at Guantanamo and pressured him to extract intelligence from interrogations.
- The NSC principals who authorized specific interrogation techniques to be used on some detainees included Vice President Cheney, Condoleezza Rice, George Tenet, Colin Powell, and John Ashcroft.
- Secretary Rumsfeld expanded the range of permissible interrogation tactics.
- Secretary Rumsfeld decided that military intelligence would control Guantanamo.
- Rumsfeld appointed General Miller to head Guantanamo and later transferred him to Abu Ghraib.
- George Tenet authorized CIA personnel to use harsh techniques on detainees.
- Stephen Cambone sent General Miller to change interrogation policy at Abu Ghraib.
- General Miller decided that Military Intelligence priorities would prevail over Military Police control.
- General Karpinski did not ensure that her MP troops were well trained or supplied.
- General Sanchez expanded the range of interrogation techniques allowed at Abu Ghraib.
- Major General Barbara Fast, the senior military intelligence officer in Iraq, brought abusive techniques from Afghanistan to Iraq.
- Colonel Pappas ran Abu Ghraib with an emphasis on using harsh interrogation techniques to extract actionable intelligence.
- Members of the 205th Military Intelligence directed MPs to "set the conditions" for interrogations.
- Members of the 372nd Military Police Company committed the abusive acts that were photographed at Abu Ghraib.

Each of the above actions was partially responsible for the abuse and torture committed by U.S. personnel. The proximate causes of the abuse and torture were the low-ranking individuals who actually performed the actions, and they are responsible for their behavior. But most of their actions would not have occurred without the previous actions of their superiors to encourage harsh interrogations.

Although not directly in the chain of command, a number of other administration officials were major facilitators in the creation of harsh interrogation and torture policy. Vice President Cheney was the driving force behind much of national security policy and specifically interrogation policy. He engineered President Bush's signature on the November 13, 2001, Military Order.[57] His counsel and later chief of staff, David Addington, provided the legal expertise for interrogation policy at the top, and he played a powerful role in enforcing Cheney's decisions, often by invoking the president's commander-in-chief authority. John Yoo, working in the Office of Legal Counsel, drafted (with Addington's participation) some of the key memos in the attempt to legalize harsh interrogation techniques (such as the November 2001 Military Order, the Geneva Conventions suspension memo, and the Bybee memos of August 1, 2002). Director of the Office of Legal Counsel Jay S. Bybee (now a federal judge) signed the infamous memos on torture. William J. Haynes, counsel to Secretary Rumsfeld, drafted the December 2, 2002, memo on interrogation techniques that Rumsfeld signed, and his office sought out SERE techniques and how they could be applied to interrogations.

The legal judgments of administration lawyers were crucial to the establishment of interrogation policy. The approach of the Bush administration to its lawyers was "show us how far we can go without crossing the line into torture." By purporting to establish legally that any abuse or infliction of pain not approaching organ failure or death did not break the law, the lawyers gave free rein to interrogators to use extremely abusive and harsh methods. The use of these methods of interrogation and treatment of detainees metastasized into behavior that far exceeded the formal written policies and resulted in the deaths of many detainees.

The point of this analysis is not to attempt to assign legal culpability (and no such allegations are intended), but rather to demonstrate that U.S. civilian and military officials neglected their duty to ensure that crimes were not committed or to take disciplinary action once these crimes were brought to their attention.

Even though many individuals fell short of the high standards expected of them, it must also be kept in mind that at many points in the series of actions, courageous individuals objected to the policies that led to abuse and torture:

- Secretary Powell objected to excluding detainees from the Geneva Conventions (though he did participate in the NSC Principals meetings).
- William Taft wrote a memo to Gonzales objecting to his judgment on Geneva.
- JAG officers objected to ignoring the Geneva Conventions.
- Some U.S. officials at Guantanamo objected to the additional techniques of interrogation approved by Rumsfeld.
- FBI Agent Jim Clemente tried to stop the abuse of al Qahtani at Guantanamo, but was overruled by General Miller and his deputy.

- Spike Bowman, senior counsel for national security for at the FBI, called the DOD General Counsel's office in the Pentagon about the abuse at Guantanamo, but his calls were not heeded.
- Military service lawyers objected to a draft of Rumsfeld's December 2, 2002, memo.
- Alberto Mora objected strenuously to reports of treatment of detainees and the Rumsfeld memo of December 2. He later left the Navy.
- David Kay, leader of the U.S. Iraq Survey Group that searched for Saddam's WMD, refused to comply with pressure from General Abizaid to use more "robust interrogation methods" in his search for WMD in Iraq.[58]
- General Taguba took his assignment seriously and reported thoroughly on the abuses at Abu Ghraib.
- An MP captain at Abu Ghraib refused to have his MPs keep prisoners up for twenty-four hours prior to interrogation at the request of military intelligence officers.[59]
- Navy dog handler William J. Kimbro refused to allow his dog to be used to terrorize prisoners at Abu Ghraib.[60]
- Specialist Joseph M. Darby turned in to military law enforcement a CD containing the infamous Abu Ghraib photographs.
- Captain Ian Fishback, after seventeen months of attempts to get interrogation guidance from his superiors, wrote an open letter to Senator John McCain.
- Lieutenant Colonel Stephen E. Abraham resigned from his position conducting CSRT hearings at Guantanamo because of command pressure.
- Morris D. Davis and Lieutenant Colonel Darrel Vandeveld resigned their positions as prosecutors in military commissions at Guantanamo because of deficiencies in due process.

Also, many private sector lawyers courageously (especially at the beginning) undertook the defense of Guantanamo inmates, despite the opprobrium heaped on them and roadblocks thrown up by the military.

War Crimes?

The United States War Crimes Act (18 U.S.C. Sec. 2441) provided that "Whoever, whether inside or outside the United States, commits a war crime ... shall be fined under this title or imprisoned for life or any term of years, or both, and if death results to the victim, shall also be subject to the penalty of death." The law defined a war crime as "a grave breach" of the Geneva Conventions or conduct "which constitutes a violation of common Article 3" of the Geneva Conventions. The Military Commissions Act of 2006, however, repealed references to the Geneva Conventions and replaced them with a list of egregious actions and any action that would "amount to cruel, inhuman, or degrading treatment prohibited by section 1003 of the Detainee

Treatment Act of 2005 (Sec. 948r)." Left out of the MCA was "outrageous and humiliating" treatment that was prohibited in Common Article 3, which forbade "Violence to life and person, in particular murder of all kinds, mutilation, cruel treatment and torture" and "outrages upon personal dignity, in particular humiliating and degrading treatment."[61] According to the MCA, "outrageous and humiliating" treatment would not constitute a war crime. Under the administration's interpretation the new law would forbid only techniques that "shock the conscience."

Both international and U.S. officials have concluded that the treatment of some detainees by the United States during the war on terror constituted war crimes. In an investigative report, the International Committee of the Red Cross concluded that the CIA had tortured Abu Zubayda and that its treatment of some detainees constituted war crimes. The report was given to the CIA and was given to President Bush in 2007.[62]

General Antonio Taguba, who wrote the first Army report on Abu Ghraib, has since his retirement concluded that the United States is guilty of war crimes. In the preface to the 2008 report by the Physicians for Human Rights, *Broken Laws, Broken Lives,* he stated:

> This report tells the largely untold human story of what happened to detainees in our custody when the Commander-in-Chief and those under him authorized a systematic regime of torture. This story is not only written in words: It is scrawled for the rest of these individual's lives on their bodies and minds.
>
> After years of disclosures by government investigations, media accounts, and reports from human rights organizations, there is no longer any doubt as to whether the current administration has committed war crimes. The only question that remains to be answered is whether those who ordered the use of torture will be held to account.[63]

It is also possible that the lawyers who claimed to justify the harsh interrogations and torture by constructing legal arguments that skirted the law in order to allow techniques approaching torture may be implicated in war crimes.[64] Even FBI personnel were so concerned at what they saw at Guantanamo that they opened a "war crimes" file, but they were later ordered to close the file.[65] The FBI concerns were expressed to top levels of the Departments of Defense and Justice and the National Security Council.

General P.X. Kelley, Commandant of the Marine Corps from 1983 to 1987, criticized President Bush's interpretation of Common Article 3 of the Geneva Conventions in June 2007 via his memo authorized by the Military Commissions Act. He argued that the president's order "cannot even arguably be reconciled with America's clear duty under Common Article 3 to treat all detainees humanely and to avoid any acts of violence against their person." He argued that U.S. troops depend on the protections of the Geneva Conventions and that Bush's reinterpretation of CA 3 undermines these protections. He concluded with a warning to the president: "Policymakers should also keep in mind that violations of Common Article 3 are 'war crimes' for which everyone involved—potentially up to and including the president of the United States—may be tried in any of the other 193 countries that are parties to the conventions."[66]

Remedies

The abuses detailed in this book have done enormous harm to the reputation of the United States throughout the world and have probably added many to the ranks of terrorists who would do harm to the United States and its citizens. While some tactical intelligence may have been gained from the harsh interrogation techniques, much inaccurate information was also forced from detainees who were willing to say anything in order to stop the pain. In addition, any intelligence benefit achieved has been far outweighed by the opprobrium of the international community and the damage to the professionalism of the U.S. Army. As Colonel Steven M. Kleinman said, "As a result [of torture], adversaries and allies alike have accused this nation of gross violations of the Geneva Conventions and of violating the basic human rights of detainees in our custody. The geostrategic consequences are likely to last decades."[67]

Former General Counsel to the Navy Alberto Mora testified that "there are serving U.S. flag-rank officers who maintain that the first and second identifiable causes of U.S. combat deaths in Iraq—as judged by their effectiveness in recruiting insurgent fighters into combat—are, respectively, the symbols of Abu Ghraib and Guantanamo."[68] In early 2009, Admiral Mike Mullen, chairman of the Joint Chiefs of Staff, declared: "trust is the coin of the realm.... That's why images of prisoner maltreatment at Abu Ghraib still serve as recruiting tools for al-Qaeda."[69]

These judgments were reinforced by Bush appointee Susan J. Crawford, the convening authority for the military commissions at Guantanamo who dismissed charges against Mohammed al-Qahtani, when she publicly concluded that "we tortured al-Qahtani. His treatment met the legal definition of torture.... It did shock me. I was upset by it. I was embarrassed by it. If we tolerate this and allow it, then how can we object when our servicemen and women, or others in foreign service, are captured and subjected to the same techniques? How can we complain? Where is our moral authority to complain? Well, we may have lost it."[70]

It is crucial to the United States and important for the rest of the world that we confront the reality of our interrogation practices, make what reparation we can, and move beyond this sad episode in our history. If we do not honestly confront our actions, we cannot claim to have learned from our mistakes and again act as a beacon for freedom on the world stage. That is why the issues dealt with in this book are so important. Pretending that these events did not happen or that the torture was merely the criminal mistakes of a few sadistic individuals at the bottom of the military and CIA hierarchy will only exacerbate the problem.

If, however, the United States publicly confronts what it has done to detainees in the war on terror and repudiates those actions that were unwarranted, illegal, and against international law, we will be able to turn international attention to the many positive actions that the United States is taking throughout the world. We will be able to return to our appropriate role as a world leader that respects human rights and speaks with authority when it condemns torture and abuse in other countries. We need to return to our birthright of freedom and liberty and to our position as leader of the world in the pursuit of human rights.

Some will say that uncovering and publicizing the crimes that have been committed will only provide more material for our enemies to use against us. But there is already quite enough evidence, which our enemies have been using to criticize us. The only way to deal with this malignancy is to excise it and cauterize the wound. It will be a painful process, but it will allow us to get this deplorable period of U.S. policy behind us.

Between the opening of Guantanamo on January 11, 2002, and 2009, fewer than thirty detainees were charged with crimes and only two were convicted (Hamdan and Hicks). More than five hundred detainees were released without ever having been charged, and the United States has refused to apologize or compensate these people in any way. One detainee from Afghanistan received a document that is probably typical of those received by others. It was dated October 7, 2006, and it read: "An Administrative Review Board has reviewed the information about you that was talked about at the meeting on 02 December 2005 and the deciding official in the United States has made a decision about what will happen to you. You will be sent to the country of Afghanistan. Your departure will occur as soon as possible."[71] After three or four years of incarceration and possible "enhanced interrogation," without evidence of wrongdoing on the part of the detainee, common human decency would dictate that those who were innocent of any wrongdoing be compensated in some way, even though no monetary compensation could make up for the lost years of one's life.

As the Bush administration left office, its officials continued to argue that the interrogation techniques they used were successful and necessary to protect U.S. national security. Vice President Cheney said "If it hadn't been for what we did—with respect to the terrorist surveillance program, or enhanced interrogation techniques for high-value detainees, the Patriot Act, and so forth—then we would have been attacked again."[72] Outgoing head of the CIA Michael Hayden asserted that the harsh interrogation techniques were successful in obtaining valuable intelligence information. "These techniques worked. Do not allow others to say it didn't work. It worked."[73]

Positing for the sake of argument that the harsh interrogation techniques produced some "valuable intelligence information," several questions remain. Was the information obtained worth the twisting of U.S. laws to justify the techniques? Was it worth setting the precedents of harsh interrogations and torture as legitimate in the United States? Was it worth the international opprobrium expressed toward the United States from both its allies and adversaries? Was it worth the implicit agreement that, when our own soldiers are captured, that they may be treated the same way we treated our detainees? Was the claim that the torture "saved lives" worth the violation of universal moral prohibitions against torture? If it is accepted that "saving lives" justifies torture, then virtually any tactical combat situation can justify torture. No "ticking time bomb" scenarios were adduced to justify the torture that U.S. personnel inflicted on detainees. Vice President Cheney implicitly or explicitly answered "yes" to all of the above questions. His summary conclusion was that "the United States needs to be not so much loved as it needs to be respected. Sometimes, that requires us to take actions that generate controversy. I'm not at all sure that that's what the Obama administration believes."[74]

Within forty-eight hours of becoming president, Barak Obama issued an executive order intended to reverse some of the Bush administration policies of the previous eight years. It declared that Common Article 3 of the Geneva Conventions was a "minimum baseline" for the treatment of prisoners. It ordered that all detained "persons shall in all circumstances be treated humanely and shall not be subjected to violence to life and person," including outrages on their personal dignity and humiliating and degrading treatment. "From this day forward" all U.S. interrogations would have to be consistent with Army Field Manual 2–22.3 (2006). No interpretation of the law "issued by the Department of Justice between September 11, 2001, and January 20, 2009," could be relied upon with respect to interrogation.[75] The executive order also declared that all regulations inconsistent with the January 22, 2009, order issued by or to the CIA with regard to interrogation, from September 11, 2001, to January 20, 2009 (the last day of the Bush administration), were revoked. In addition, any then operating CIA detention facilities were to be closed as "expeditiously as possible." President Obama also issued an executive order that mandated the closing of the Guantanamo Bay detention facility "as soon as practicable, and no later than 1 year from the date of this order."[76]

Some commentators argued that officials of the Bush administration clearly broke the law and should be prosecuted for their crimes.[77] Mark J. McKeon, a lawyer who worked on the indictment of Slobodan Milosevic for war crimes, argued that the United States must take its own actions seriously:

> While at the Hague, I felt myself standing in a long line of American prosecutors working for a world where international standards restricted what one nation could do to another during war, stretching back to at least Justice Robert Jackson at the Nuremberg trials. Those standards protected our own soldiers and citizens. They were also moral and right.... We cannot expect to regain our position of leadership in the world unless we hold ourselves to the same standards that we expect of others. That means punishing the most senior government officials responsible for these crimes. We have demanded this from other countries that have returned from walking on the dark side; we should expect no less from ourselves.[78]

The analysis in this book, especially Chapter Five, presents a plausible argument that U.S. officials violated the Geneva Conventions and broke U.S. and international law. Prosecuting these officials, however, would be difficult and probably counterproductive to confronting the failures of U.S. interrogation policy during the war on terror. The Bybee I memo of August 1, 2002, however flawed, purported to redefine torture in such a way as to allow most interrogation techniques approved by Secretary Rumsfeld, Director Tenet, and other U.S. officials. Since the Office of Legal Counsel of the Justice Department is the authoritative interpreter of U.S. law for the executive branch, it would be difficult to convict an interrogator or policymaker who in good faith relied on the OLC's interpretation of the law.

In addition, the Military Commissions Act of 2006 amended the War Crimes Act and applied its provisions retroactively. The War Crimes Act was changed so that only specific actions (the most egregious types of torture and abuse) could be prosecuted, whereas the law previously allowed prosecution of any violation of Common Article 3. Thus prosecution of individual interrogators or policymakers was rendered problematic, given changes to the law. The MCA also allows the defense against charges of lawbreaking specified in the Detainee Treatment Act of 2005, Section 1004 of which provides that if a person thought his actions were lawful or relied on counsel to that effect (e.g., the Bybee I and II memos), it would constitute a defense of his actions.[79] These changes in the law make it highly unlikely that the prosecution of government personnel who were using approved interrogation techniques could be convicted.

There is also the possibility that if persons were prosecuted for breaking laws against torture, the above legal provisions would prove sufficient to win acquittals. If this happened, the broader public and international community might conclude that the illegal actions were allowed and the abuses condoned by the United States. This might be the result even if the person did, in fact, take actions that were admittedly torture. A court judgment of innocence could easily be presented publicly as vindication of the policies that critics of the Bush administration denounced.

The abuse and torture of detainees that were not directly related to specific interrogation techniques approved by Bush administration officials, however, can more easily be prosecuted in civil courts or through the Uniform Code of Military Justice. The Army has, in fact, prosecuted a number of low-level enlisted soldiers for their participation in the horrors of Abu Ghraib. The Nuremberg defense that "I was only following orders" was not sufficient to exculpate them. Nevertheless, as the analysis in this book has shown, their superiors throughout the chain of command, up to President Bush, were significantly involved in creating and implementing the policies that led to the torture and abuse of numerous individuals.

But in dealing with the application of approved techniques of interrogation or their formulation in policy, criminal prosecution would be difficult and politically contentious. Any prosecution of former members of the Bush administration would be met with assertions that the prosecutions were merely politically partisan attacks by Democrats seeking to discredit the Bush administration. Trials would be politically divisive and likely to take years to conduct, and they likely would not result in any definitive resolution of the matter. In addition, any criminal trial would cause former members of the Bush administration to conceal as much as possible any evidence that might be used against them. Thus a political decision not to prosecute Bush administration officials might be a prudent policy.

Conclusion

What is most important for the United States is to uncover what has been done in its name, admit our mistakes, and get beyond this unfortunate episode in U.S. public policy. Putting the torture behind us, however, necessarily entails uncovering what has happened, putting it in the public record in an authoritative way, denouncing the worst transgressions, and ensuring that they do not happen again. Thus the best way forward would be for a combination of congressional investigations and/or narrowly focused independent commissions comparable to the 9/11 commission. Congress could use its subpoena power and grants of immunity to compel testimony and obtain records of policymaking and implementation. An independent nonpartisan commission of military lawyers, ethicists, and former military leaders could clear the air by issuing an account of what happened and how it happened. The records of military investigations cited earlier in this book have already laid an important evidentiary basis for such an investigation.

Such investigations and reports would allow the United States to understand how its policies led to the abuse and torture that did occur and illuminate the path to ensure that it does not happen again. Such a public display of honesty would do much to restore the reputation of the United States in the eyes of the rest of the civilized world and demonstrate that we once again will practice what we preach. Such actions would also undermine the terrorist "narrative" that the United States is waging a lawless war on the Muslim world and would provide a "positive alternative—i.e., a narrative of equality, justice, and commitment to the rule of law" that will support the broader counterterrorism strategy of the United States.[80]

This path would not take a "truth and reconciliation" approach because it would not be intended to reconcile former enemies, but as legal scholar Jack Balkin argues, "rather, we need to renew our commitment to human rights and the rule of law and prevent future abuses. Our aim is not truth and reconciliation, it is truth and repudiation."[81] As Abraham Lincoln said after his reelection in 1864: "In any future great national trial, compared with the men of this, we shall have as weak and as strong, as silly and as wise, as bad and as good. Let us therefore study the incidents in this as philosophy to learn wisdom from and none of them as wrongs to be avenged."[82] On April 16, 2009, President Obama echoed Lincoln's words: "This is a time for reflection, not retribution. I respect the strong views and emotions that these issues evoke. We have been through a dark and painful chapter in our history. But at a time of great challenges and disturbing disunity, nothing will be gained by spending our time and energy laying blame for the past."[83]

With luck and determination, the United States can learn from this painful era of U.S. history and will in the future heed Nietzsche's admonition: "He who fights with monsters should be careful lest he thereby become a monster."[84] As U.S. interrogator Matthew Alexander concluded, "Murderers like Zarqawi can kill us, but they can't force us to change who we are. We can only do that to ourselves ... Americans, including officers like myself, must fight to protect our values not only from al-Qaeda but also from those within our own country who would erode them."[85]

Notes

Chapter 1: U.S. Detainee Policy

1. Lieber Code of 1863, General Orders 100, "Instructions for the Government of Armies of the United States in the Field," found at http://www.civilwarhome.com/liebercode.htm, accessed December 6, 2008.

2. Jane Mayer, *The Dark Side* (New York: Doubleday, 2008), p. 10.

3. From Philip Zelikow's testimony before the Senate Judiciary Committee, May 13, 2009; quoted by Carrie Johnson, "Ex-Official Testifies About Efforts to Halt Harsh Tactics," *Washington Post*, May 14, 2009, p. A 4.

4. The word "detainee" is used to denote a person under the control of a government during wartime who is not a prisoner of war. The word is used in Article IV of the Geneva Conventions, which covers civilians and non-combatants. With respect to the incarceration of suspected terrorists by the U.S. military, the word "prisoner" is also appropriate, especially for persons kept imprisoned for several years.

5. Robert H. Jackson, "Crimes in the Conduct of War," Opening Speech for the Prosecution at Nuremberg, quoted in Daniel B. Prieto, "War About Terror: Civil Liberties and National Security After 9/11," *Council on Foreign Relations Working Paper*, February 2009, p. 5.

6. For an excellent analysis of the implications of using the war frame, see Richard M. Pious, *The War on Terrorism and the Rule of Law* (Los Angeles: Roxbury, 2006).

7. The term "enemy combatant" was used by the Bush administration to mean illegal enemy combatants. The formal definition of the Department of Defense was: "an individual who was part of or supporting Taliban or al Qaida forces, or associated forces that are engaged in hostilities against the United States or its coalition partners. This includes any person who has committed a belligerent act or has directly supported hostilities in aid of enemy armed forces." See *Kiyemba, et al. v. Obama*, Court of Appeals of the District of Columbia, No. 08-5424 (February 18, 2009), p. 12.

8. Frontline, "The Dark Side," http://www.pbs.org/wgbh/pages/frontline/darkside/view/.

9. Bush press conference, Sept. 6, 2006, "President Discusses Creation of Military Commissions to Try Suspected Terrorists." White House website, accessed November 29, 2008.

10. John H. Langbein, *Torture and the Law of Proof* (Chicago: University of Chicago Press, 1976, 2006), p. 3. This section is largely based on Langbein's scholarship.

11. Joseph Perez, *The Spanish Inquisition: A History* (London: Profiles Books, 2002), pp. 1–20. This section is based primarily on Perez's book.

12. ibid., p. 135.

13. Langbein, *Torture and the Law of Proof,* pp. 144–6.

14. See Edward Burman, *The Inquisition: The Hammer of Heresy* (Gloustershire, UK: Sutton Publishing, 2004), p. 58.

15. Perez, *The Spanish Inquisition*, p. 163–7.

16. Langbein, *Torture and the Law of Proof*, p. 3.

17. John H. Langbein, "The Legal History of Torture," in Sandford Levinson, ed., *Torture: A Collection* (New York: Oxford University Press, 2004), pp. 96–97.

18. Langbein, *Torture and the Law of Proof*, p. 59.

19. Langbein, "The Legal History of Torture," pp. 94–128.

20. ibid., p, 82.

21. ibid., p. 135.

22. ibid., p. 100.

23. Quoted by James Norton, "The Lack of Human Decency at Guantanamo Bay Undermines a Legacy of Just Treatment," *Christian Science Monitor,* found at http://www.csmonitor.com/2006/0614/p09s02-coop.html, accessed December 6, 2008.

24. "Treaty Between His Majesty the King of Prussia and the United States of America, Art. 24 (1785)," quoted in Joseph Margulies, *Guantanamo and the Abuse of Presidential Power* (New York: Simon and Schuster, 2006), p. 73.

25. "Lieber Code of 1863, General Orders 100, 'Instructions for the Government of Armies of the United States in the Field,'" found at http://www.civilwarhome.com/liebercode.htm, accessed December 6, 2008.

26. "Court-Martial of Major Edwin F. Glenn, Samar, Philippines, April 1902," quoted in Margulies, *Guantamamo and the Abuse of Presidential Power,* p. 74.

27. Willie Nellessen, former POW at Camp Hearne, 1943–45, "Foreword," in Michael R. Waters, *Lone Star Stalag* (College Station, TX: Texas A&M University Press, 2004), p. ix.

28. Margulies, *Guantanamo,* pp. 74–80.

29. The record of the CIA in the interrogation of prisoners is more blurred. The CIA developed the KUBARK manual in the 1960s and trained forces in other nations in the use of coercive interrogation techniques. During the Vietnam War, the CIA cooperated with South Vietnamese forces in carrying out the Phoenix program that assassinated Viet Cong leaders and probably participated in the torture of captives. During the Cold War, the CIA also developed programs of harsh interrogation tactics that were used to train foreign intelligence agencies, for instance in Iran and Latin America. Thus agencies of the U.S. government had been involved in torture before the Bush administration, though there is no evidence that these practices were initiated by systematic policies at the highest levels of government or discussed at National Security Council Principals Meetings. For details, see Alfred W. McCoy, *A Question of Torture* (New York: Henry Holt, 2006), pp. 60–80.

Chapter 2: Policymaking on Torture

1. Quoted in Jane Mayer, "The Memo," *The New Yorker*, February 27, 2006.

2. Quoted by Karen Greenberg, *The Least Worst Place: Guantanamo's First 100 Days* (New York: Oxford University Press 2009), p. 50.

3. Joby Warrick, "CIA Played Larger Role in Advising Pentagon," *Washington Post*, June 18, 2008, p. 1.

4. Jack Goldsmith, *The Terror Presidency* (New York: Norton, 2007), p. 131.

5. "Memorandum Opinion for the Deputy Counsel to the President, 'The President's Constitutional Authority to Conduct Military Operations Against Terrorists and Nationals

Supporting Them,' from: John C. Yoo, Deputy Assistant Attorney General, Office of Legal Counsel" (September 25, 2001), in Karen J. Greenberg and Joshua L. Dratel, eds., *The Torture Papers: The Road to Abu Ghraib* (Cambridge: Cambridge University Press, 2005), p. 3.

6. "Detention, Treatment, and Trial of Certain Non-Citizens in the War Against Terrorism," found at: http://www.whitehouse.gov/news/releases/2001/11/20011113-27.html.

7. Section 3 (e), "Detention, Treatment, and Trial of Certain Non-Citizens in the War Against Terrorism," November 13, 2001.

8. Karen Greenberg, *The Least Worst Place: Guantanamo's First 100 Days* (New York: Oxford University Press, 2009), p. 2.

9. Barton Gellman and Jo Becker, "A Different Understanding with the President," *Washington Post*, June 24, 2007, p. 10.

10. Jane Mayer, *The Dark Side* (New York: Doubleday, 2008), p. 80.

11. Gellman and Becker, "A Different Understanding with the President," p. 10.

12. ibid.

13. ibid., p. 1.

14. *Hamdan v. Rumsfeld* (2006), No. 05–184, Slip Opinion.

15. "Memorandum for William J. Haynes II, General Counsel, DOD: from John Yoo, RE: Application of Treaties and Laws to al Qaeda and Taliban Detainees" (January 9, 2002), in Greenberg and Dratel, eds., *The Torture Papers*, pp. 38–79.

16. Quoted in Karen deYoung, *Soldier: The Life of Colin Powell* (New York: Knopf, 2006), p. 367.

17. "Memorandum from William H. Taft IV to John C. Yoo, 'Your Draft Memorandum of January 9,'" (January 11, 2002), found at www.newyorker.com/online/contents/articles/050214on_onlineonly02. Quoted in deYoung, *Soldier*, p. 368–69.

18. deYoung, *Soldier*, p. 367.

19. "Memorandum for Chairman of the Joint Chiefs of Staff (January 19, 2002), Subject: Status of Taliban and Al Qaeda," in Greenberg and Dratel, eds., *The Torture Papers*, p. 80.

20. Philippe Sands, *Torture Team* (New York: Palgrave, 2008), p. 32.

21. ibid.

22. Lt. Gen. Ricardo Sanchez with Donald T. Phillips, *Wiser in Battle: A Soldier's Story* (New York: Harper, 2008), p. 144.

23. Douglas Feith, *War and Decision: Inside the Pentagon at the Dawn of the War on Terrorism* (New York: Harper, 2008), p. 161.

24. ibid., p. 162.

25. Sands, *Torture Team*, p. 33.

26. Feith, *War and Decision*, p. 162.

27. Sands, *Torture Team*, p. 33.

28. ibid., p. 35.

29. ibid., p. 90.

30. ibid., p. 182.

31. "Memorandum for Alberto R. Gonzales, Counsel to the President, and William J. Hayens II, General Counsel of the Department of Defense from Assistant Attorney General Jay S. Bybee, RE: *Application of Treaties and Laws to al Qaeda and Taliban Detainees*" (January 22, 2002), in Greenberg and Dratel, eds., *The Torture Papers*, pp. 81–121.

32. "Memorandum for the President (25 January 2002) from Alberto R. Gonzales, subject: Decision RE application of the Geneva Convention on Prisoners of War to the Conflict with al Qaeda and the Taliban," in Greenberg, *The Least Worst Place*, pp. 118–21. According to *Newsweek*, the memo was "actually" written by David Addington, Vice President Cheney's

legal aide. Daniel Klaidman, "Homesick for Texas," *Newsweek*, July 12, 2004, p. 32. Gonzales was criticized in the press for saying that the "new paradigm" renders the Geneva limitations "quaint." But the context of his use of the word "quaint" is not as damning as excerpting the word makes it seem. The end of the sentence reads: "renders quaint some of its provisions requiring that captured enemy be afforded such things as commissary privileges, scrip (i.e., advance of monthly pay), athletic uniforms, and scientific instruments." Whether Gonzales correctly characterized the Geneva requirements is a separate issue.

33. DeYoung, *Soldier*, p. 369.

34. "Memorandum TO: Counsel to the President and Assistant to the President for National Security Affairs, FROM: Colin L. Powell (26 January 2002). SUBJECT: Draft Decision Memorandum for the President on the Applicability of the Geneva Convention to the Conflict in Afghanistan," pp. 2, 4, in Greenberg and Dratel, eds., *The Torture Papers*, pp. 122–25. Many of the memoranda and oral directives included statements that detainees were to be treated "humanely" despite the more aggressive interrogation techniques to which they could be subjected. The problem was that if the detainees were in fact treated humanely, it would be more difficult to extract information from them. Thus these statements must have been considered to be *pro forma*, while the overall thrust of the directives was that detainees were to be subject to more aggressive interrogation techniques that were outside the Geneva Convention limits.

35. "Memorandum TO: Counsel to the President and Assistant to the President for National Security Affairs, FROM: Colin L. Powell (26 January 2002). SUBJECT: Draft Decision Memorandum for the President on the Applicability of the Geneva Convention to the Conflict in Afghanistan 'Comments' on the Memorandum of January 25, 2002,'" appended to memorandum.

36. DeYoung, *Soldier*, p. 368; Douglas Feith puts the date of this meeting at February 4.

37. DeYoung, *Soldier*, p. 370.

38. "Memorandum for the Vice President, et al., Subject: Humane Treatment of al Qaeda and Taliban Detainees (February 7, 2002), signed by President Bush," in Greenberg and Dratel, eds., *The Torture Papers*, pp. 134–35.

39. For a detailed analysis of the legal issues involved in the treatment of prisoners and the international and legal obligations of the United States regarding detainees, see: Robert K. Goldman and Brian D. Tittemore, "Unprivileged Combatants and the Hostilities in Afghanistan: Their Status and Rights Under International Humanitarian and Human Rights Law" (Washington, D.C.: American Society of International Law Task Force Paper, 2002). See also: Jennifer K. Elsea, "Lawfulness of Interrogation Techniques under the Geneva Conventions," *Congressional Research Service Report to Congress* (RL32567), September 8, 2004; Elsea, "U.S. Treatment of Prisoners in Iraq: Selected Legal Issues," *Congressional Research Service Report for Congress* (RL32395), December 2, 2004; and L.C. Green, *The Contemporary Law of Armed Conflict* (New York: Manchester University Press, 1993).

40. Schlesinger Report, p. 29.

41. Sanchez, *Wiser in Battle*, p. 144.

42. In June of 2004 Alberto Gonzales tried to minimize the importance or the legal status of administration memos about torture, saying they were "unnecessary, over-broad discussions" and "not relied upon" by policymakers. Quoted in Dana Milbank, "The Administration vs. the Administration," *Washington Post*, June 29, 2004, p. A21. But the previous year he placed strong emphasis on the legal importance of Office of Legal Counsel opinions. "OLC's interpretation of this legal issue [Geneva Conventions applicability to al Qaeda] is definitive. The Attorney General is charged by statute with interpreting the law for the Executive Branch. This interpretive authority extends to both domestic and international law. He has, in turn, delegated this

role to OLC." "Memorandum for the President, From: Alberto R. Gonzales; Subject: Decision Re Application of the Geneva Convention on Prisoners of War to the Conflict with al Qaeda and the Taliban" (25 January 2002).

43. Goldsmith, *Terror Presidency,* p. 206.

44. ibid., p. 167.

45. ibid.

46. "Memorandum for Alberto R. Gonzales, counsel to the President, 'Standards of Conduct for Interrogation under 18 U.S.C. Sc. 2340–2340A'" (August 1, 2002), in Greenberg and Dratel, eds., *The Torture Papers,* p. 172. According to *Newsweek,* the memo was written in close consultation with White House lawyers. Klaidman, "Homesick for Texas," p. 32.

47. Page 1 of Bybee memo, in Greenberg and Dratel, eds., *The Torture Papers,* p. 172.

48. Pages 15, 28 of Bybee memo, in Greenberg and Dratel, eds., *The Torture Papers,* p. 185.

49. Pages 3–4 of Bybee memo, in Greenberg and Dratel, eds., *The Torture Papers,* p. 174.

50. On December 30, 2004, the Bybee memo was superseded "in its entirety" by "Memorandum for James B. Comey, Deputy Attorney General from Acting Assistant Attorney General Daniel Levin Re: Legal Standards Applicable Under 18 U.S.C. par. 2340–2340A." The memo did not address the commander-in-chief powers of the president because it was "unnecessary" (p. 2). John Yoo argues that this memo made no difference, but that "the differences in the memos was for appearances' sake." (See Footnote No. 8). He also argues that the memo should not have been withdrawn. See John Yoo, *War by Other Means* (New York: Atlantic Monthly Press, 2005), pp. 177–87.

51. Bybee memo, p. 22, in Greenberg and Dratel, eds., *The Torture Papers,* p. 191.

52. ibid., p. 212.

53. Goldsmith, *Terror Presidency,* pp. 210, 212.

54. Bybee memo, p. 33, in Greenberg and Dratel, eds., *The Torture Papers,* p. 202.

55. ibid., p. 200.

56. ibid., p. 207.

57. Jane Mayer, "Outsourcing Torture," *New Yorker,* February 14, 2007, website, p. 8 of 14. John Yoo's belief in the legal right of the president to order torture was quite broad. When asked by Doug Cassel (director of the Notre Dame Law School Center for Civil and Human Rights) if it would be legal for the president to order that the testicles of a child of a suspect be crushed in order to get a suspect to talk, Yoo replied: "I think it depends on why the president thinks he needs to do that." Yoo could have replied that such an act would be morally wrong but that the president had the legal authority to do it, but he didn't. Nat Hentoff, "Don't Ask, Don't Tell," *Village Voice,* January 27, 2006, http://www.villagevoice.com/news/0605,hentoff,71946,6.html.

58. Bybee memo, August 1, 2002, p. 34.

59. Goldsmith, *Terror Presidency,* p. 205.

60. "Memorandum for John Rizzo, Acting General Counsel of the Central Intelligence Agency from Jay S. Bybee, Assistant Attorney General, Office of Legal Council, Department of Justice (August 1, 2002); Subject: "Interrogation of al Qaeda Operative," found at: http://documents.nytimes.com/justice-department-memos-on-interrogation-techniques#p=1.

61. ibid., p. 144.

62. ibid., p. 155.

63. ibid., p. 144.

64. ibid., p. 155.

65. David Rose, *Guantanamo: America's War on Human Rights* (London: Faber and Faber, 2004), p. 94.

66. Karen J. Greenberg, "When Gitmo Was (Relatively) Good," *Washington Post,* January 25, 2009, p. B1.

67. Sands, *Torture Team,* p. 42.

68. Quoted in Greenberg, *The Least Worst Place,* p. 168.

69. Greenberg, "When Gitmo Was (Relatively) Good," p. B1.

70. Sands, *Torture Team,* p. 43.

71. ibid., p. 44.

72. ibid., p. 46.

73. "Press Briefing by White House Counsel Judge Alberto Gonzales [and others]," June 22, 2004, http://www.whitehouse.gov/news/releases/2004/06/20040622-14.html, accessed December 6, 2008.

74. "Memorandum from JPRA Chief of Staff for Office of the Secretary of Defense General Counsel, Subject: Exploitation (July 25, 2002). From Senate Armed Services Committee Hearing on 'The Origins of Aggressive Interrogation Techniques'" [TAB 1], available at: http://Levin .Senate.gov/newsroom/supporting/2008/documents.sasc.061708.pdf.

75. See the opening statement of Senator Carl Levin at hearings on treatment of detainees, at: http://Levin.Senate.gov/newsroom/supporting/2008/documents.sasc.061708.pdf. This account follows the chronology presented in the Levin opening statement.

76. The "waterboard" is explained: "Subject is interrogated while strapped to a wooden board ... Up to 1.5 gallons of water is slowly poured directly onto the subject's face from a height of 12–24 inches. In some cases, a wet cloth is placed over the subject's face ... This tactic instills a feeling of drowning and quickly compels cooperation." "Physical Pressures used in Resistance Training and Against American Prisoners and Detainees," (July 25, 2002). From Senate Armed Services Committee Hearing on "The Origins of Aggressive Interrogation Techniques," [TAB 3]. Available at: http://Levin.Senate.gov/newsroom/supporting/2008/documents.sasc.061708 .pdf.Waterboarding will be discussed further in Chapter Four.

77. "Physical Pressures Used in Resistance Training and Against American Prisoners and Detainees, (July 25, 2002)." From Senate Armed Services Committee Hearing on "The Origins of Aggressive Interrogation Techniques," [TAB 3], available at: http://Levin.Senate.gov/newsroom/supporting/2008/documents.sasc.061708.pdf.

78. "Operational Issues Pertaining to the Use of Physical/Psychological Coercion in Interrogation," quoted in Peter Finn and Joby Warrick, "In 2002, Military Agency Warned Against 'Torture,'" *Washington Post,* April 25, 2009, p. 1. See also Senate Armed Services Committee, "Inquiry into the Treatment of Detainees in U.S. Custody," Executive Summary (April 2009), p. xxv, http://levin.senate.gov/newsroom/supporting/2008/detainees.121108.pdf, accessed April 26, 2009.

79. Diane Beaver said that the interrogators at Guantanamo also got some ideas from the television show *24,* which she said was "hugely popular" among the interrogators. Sands, *Torture Team,* p. 62. The Secretary of Homeland Security, Michael Chertoff, lent the prestige of his office to the message of the TV program by visiting the actors when they were filming an episode in Washington, D.C. Amy Argetsinger and Roxanne Roberts, "The Reliable Source," *Washington Post,* November 5, p. C3 and November 8, p. 3C.

80. Sands, *Torture Team,* p. 47; Dunlavey added: "It's possible that someone was sent to my Task Force and came up with these great ideas." Sands, *Torture Team,* p. 47.

81. ibid.

82. ibid., p. 74.

83. ibid., p. 64.

84. ibid., p. 61.

85. "E-mail between DoD CITF Personnel, Subject: FW: Counter Resistance Strategy Meeting Minutes" [Minutes of an October 2, 2002, meeting at Guantanamo Bay, Cuba [TAB 7] (October 24, 2002). (Note: "All questions and comments have been paraphrased.") Fredman said that "the CIA has employed aggressive techniques on less than a handful of suspects since 9/11."

86. "E-mail between DoD CITF Personnel, Subject: FW: Counter Resistance Strategy Meeting Minutes" [Minutes of an October 2, 2002, meeting at Guantanamo Bay, Cuba [TAB 7] (October 24, 2002). (Note: "All questions and comments have been paraphrased.") Available at: http://Levin.Senate.gov/newsroom/supporting/2008/documents.sasc.061708.pdf

87. Sands, *Torture Team,* pp. 46–47

88. "From Jerald Phifer, STC, USA, Director; J2; For Commander, Joint Task Force 170, subject: Request for approval of Counter-Resistance Strategies" (October 11, 2002), in Greenberg and Dratel, eds., *The Torture Papers,* p. 227.

89. Sands, *Torture Team,* p. 49.

90. ibid., pp. 65–71.

91. "From: Diane E. Beaver, LTC, USA, Staff Judge Advocate; Memorandum for Commander, Joint Task Force 170; subject: Legal Brief on Proposed Counter-Resistance Strategies" (October 11, 2002).

92. Cover memo for legal brief with same cite as brief itself, in Greenberg and Dratel, eds., *The Torture Papers,* p. 226.

93. Sands, *Torture Team,* p. 66.

94. "From James T. Hill, General, US Army; Memorandum for Chairman of the Joint Chiefs of Staff; subject: Counter-Resistance Techniques" (October 25, 2002), in Greenberg, *The Least Worst Place,* p. 223, and in Sands, *Torture Team,* p. 82.

95. Sands, *Torture Team,* p. 83.

96. ibid., p. 86.

97. ibid., p. 92.

98. "Memorandum from Headquarters U.S. Air Force to Joint Staff: Review of SOUTHCOM/GTMO Request for Techniques" (November 4, 2002) [TAB 10], available at: http://Levin.Senate.gov/newsroom/supporting/2008/documents.sasc.061708.pdf

99. "Memorandum from Criminal Investigative Task Force (CITF) to Joint Staff: Review of SOUTHCOM/GTMO Request for Techniques" (November 4, 2002) [TAB 11], available at: http://Levin.Senate.gov/newsroom/supporting/2008/documents.sasc.061708.pdf

100. "Memorandum from Criminal Investigative Task Force (CITF) to Joint Staff: Review of SOUTHCOM/GITMO Request for Techniques" (November 7, 2002) [TAB 12], available at: http://Levin.Senate.gov/newsroom/supporting/2008/documents.sasc.061708.pdf.

101. "Memorandum from Headquarters United States Marine Corps to Joint Staff: Review of SOUTHCOM/GTMO Request for Techniques" (November 4, 2002) [TAB 14], available at: http://Levin.Senate.gov/newsroom/supporting/2008/documents.sasc.061708.pdf.

102. Sands, *Torture Team,* p. 92.

103. ibid., p. 219.

104. ibid., p. 92; see also David E. Graham, "Down a Slippery Slope," *Miller Center Report,* University of Virginia (Fall/Winter 2005), pp. 26, 31.

105. "From John Rankin, to Officer in Charge, Subject: After Action Report Joint Task Force Guantanamo Bay" (January 15, 2003). From Senate Armed Services Committee Hearing on "The Origins of Aggressive Interrogation Techniques," [TAB 19], available at: http://Levin.Senate.gov/newsroom/supporting/2008/documents.sasc.061708.pdf.

106. See Scott Shane, "China Inspired Interrogations at Guantanamo," *New York Times,* July 2, 2008, p. 1.

107. Steven M. Kleinman, Colonel, US Air Force, "Statement before the United States Senate Committee on Armed Services, Hearing on the Treatment of Detainees in U.S. Custody," (September 25, 2008). Found on the Senate Armed Services Committee website: http://armedservices.senate.gov/statemnt/2008/September/Moulton%2009-25-08.pdf.

108. Graham, "Down a Slippery Slope," p. 31.

109. ibid., p. 30.

110. Sands, *Torture Team*, p. 92.

111. Mayer, *Dark Side*, p. 223.

112. "JTF GTMO 'SERE' Interrogation Standard Operating Procedures" (December 18, 2002) [TAB 16], first page and extracts, at: http://levin.senate.gov/newsroom/release.cfm?id=299242]

113. "JTF GTMO 'SERE' Interrogation Standard Operating Procedures" (December 18, 2002) [TAB 16], first page and extracts, at: http://Levin.Senate.gov/newsroom/supporting/2008/documents.sasc.061708.pdf.

114. Sands, *Torture Team*, pp. 108–9.

115. ibid., p. 135.

116. ibid., p. 118. Bowman made several calls to former colleagues in the Office of the Secretary of Defense, but was not successful in getting his concerns raised or acted upon. Interview with Marion (Spike) Bowman, Washington (February 26, 2009).

117. ibid., p. 119.

118. ibid., p. 120.

119. "E-mail between DoD CITF Personnel, Subject: FW: Counter Resistance Strategy Meeting Minutes [Minutes of an October 2, 2002, meeting at Guantanamo Bay, Cuba" [TAB 7] (October 24, 2002). (Note: "All questions and comments have been paraphrased.") Fredman said that "the CIA has employed aggressive techniques on less than a handful of suspects since 9/11." See also Joby Warrick, "CIA Played Larger Role in Advising Pentagon," *Washington Post*, June 18, 2008, p. 1; Mark Mazzetti and Scott Shane, "Notes Show Confusion on Interrogation Methods," *New York Times*, June 18, 2008, website.

120. Sands, *Torture Team*, pp. 125–26, 129.

121. "MEMORANDUM FOR INSPECTOR GENERAL, DEPARTMENT OF THE NAVY, Subj: STATEMENT FOR THE RECORD: OFFICE OF GENERAL COUNSEL INVOLVEMENT IN INTERROGATION ISSUES; Ref: NAVIG Memo 5021 Ser 00/017 of 18 Jun 04" (July 7, 2004), p. 4.

122. Sands, *Torture Team*, p. 129.

123. Jane Mayer, "The Memo," *New Yorker*, February 27, 2006, p. 3 of 14 on webpage.

124. ibid.

125. Sands, *Torture Team*, p. 129.

126. ibid., p. 133.

127. Jane Mayer, "The Memo," *New Yorker*, February 27, 2006, p. 2 of 14 on webpage.

128. ibid., p. 5 of 14 on webpage.

129. ibid., p. 4 of 14 on webpage.

130. "MEMORANDUM FOR INSPECTOR GENERAL," Ref: NAVIG Memo 5021 Ser 00/017 of 18 Jun 04" (July 7, 2004), p. 4. It was signed by Alberto J. Mora and labeled: "SECRET—Unclassified upon removal of attachments."

131. Page 6 of Mora Memo. The memorandum is reproduced in Greenberg and Dratel, eds., *The Torture Papers* p. 236. The typed date is November 27, 2002, but the stamped date when it was signed by Rumsfeld was December 2. "Action Memo, For: Secretary of Defense, From: William J. Haynes II, Subject: Subject: Counter-Resistance Techniques."

132. "MEMORANDUM FOR INSPECTOR GENERAL," Ref: NAVIG Memo 5021 Ser 00/017 of 18 Jun 04" (July 7, 2004), pp. 6–7.

133. "MEMORANDUM FOR INSPECTOR GENERAL," Ref: NAVIG Memo 5021 Ser 00/017 of 18 Jun 04" (July 7, 2004), p. 11; Philippe Sands, *Torture Team*, 138.

134. "MEMORANDUM FOR INSPECTOR GENERAL," Ref: NAVIG Memo 5021 Ser 00/017 of 18 Jun 04" (July 7, 2004), pp. 12–13.

135. Sands, *Torture Team*, p. 140; Haynes denies remembering this event.

136. Jane Mayer, "The Memo," *New Yorker*, February 27, 2006, p. 9 of 14 on webpage.

137. Major General Jack Rives, USAF Deputy Judge Advocate General, "Memorandum for SAF/GC, From AF/JA, Subject: "Final Report and Recommendations of the Working Group to Assess the Legal, Policy and Operational Issues Relating to Interrogation of Detainees Held by the U.S. Armed Forces in the War on Terrorism" (February 5, 2003). Major General Thomas J. Romig, US Army Judge Advocate General, "Memorandum for General Counsel of the Department of the Air Force, Subject: Draft Report and Recommendations of the Working Group to Assess the Legal, Policy and Operational Issues Relating to Interrogation of Detainees Held by the U.S. Armed Forces in the War on Terrorism" (March 3, 2003).

138. Kevin M. Sandkuhler, Brigadier General, USMC, Staff Judge Advocate to CMC, "Memorandum for General Counsel of the Air Force, Subj: Working Group Recommendations on Detainee Interrogations" (February 27, 2003).

139. "Draft, Working Group Report on Detainee Interrogations in the Global War on Terrorism: Assessment of Legal, Historical, Policy, and Operational Considerations" (March 6, 2003), reprinted in Greenberg and Dratel, eds., *The Torture Papers*, p. 241.

140. The memos include: Jack Rives, Major General, USAF, Deputy Judge Advocate General, "Memorandum for SAF/GC, From AF/JA, Subject: 'Final Report and Recommendations of the Working Group to Assess the Legal, Policy and Operational Issues Relating to Interrogation of Detainees Held by the U.S. Armed Forces in the War on Terrorism'" (February 5, 2003); Kevin M. Sandkuhler, Brigadier General, USMC, Staff Judge Advocate to CMC, Memorandum for General Counsel of the Air Force, Subj: Working Group Recommendations on Detainee Interrogations" (February 27, 2003); Thomas J. Romig, Major General, US Army, Judge Advocate General, "Memorandum for General Counsel of the Department of the Air Force, Subject: Draft Report and Recommendations of the Working Group to Assess the Legal, Policy and Operational Issues Relating to Interrogation of Detainees Held by the U.S. Armed Forces in the War on Terrorism" (March 3, 2003). The memoranda are printed in Congressional Record, Senate, July 25, 2005, pp. S8794-S8796.

141. Jack Rives, Major General, USAF, Deputy Judge Advocate General, "Memorandum for SAF/GC, From AF/JA, Subject: 'Final Report and Recommendations of the Working Group to Assess the Legal, Policy and Operational Issues Relating to Interrogation of Detainees Held by the U.S. Armed Forces in the War on Terrorism'" (February 5, 2003).

142. Thomas J. Romig, Major General, US Army, Judge Advocate General, "Memorandum for General Counsel of the Department of the Air Force, Subject: Draft Report and Recommendations of the Working Group to Assess the Legal, Policy and Operational Issues Relating to Interrogation of Detainees Held by the U.S. Armed Forces in the War on Terrorism" (March 3, 2003).

143. Mayer, "The Memo," p. 10 of 14.

144. "MEMORANDUM FOR INSPECTOR GENERAL," Ref: NAVIG Memo 5021 Ser 00/017 of 18 Jun 04" (July 7, 2004), p. 17.

145. "MEMORANDUM FOR INSPECTOR GENERAL," Ref: NAVIG Memo 5021 Ser 00/017 of 18 Jun 04" (July 7, 2004), p. 19.

146. In January of 2006, with his military career effectively ended, Mora retired as general counsel of the Navy to become WalMart's general counsel for international operations. In May 2004, when military lawyers became aware of the final approved working group report (dated April 4, 2003), six military lawyers took the very unusual step of taking their concerns to the New York City Bar Association's Committee on International Human Rights. They were concerned about "a real risk of disaster," a concern that later proved to be prescient. Andrew Rosenthal, "Legal Breach: The Government's Attorneys and Abu Ghraib," *New York Times,* December 30, 2004, p. A22. John Barry, Michael Hirsh, and Michael Isikoff, "The Roots of Torture," *Newsweek,* May 24, 2004, pp. 28–34; Seymour M. Hersh, "The Gray Zone," *New Yorker,* May 24, 2004, p. 42.

147. "Working Group Report on Detainee Interrogations in the Global War on Terrorism: Assessment of Legal, Historical, Policy, and Operational Considerations" (April 4, 2003), reprinted in Greenberg and Dratel, eds., *The Torture Papers,* p. 286.

148. ibid., pp., 341–42.

149. ibid., pp. 342–43.

150. "Memorandum for the Commander, US Southern Command (April 16, 2003), Subject Countger-Resistance Techniques in the War on Terrorism, signed by Donald Rumsfeld," Greenberg, *The Least Worst Place,* p. 360.

151. Sands, *Torture Team,* p. 48.

152. This account is based on Joby Warrick, "CIA Tactics Endorsed in Secret Memos," *Washington Post,* October 15, 2008, p. 1.

153. R. Jeffrey Smith and Peter Finn, "Harsh Methods Approved as Early as Summer 2002," *Washington Post,* April 28, 2009, p. A6.

154. "Memorandum for John Rizzo, Acting General Counsel of the Central Intelligence Agency from Jay S. Bybee, Assistant Attorney General, Office of Legal Council, Department of Justice (August 1, 2002); Subject: "'Interrogation of al Qaeda Operative,'" found at: http://documents.nytimes.com/justice-department-memos-on-interrogation-techniques#p=1.

155. Warrick, "CIA Tactics Endorsed in Secret Memos," p. 1.

156. Dan Eggen, "Bush Approved Meetings on Interrogation Techniques," *Washington Post,* April 12, 2008, p. A03.

157. Jan Crawford Greenburg, Howard L. Rosenberg, and Ariane de Vogue, "Bush Aware of Advisers' Interrogation Talks," (April 11, 2008), http://abcnews.go.com/TheLaw/LawPolitics/story?id=4635175.

158. Dan Froomkin, "Bush OK'd Torture Meetings, *Washington Post,* April 14, 2008, website.

159. Greenburg, Rosenberg, and de Vogue, "Bush Aware of Advisers' Interrogation Talks," at: http://abcnews.go.com/TheLaw/LawPolitics/story?id=4635175.

160. Quoted by Mayer, "The Dark Side," p. 153.

161. Joby Warrick, "Top Officials Knew in 2002 of Harsh Interrogations," *Washington Post,* September 25, 2008, p. A7.

162. Mayer, "The Memo," p. 5 of 14.

163. ibid.

Chapter 3: The Implementation of Policy

1. "Interview of the vice president by Scott Hennen, WDAY at Radio Day at the White House," The Vice President's Office. White House website: October 24, 2006, www.whitehouse.gov/news/releases/2006/10/print/20061024-7.html. See also Dan Eggen, "Cheney's Remarks Fuel

Torture Debate," *Washington Post,* October 27, 2006, p. A9; Neil A. Lewis, "Furor Over Cheney Remark on Tactics for Terror Suspects," *New York Times,* October 28, 2006, p. A8.

2. "Memorandum for John A. Rizzo, Senior Deputy General Counsel, CIA (May 30, 2005) from Steven G. Bradbury, Principle Deputy Assistant Attorney General; Re: "Application of United States Obligations Under Article 16 of the Convention Against Torture to Certain Techniques that May Be Used in the Interrogation of High Value al Qaeda Detainees," p. 37. Found at: http://documents.nytimes.com/justice-department-memos-on-interrogation-techniques#p=1.

3. E-mail between DoD CITF Personnel, Subject: FW: Counter Resistance Strategy Meeting Minutes [Minutes of an October 2, 2002, meeting at Guantanamo Bay, Cuba [Tab 7] (October 24, 2002. (Note: "All questions and comments have been paraphrased.") Fredman said that "The CIA has employed aggressive techniques on less than a handful of suspects since 9/11."

4. Joanne Mariner, "Welcome to the Least Worst Place," *FindLaw,* March 28, 2007, website.

5. Andy Worthington, *The Guantanamo Files* (London: Pluto Press, 2007), p. 126.

6. "Letter from Shafiq Rasul and Asif Iqbal to Members of the Senate Armed Services Committee (May 13, 2004)," in Michael Ratner and Ellen Ray, *Guantanamo: What the World Should Know* (White River Junction, Vermont: Chelsea Green Publishing, 2004), pp. 150–58.

7. Andy Worthington, *The Guantanamo Files* (London: Pluto Press, 2007), p. 126.

8. ibid.

9. ibid.

10. "News Conference of Secretary of Defense Rumsfeld," January 27, 2002, available at: http://www.defenselink.mil/transcripts/2002/t01282002_t0127enr.html.

11. "President Bush, Prime Minister Blair Discuss War on Terror, Press Conference," July 17, 2003, available at: http://www.whitehouse.gov/news/releases/2003/07/20030717-9.html.

12. Donna Miles, "Bush: Guantanamo Detainees Receiving Humane Treatment," Department of Defense, American Forces Press Service (June 20, 2005), available at: http://www.defenselink.mil/news/newsarticle.aspx?id=16359, accessed April 2, 2005. Although this statement was made in 2005, it represents the tone of President Bush's attitude since 9/11. By 2005 it had been demonstrated that many detainees were innocent and posed no threat to the United States.

13. Fox News, "Rumsfeld: Afghan Detainees at Gitmo Bay Will Not Be Granted POW Status," January 28, 2002, available at: http://www.foxnews.com/story/0,2933,44084,00.html.

14. Josh White and Robin Wright, "After Guantanamo 'Reintegration for Saudis,'" *Washington Post,* December 10, 2007, pp. 1, 16.

15. Benjamin Wittes, *Law and the Long War* (New York: Penguin Press, 2008), p. 78.

16. Quoted by Karen Greenberg, *The Least Worst Place* (New York: Oxford University Press, 2009), p. 160.

17. ibid., p. 161.

18. Quoted by Jane Mayer, *The Dark Side* (New York: Doubleday, 2008), p. 183.

19. Mark Denbeaux and Joshua Denbeaux, "Report on Guantanamo Detainees: A Profile of 517 Detainees through Analysis of Department of Defense Data," (April 2005), available at: http://law.shu.edu/aaafinal.pdf. The text of U.S. offers of $4285 and millions at end of Report No. 1, pp. 1, 2.

20. Wittes, *Law and the Long War,* pp. 87–95.

21. Rasul, letter to the Senate Armed Services Committee, in Ratner and Ray, *Guantanamo,* p. 151.

22. See, for example: Andy Worthington, *The Guantanamo Files* (London: Pluto Press, 2007); Clive Stafford Smith, *Bad Men* (London: Weidenfeld and Nicolson, 2007); Murat Kurnaz, *Five Years of My Life* (New York: Palgrave, 2007); and Moazzam Begg, *Enemy Combatant* (London: Pocket Books, 2006).

23. Quoted in David Rose, *Guantanamo: America's War on Human Rights* (London: Faber and Faber, 2004), p. 71.

24. Testimony of Murat Kurnaz, Committee on Foreign Affairs, Subcommittee on International Organizations, Human Rights, and Oversight, Rayburn House Office Building, Room 2172 (May 20, 2008).

25. This account is based on: Testimony of Murat Kurnaz, Committee on Foreign Affairs, Subcommittee on International Organizations, Human Rights, and Oversight, Rayburn House Office Building, Room 2172 (May 20, 2008).

26. This account is based on Jumah al Dossari, "I'm Home, but Still Haunted by Guantanamo," *Washington Post*, August 17, 2008, p. B4.

27. ibid.

28. Rose, *Guantanamo*, pp. 72–3.

29. Office of the Inspector General, Department of Justice, *A Review of the FBI's Involvement in and Observations of Detainee Interrogations in Guantanamo Bay, Afghanistan, and Iraq,* unclassified version made public (May 2008), p. 86.

30. Phillippe Sands, *Torture Team* (New York: Palgrave Macmillan, 2008), p. 224.

31. Report by Vice Admiral Albert T. Church, III, Executive Summary (March 2005), p. 14.

32. Peter Finn, "4 Cases Illustrate Guantanamo Quandaries," *Washington Post* (February 16, 2009), p. A1.

33. Chris Mackey and Greg Miller, *The Interrogators* (Boston: Little Brown, 2004), p. 285.

34. ibid., p. 476.

35. ibid.

36. ibid., p. 477.

37. Opening statement by Senator Carl Levin, Senate Armed Services Committee Hearing on "The Origins of Aggressive Interrogation Techniques," available at: http://Levin.Senate.gov/newsroom/supporting/2008/documents.sasc.061708.pdf, p. 9.

38. ibid., p. 10.

39. Naval Inspector General, Vice Admiral Albert T. Church, III, "Executive Summary" (unclassified summary of longer report completed February 2005), http://www.defenselink.mil/news/Mar2005/d20050310exe.pdf.

40. MG George R. Fay, "AR 15-6 Investigation of the Abu Ghraib Detention Facility and 205th Military Intelligence Brigade," in Greenberg and Dratel, *The Torture Papers,* p. 1037. Major General George R. Fay, Investigating Officer, "Investigation of the Abu Ghraib Detention Facility and 205th Military Intelligence Brigade" (hereinafter the Fay Report), in Greenberg and Dratel, *The Torture Papers,* pp. 1116–17. See also Senate Armed Services Committee, "Executive Summary," pp. 22–23, "Into the Treatment of Detainees in U.S. Custody," (April 2009), http://levin.senate.gov.

41. newsroom/supporting/2008/detainees.121108.pdf, accessed April 26, 2009.

42. MG George R. Fay, "AR 15-6 Investigation of the Abu Ghraib Detention Facility and 205th Military Intelligence Brigade," in Greenberg and Dratel, *The Torture Papers,* p. 1037–38.

43. James R. Schlesinger, chair, *Final Report of the Independent Panel to Review Department of Defense Detention Operations,* in Steven Strasser, ed., *The Abu Ghraib Investigations* (New York: Public Affairs, 2004), p. 35.

44. Naval Inspector General, Vice Admiral Albert T. Church, III, "Executive Summary" (unclassified summary of longer report completed February 2005), available at: http://www.defenselink.mil/news/Mar2005/d20050310exe.pdf, p. 6.

45. ibid.

46. Mayer, *The Dark Side*, p. 225.

47. Tim Golden, "In U.S. Report, Brutal Details of 2 Afghan Inmates' Deaths," *New York Times*, May 20, 2005.

48. Paul Bremer, *My Year in Iraq* (New York: Threshold Editions, 2006), p. 134.

49. Interview by Leon Wordon, "Newsmaker Interview: Brig. Gen. Janis Karpinski," *Signal Newspaper of Santa Clara, CA*, July 4, 2004.

50. Quoted by Michiko Kakutani, "How Abu Ghraib Became the Anything-Goes Prison," *New York Times*, May 14, 2008, *NY Times* website.

51. Mark Marzzetti, Julian E. Barnes, and Edward T. Pound, "Inside the Iraq Prison Scandal," *U.S. News and World Report*, May 24, 2004, p. 22. See the elaboration of Karpinski on the Miller takeover of Abu Ghraib in her interview by Leon Wordon, "Newsmaker Interview: Brig. Gen. Janis Karpinski," *Signal Newspaper of Santa Clara, CA*, July 4, 2004, posted on Truthout .org, accessed July 10, 2004.

52. Schlesinger Report, p. 8. See also Mark Marzzetti, Julian E. Barnes, and Edward T. Pound, "Inside the Iraq Prison Scandal," *U.S. News and World Report*, May 24, 2004, p. 22.

53. Interview by Leon Wordon, "Newsmaker Interview: Brig. Gen. Janis Karpinski," *Signal Newspaper of Santa Clara, CA*, July 4, 2004.

54. Taguba Report, "Assessment of DoD Counter-Terrorism Interrogation and Detention Operations I Iraq (MG Miller's Assessment)," No. 2. See also Mark Marzzetti, Julian E. Barnes, and Edward D. Pound, "Inside the Iraq Prison Scandal," *U.S. News and World Report*, May 24, 2004, p. 22.

55. Taguba Report, "10 Comments on MG Miller's Assessment," Sections 1 and 2.

56. James R. Schlesinger, chair, "Final Report of the Independent Panel to Review Department of Defense Detention Operations," in Steven Strasser, ed., *The Abu Ghraib Investigations* (New York: Public Affairs, 2004), pp. 1–101.

57. See the DOD IG report, JPRA, and Steven M. Kleinman, Colonel, US Air Force, "Statement before the United States Senate Committee on Armed Services, Hearing on the Treatment of Detainees in U.S. Custody," (September 25, 2008). Found on the Senate Armed Services Committee website: http://armed-services.senate.gov/statemnt/2008/September/Moulton%2009-25-08.pdf.

58. Schlesinger, "Final Report of the Independent Panel to Review Department of Defense Detention Operations," in Strasser, ed., *The Abu Ghraib Investigations*, p.11.

59. Scott Higham, Josh White, and Christian Davenport, "A Prison on the Brink," *Washington Post*, May 9, 2004, pp. 1, A17.

60. R. Jeffrey Smith and Josh White, "General Granted Latitude At Prison," *Washington Post*, June 12, 2004, pp. 1, A18.

61. *Washington Post* Foreign Service, "Memo Appealed for Ways to Break Iraqi Detainees," August 23, 2004, A12. See also Mark Danner, *Torture and Truth* (New York: New York Review Books, 2004), p. 33.

62. Opening statement of Senator Carl Levin at hearings on treatment of detainees, p. 10, available at: http://Levin.Senate.gov/newsroom/supporting/2008/documents.sasc.061708 .pdf.

63. Wordon, "Newsmaker Interview: Brig. Gen. Janis Karpinski."

64. Memorandum for Commander, U.S. Central Command, Subject: CJTF-7 Interrogation and Counter-Resistance Policy (14 September 2003), signed by General Sanchez. http://www.scvhistory.com/scvhistory/signal/iraq/reports/sanchez-memo-091403.pdf.

65. From Richard S. Sanchez, Memorandum for Commander, U.S. Central Command, Subject: L CJTF-7 Interrogation and Counter-Resistance Policy (September 14, 2003), available at: http://www.scvhistory.com/scvhistory/signal/iraq/reports/sanchez-memo-091403.pdf (accessed July 8, 2008). Memorandum for C2 and C3, Combined Joint Task Force Seven, Baghdad, Iraq 09335, Commander, 205th Military Intelligence Brigade, Subject CJTF-7 Interrogation and Counter-Resistance Policy (September 14, 2003).

66. Smith and White, "General Granted Latitude at Prison," pp. 1, A18. General Sanchez has denied approving the use of dogs, sleep deprivation, or noise. Jackson Diehl, "Officers' Unheroic Example," *Washington Post*, July 19, 2004, p. A17.

67. Schlesinger Report, pp. 8–9.

68. ibid., p. 9.

69. Worden, "Newsmaker Interview: Brig. Gen. Janis Karpinski."

70. Taguba Report, Part III, Sec. C.8.A.1.

71. ibid., Part I, Sec. 11b.

72. ibid., Part I, Sec. 11.

73. ibid., Part I, Sec. 12.

74. Mayer, *The Dark Side*, pp. 252–57.

75. Schlesinger Report, p. 34.

76. Kleinman, "Statement before the United States Senate Committee on Armed Services, Hearing on the Treatment of Detainees in U.S. Custody." Found on the Senate Armed Services Committee website: http://armed-services.senate.gov/statemnt/2008/September/Moulton%2009-25-08.pdf.

77. U.S. Army Field Manual 34–52, *Intelligence Interrogation*, available at: http://www.fas.org/irp/doddir/army/fm34–52.pdf.

78. Phifer memo of October 11, 2002, listing techniques reprinted in Greenberg and Dratel, eds., *The Torture Papers*, p. 227–28. Haynes memo recommended that all of Categories I and II be approved, but only technique no. 4 in Category III (grabbing, poking, and pushing), reprinted in Greenberg and Dratel, eds., *The Torture Papers*, p. 236.

79. See Sands, *Torture Team*.

80. From Jerald Phifer, STC, USA, Director; J2; For Commander, Joint Task Force 170, subject: Request for approval of Counter-Resistance Strategies (October 11, 2002), in Greenberg and Dratel, eds., *The Torture Papers*, p. 227.

81. Action Memo, For: Secretary of Defense, From: William J. Haynes II, Subject: Counter-Resistance Techniques (November 27, 2002, stamped as approved: December 2, 2002); reproduced in Greenberg and Dratel, eds., *The Torture Papers*, p. 236.

82. "Detainee Interrogations in the Global War on Terrorism: Assessment of Legal, Historical, Policy, and Operational Considerations" (April 4, 2003), reprinted in Greenberg and Dratel, eds., *The Torture Papers*, p. 286.

83. "Detainee Interrogations in the Global War on Terrorism: Assessment of Legal, Historical, Policy, and Operational Considerations" (April 4, 2003), reprinted in Greenberg and Dratel, eds., *The Torture Papers*, pp. 286, 347, 357–58.

84. "Memorandum for the Commander, U.S. Southern Command, From: Donald Rumsfeld" (signed April 16, 2003), in Greenberg and Dratel, eds., *The Torture Papers*, pp. 360–63

85. "JTF GTMO 'SERE' Interrogation Standard Operating Procedure" Subj: Guidelines

for Employing ("SERE" crossed out) Management Techniques During Detainee Interrogations (December 18, 2002). From Senate Armed Services Committee Hearing on "The Origins of Aggressive Interrogation Techniques," available at: http://Levin.Senate.gov/newsroom/supporting/2008/documents.sasc.061708.pdf

86. Scott A. Allen, MD; Josiah D. Rich, MD, MPH; Robert C. Bux, MD; Bassina Farbenblum; Matthew Berns; and Leonard Rubenstein, "Deaths of Detainees in U.S. Custody in Iraq and Afghanistan from 2002 to 2005," (December 5, 2006), posted at: http://www.medscape.com/viewarticle/547787. See also, ACLU, "Autopsy Reports Reveal Homicides of Detainees in U.S. Custody," (November 25, 2005), posted at: http://action.aclu.org/torturefoia/released/102405/, and Human Rights First, "Torture: Quick Facts," posted at: http://www.humanrightsfirst.org/us_law/etn/misc/factsheet.htm.

87. Douglas Jehl and Eric Schmitt, "U.S. Military Says 26 Inmate Deaths May be Homicide," *New York Times*, March 16, 2005, p. 1.

88. Mayer, *The Dark Side*, p. 275.

89. Antonio M. Taguba, "Article 15–6 Investigation of the 800th Military Policy Brigade," (February 26, 2003), (hereinafter the "Taguba Report"), Part I, Sec. 2, No. 5. The report is printed in Greenberg and Dratel, eds., *The Torture Papers*, pp. 405–65.

90. Taguba Report, Part I, Sec. 2, No. 6.

91. ibid., No. 8.

92. ibid., No. 10.

93. Major General George R. Fay, Investigating Officer, "Investigation of the Abu Ghraib Detention Facility and 205th Military Intelligence Brigade" (hereinafter the Fay Report), in Steven Strasser, ed., *The Abu Ghraib Investigations* (New York: Public Affairs, 2004), pp. 109–71.

94. Eric Schmitt, "Army Report Says Flaws in Detention Didn't Cause Abuse," *New York Times*, July 23, 2004, *NY Times* website.

95. Selections quoted in the *Washington Post*, July 23, 2004, p. A14. See also the editorial, "An Army Whitewash," *Washington Post*, July 24, 2004, p. A20, and editorial, "Abu Ghraib, Whitewashed," *New York Times*, July 24, 2004.

96. Department of the Army, "Memorandum for Commander 104th Military Intelligence Battalion, 4th Infantry Division, (November 9, 2003), Subject: Rebuttal of [blank] to Written Reprimand," reproduced in Jameel Jaffer and Amrit Singh, *Administration of Torture* (New York: Columbia University Press, 2007), pp. A-292–A-294.

97. "Statement under oath of [redacted], (2004/05/13), A/302nd Military Intelligence Battalion, Heidelberg, Germany," reprinted in Jaffer and Singh, *Administration of Torture*, p. 319.

98. Office of the Inspector General, Department of Justice, "A Review of the FBI's Involvement in and Observations of Detainee Interrogations in Guantanamo Bay, Afghanistan, and Iraq," unclassified version made public (May 2008), pp. 171–201.

99. See Eric Lichtblau and Scott Shane, "Report Details Dissent On Guantanamo Tactics," *New York Times*, May 21, 2008, p. A17.

100. Office of the Inspector General, Department of Justice, "A Review of the FBI's Involvement," p. 181.

101. Mayer, *The Dark Side*, p. 3.

102. Office of the Inspector General, Department of Justice, "A Review of the FBI's Involvement," p. 102–3. Other FBI-specific accounts of torture can be found in Jaffer and Singh, *Administration of Torture* pp. A-279–A-281; accounts of hostage-taking, p. A-94.

103. Office of the Inspector General, Department of Justice, "A Review of the FBI's Involvement," p. 370.

104. Neil A. Lewis, "Red Cross Found Abuses at Abu Ghraib Last Year," *New York Times,* May 11, 2004, p. A11.

105. "Report of the International Committee of the Red Cross (ICRC) on the Treatment by the Coalition Forces of Prisoners of War and other Protected Persons by the Geneva Conventions in Iraq During Arrest, Internment and Interrogation," (February 2004). Posted at www .globalsecurity.org, accessed July 12, 2004, in Greenberg and Dratel, eds., *The Torture Papers,* pp. 383–404.

106. ICRC Report, Executive Summary.

107. ibid., Sec. 3.1.

108. ibid., Sec. 3.2.

109. ibid., Sec. 1, paragraph 7.

110. The severe mistreatment of the Reuters employees is detailed in Mark Danner, "The Logic of Torture," *New York Review,* June 24, 2004, p. 71.

111. "Memorandum for John Rizzo, Acting General Counsel of the Central Intelligence Agency from Jay S. Bybee, Assistant Attorney General, Office of Legal Council, Department of Justice (August 1, 2002); Subject: "Interrogation of al Qaeda Operative," http://documents .nytimes.com/justice-department-memos-on-interrogation-techniques#p=1.

112. "Memorandum for John A. Rizzo, Senior Deputy General Counsel, CIA (May 10, 2005) from Steven G. Bradbury, Principle Deputy Assistant Attorney General; Re: 'Application of 18 U.S.C. sections 2340-2340A to Certain Techniques That May Be Used in the Interrogation of High Value al Qaeda Detainee,'" http://documents.nytimes.com/justice-department-memos-on-interrogation-techniques#p=1.

113. ibid., pp. 1–2 and footnote 3.

114. "The detainee's hands are generally between the level of his heart and his chin. In some cases the detainee's hands may be raised above the level of his head, but only for a period of up to two hours. All of the detainee's weight is borne by his legs and feet during standing sleep deprivation. You have informed us that the detainee is not allowed to hang from or support his body weight with the shackles." ibid., p. 11.

115. "Memorandum for John A. Rizzo, Senior Deputy General Counsel, CIA (May 10, 2005) from Steven G. Bradbury, Principle Deputy Assistant Attorney General; Re: 'Application of 18 U.S.C. sections 2340-2340A to the Combined Use of Certain Techniques in the Interrogation of High Value al Qaeda Detainees,'" http://documents.nytimes.com/justice-department-memos-on-interrogation-techniques#p=1.

116. Quoting a CIA document, Bradbury says that walling "is one of the most effective interrogation techniques because it wears down the [detainee] physically, heightens uncertainty in the detainee about what the interrogator may do to him, and creates a sense of dread when the [detainee] knows he is about to be walled again." ibid., p. 6.

117. Quoted in Danner, "US Torture," p. 5 of online version.

118. International Committee of the Red Cross, *Report on the Treatment of Fourteen "High Value Detainees" in CIA Custody,* posted at: http://www.nybooks.com/icrc-report.pdf, accessed April 14, 2009. This account and all of the quotations from the report are based on that report and on Mark Danner, "US Torture: Voices from the Black Sites," *New York Review of Books* 56, No. 6 (April 9, 2009), http://www.nybooks.com/articles/22530, accessed on March 15, 2009. Danner obtained a copy of the report before it was leaked to the press. Each page of the report had these lines at the bottom of the page: "This report is strictly confidential and intended only for the Authorities to whom it is presented. It may not be published, in full or in part, without the consent of the International Committee of the Red Cross." Nevertheless, the report was leaked in early April 2009.

119. ICRC, "Report," p. 2; and quoted in Danner, "US Torture," p. 6 of online version.

120. From Danner, "US Torture," p. 6 of online version.

121. ibid., p. 13.

122. ibid., p. 14.

123. Lawrence E. Hinkle Jr. and Harold G. Wolff, "Communist Interrogation and Indoctrination of 'Enemies of the State,'" *A.M.A. Archives of Neurology and Psychiatry* 76, No. 2 (August 1956), p. 134. Cited in Mark Danner, "The Red Cross Torture Report: What it Means," *New York Review of Books* 56, no. 7 (April 30, 2009), endnote 12.

124. Quoted in Danner, "US Torture," p. 16 of online version.

125. Jan Crawford Greenburg, Howard L. Rosenberg, and Ariane de Vogue, "Sources: Top Bush Advisors Approved 'Enhanced Interrogation,'" *ABC News* (April 9, 2008), quoted in Danner, "US Torture," p. 12 of online version. The Bybee II memo describes a "prototypical interrogation" in which the "detainee begins his first interrogation session stripped of his clothes, shackled, and hooded, with the walling collar over his head and around his neck." The sessions gradually escalate to waterboarding. This process "may last 30 days" and, with permission, may go on another 30 days.

126. Quoted in Danner, "US Torture," p. 21 of online version.

127. ibid., p. 20.

128. Bob Woodward, "Detainee Tortured, Says U.S. Official," *Washington Post*, January 14, 2009, p. 1.

129. "From: Bald, Gary M, To [deleted], Subject GTMO Special Inquiry" (August 17, 2004), reproduced copy in Jaffer and Singh.

130. "From [blank] (Div 13) (FBI) To [blank], Subject: RE: Detainee abuse claimes" (May 05, 2004), printed in Jaffer and Singh, *Administration of Torture*, pp. A-174–A-175.

131. For accounts of the SERE training at Fort Bragg, NC, and in Iraq, see Jane Mayer, *The Dark Side*, pp. 197 and 245.

132. See Joseph Perez, *The Spanish Inquisition* (London: Profile Books, 2004), pp. 146–8 and Darius Rejali, *Torture and Democracy* (Princeton, NJ: Princeton University Press, 2007), pp. 279–85.

133. *U.S. vs. Hideji Nakamura, U.S. Military Commission, Yokohama*, 1947. Cited in Evan Wallach, "Drop by Drop: Forgetting the History of Water Torture in U.S. Courts," *Columbia Journal of Transnational Law* 45, p. 468. See also: Evan Wallach, "Waterboarding Used to be a Crime," *Washington Post*, November 4, 2007, p. B1.

134. "Interview of the Vice President by Scott Hennen, WDAY at Radio Day at the White House," The Vice President's Office. White House website: October 24, 2006. www.whitehouse .gov/news/releases/2006/10/print/20061024-7.html. See also Dan Eggen, "Cheney's Remarks Fuel Torture Debate," *Washington Post*, October 27, 2006, p. A9 and Neil A. Lewis, "Furor Over Cheney Remark on Tactics for Terror Suspects," *New York Times*, October 28, 2006, p. A8.

135. "Memorandum for John Rizzo, Acting General Counsel of the Central Intelligence Agency from Jay S. Bybee, Assistant Attorney General, Office of Legal Council, Department of Justice (August 1, 2002); Subject: 'Interrogation of al Qaeda Operative,'" http://documents .nytimes.com/justice-department-memos-on-interrogation-techniques#p=1.

136. "Memorandum for John A. Rizzo, Senior Deputy General Counsel, CIA (May 10, 2005) from Steven G. Bradbury, Principle Deputy Assistant Attorney General; Re: 'Application of 18 U.S.C. sections 2340-2340A to Certain Techniques That May Be Used in the Interrogation of High Value al Qaeda Detainee,'" p. 13, http://documents.nytimes.com/justice-department-memos-on-interrogation-techniques#p=1.

137. "Memorandum for John A. Rizzo, Senior Deputy General Counsel, CIA (May 30,

2005) from Steven G. Bradbury, Principle Deputy Assistant Attorney General; Re: 'Application of United States Obligations Under Article 16 of the Convention Against Torture to Certain Techniques that May Be Used in the Interrogation of High Value al Qaeda Detainees,'" p. 37; http://documents.nytimes.com/justice-department-memos-on-interrogation-techniques#p=1.

138. "Executive Order: Interpretation of the Geneva Conventions Common Article 3 as Applied to a Program of Detention and Interrogation Operated by the Central Intelligence Agency," July 20, 2007, posted on White House website.

139. Greg Miller, "Waterboarding is Legal, White House Says," *Los Angeles Times,* February 7, 2008, http://www.latimes.com/news/nationworld/washingtondc/la-na-torture7feb07,0,212005.story.

140. Quoted in Dan Eggen, "Justice Official Defends Rough CIA Interrogations," *Washington Post,* February 17, 2008, p. A3. See also *Legal Times:* http://legaltimes.typepad.com/blt/2008/02/steven-bradbury.html.

141. Malcom Nance, personal account of waterboarding (October 31, 2007), in *Small Wars Journal,* found at: http://smallwarsjournal.com/blog.

142. Nance, quoted in Mayer, *The Dark Side,* p. 173.

143. Christopher Hitchens, "Believe Me, It's Torture," *Vanity Fair,* August 2008, website.

144. Richard E. Mezo, "Why It Was Called 'Water Torture,'" *Washington Post,* February 10, 2008, p. B7.

145. "Memorandum for John Rizzo, Acting General Counsel of the Central Intelligence Agency from Jay S. Bybee, Assistant Attorney General, Office of Legal Council, Department of Justice (August 1, 2002); Subject: 'Interrogation of al Qaeda Operative,'" p. 15, http://documents.nytimes.com/justice-department-memos-on-interrogation-techniques#p=1.

146. "Memorandum for John A. Rizzo, Senior Deputy General Counsel, CIA (May 10, 2005) from Steven G. Bradbury, Principle Deputy Assistant Attorney General; Re: 'Application of 18 U.S.C. sections 2340-2340A to Certain Techniques That May Be Used in the Interrogation of High Value al Qaeda Detainee,'" p. 42.

147. Marc Santora, "3 Top Republican Candidates Take a Hard Line on the Interrogation of Detainees," *New York Times,* November 3, 2007, p. A13.

148. Both quotes from Greg Miller, "Waterboarding is Legal, White House Says," *Los Angeles Times,* February 7, 2008, http://www.latimes.com/news/nationworld/washingtondc/la-na-torture7feb07,0,212005.story.

149. See letter to "Honorable Michael B. Mukasey" from ten U.S. Senators (October 23, 2007), at: http://www.talkingpointsmemo.com/docs/mukasey-waterboarding.

150. "To The Honorable John D. Rockefeller IV and Honorable Silvestre Reyes," signed by 30 retired generals and admirals (December 12, 2007), at http://www. huffingtonpost.com/2007/12/13/military-leaders-ignore-_n_76656.html?viet=print.

151. Otto Kreisher, "Intelligence Chiefs: Waterboarding Legal in Certain Circumstances," *Government Executive,* February 5, 2008, website.

152. Richard Esposito and Jason Ryan, "CIA Chief: We Waterboarded," *ABC News,* February 5, 2008, at: http://abcnews.go.com/print?id=4244423.

153. White House, Office of the Press Secretary, Executive Order, "Ensuring Lawful Interrogations," (January 22, 2009).

154. Quoted in Bob Woodward, *State of Denial* (New York: Simon and Schuster, 2006), p. 80.

155. *Valentine v. U.S. ex rel. Neidecker,* 299 U.S. 5, p. 9 (1936), in Louis Fisher, "Extraordinary Rendition: The Price of Secrecy," *American University Law Review* 57, p. 1412.

156. *4A Opinions of the Office of Legal Counsel* 149 (1980), in Louis Fisher, "Extraordinary Rendition: The Price of Secrecy," *American University Law Review* 57, p. 1412.

157. William G. Weaver and Robert M. Pallitto, "'Extraordinary Rendition' and Presidential Fiat," *Presidential Studies Quarterly* 36, No. 1, p. 102 (p. 7 of Blackwell online version).

158. See Louis Fisher, "Extraordinary Rendition: The Price of Secrecy," *American University Law Review* 57, p. 1415.

159. "Hearing Before the Joint Investigation of the House and Senate Intelligence Committees, 107th Congress (September 26, 2002), statement of Cofer Black, former Chief of Counterterrorist Center, CIA," http://intelligence.senate.gov/0209hrg/020926/witness.htm. Quoted by Jane Mayer, "Outsourcing Torture," *New Yorker,* February 14, 2007, website, p. 6 of 14.

160. Weaver and Pallitto, "'Extraordinary Rendition' and Presidential Fiat," p. 102, (p. 1–2 of Blackwell online version).

161. Jane Mayer, "Outsourcing Torture," website, p. 5 of 14.

162. Jane Mayer, "Outsourcing Torture," website, p. 2 of 14. For citations to the State Department reports about the human rights records and practices of these countries, see *NY Bar Report,* p. 8, footnote 14.

163. "Convention Against Torture and Other Cruel, Inhuman, or Degrading Treatment of Punishment," G.A. Res. 39/46, Annex, U.N. Doc. A/Res/39/46/Annex (December 10, 1984), in Fisher, p. 1418.

164. "Public Law 105–277 at Section 2242(a)-(b)," in Michael John Garcia, "Renditions: Constraints imposed by Laws on Torture," *Congressional Research Service Report for Congress,* January 25, 2008, p. 10.

165. Interviewed by Stephen Grey, *Ghost Plane: The Inside Story of the CIA's Secret Rendition Programme* (London: Hurst & Company, 2006), p. 36.

166. Elizabeth Bumiller, David Sanger, and Richard Stevenson, "Bush Says Iraqis Will Want G.I.'s to Stay to Help," *New York Times,* January 28, 2005, p. 1.

167. See Grey, *Ghost Plane,* p. 192, www.whitehouse.gov/news/releases/2005/04/20050428-9.html.

168. *Department of State Country Reports on Human Rights Practices for 2003* 2, pp. 1826–27 (2004), in Louis Fisher, "Extraordinary Rendition: The Price of Secrecy," *American University Law Review* 57, p. 1421. State Department reports on other countries can be found on the State Department website: http://www.state.gov/g/drl/rls/hrrpt/2003/.

169. Grey, *Ghost Plane,* p. 199–200.

170. ibid., p. 200.

171. Mayer, "Outsourcing Torture," website, p. 9 of 14.

172. See James P. Pfiffner, *Power Play: The Bush Presidency and the Constitution* (Washington: Brookings, 2008), pp. 137-138.

173. Elisabeth Rosenthal, "Italian Trial of C.I.A. Operatives Begins With Torture Testimony," *New York Times,* May 15, 2008, p. A10.

174. Committee on International Human Rights of the Association of the Bar of the City of New York and the Center for Human Rights and Global Justice, New York University Law School, "Torture by Proxy: International and Domestic Law Applicable to 'Extraordinary Renditions'" (2004), pp. 9–11. See also Commission of Inquiry into the Actions of Canadian Officials in Relation to Maher Arar, Ministry of the Attorney General, Toronto (December 12, 2006), http://www.fedpubs.com/subject/govern/arar_rcmp.htm.

175. Mayer, *Dark Side,* pp. 108–9.

176. "A Conversation with Michael Hayden," *Council on Foreign Relations* (September 7, 2007), New York City, p. 17 of transcript, http://www.cfr.org/publication/14158/.

Chapter 4: The Logic of Torture

1. Interview of the Vice President by Jonathan Kar, ABC News (December 15, 2008), Vice President's Ceremonial Office, Executive Office Building. White House website: www .whitehouse.gov/news/releases/ 2008/12/print/2008 1215-8 (accessed December 22, 2008).

2. Charles C. Krulak and Joseph P. Hoar, "It's Our Cage, Too," *Washington Post,* May 17 2007, p. A17. John Hutson also commented on the danger of allowing any form of torture: "I know from the military that if you tell someone they can do a little of this for the country's good, some people will do a lot of it for the country's better." Scott Shane, David Johnston, and James Risen, "Secret US Endorsement of Severe Interrogations," *New York Times,* October 4, 2007, p. 1.

3. Darius Rejali, *Torture and Democracy* (Princeton University Press, 2007), p. 24.

4. Ron Suskind, *The Way of the World* (New York: Harper, 2008), pp. 129–32.

5. Another variation on this scenario is a case, reported by Mark Bowden, in which a young boy was kidnapped, tied, and gagged and hidden by the kidnapper. When he was captured by police, he would not reveal where the boy was. The police thought the boy might still be alive, and threatened to bring in an interrogator to apply torture to the man to get him to reveal the location of the boy (the man revealed the location, but the boy was dead). A reasonable person might conclude that torture was justified in this instance. See Mark Bowden, "The Dark Art of Interrogation," *The Atlantic Monthly,* October 2003, www.theatlantic.com, accessed July 29, 2004.

6. Jane Mayer, "Whatever it Takes," *New Yorker,* February 19 and 26, 2007, pp. 66–82.

7. Amy Argetsinger and Roxanne Roberts, "The Reliable Source," *Washington Post,* November 5, p. C3, and November 8, p. 3C.

8. Mayer, "Whatever it Takes," p. 68.

9. ibid., p. 72.

10. See Bob Brecher, *Torture and the Ticking Bomb* (Oxford: Blackwell, 2007).

11. Charles Krauthammer, "The Truth about Torture," *The Weekly Standard,* December 5, 2005. Krauthammer later added an extension to the ticking time bomb scenario. He argued that the United States found itself in such a situation after it had captured "high-value" terrorists. Torture, he argued, would be justified for the "extraction of information from a high-value enemy in possession of high-value information likely to save lives." He said that Khalid Sheik Mohammed had answered a question about possible future attacks with "soon you will know" and that that justified torturing him to discover the plans. He did not, however, say what plans had been discovered after the 183 times KSM had been waterboarded in March of 2003. Charles Krauthammer, "Torture? No. Except …," *Washington Post,* May 1, 2009, p. A21.

12. Alan Dershowitz, "Want to Torture? Get a Warrant," *San Francisco Chronicle,* January 22, 2002.

13. Quoted in Kathleen Parker, "Is It Torture?" *Washington Post,* April 26, 2009, p. A 15.

14. For an insightful analysis and refutation of the ticking bomb scenario, see David Luban, "Liberalism, Torture, and the Ticking Bomb," *Virginia Law Review* 91, no. 6 (October 2005), p. 1425, http://www.virginialawreview.org/content/pdfs/91/1425.pdf.

15. Intelligence Science Board, *Educing Information* (National Defense Intelligence College Press, December 2006), Chapters Three and Four.

16. President Bush, Press Conference in the Rose Garden (September 15, 2006), at: http://www.whitehouse.gov/news/releases/2006/09/20060915-2.html

17. See Brecher, *Torture and the Ticking Bomb.* Much of the following discussion is based on his book.

18. Darius Rejali, *Torture and Democracy* (Princeton University Press, 2007), p. 24.

19. See the detailed analysis of interrogation methods by Mark Bowden, "The Dark Art of Interrogation," *The Atlantic Online,* October 2003, www.theatlantic.com, accessed July 30, 2004.

20. For examples where torture allegedly worked in preventing terrorist attacks, see John Yoo, *War By Other Means* (New York: Atlantic Monthly Press, 2006), p. 189–91.

21. Seymour M. Hersh, "Torture at Abu Ghraib," *The New Yorker,* May 10, 2004, p. 47. See also Tim Golden and Don Van Natta, Jr., "U.S. Said to Overstate Value of Guantanamo Detainees," *New York Times,* June 21, 2004, p. 1.

22. Sec. 4A3, Current Doctrine. The relevant portions of the Army Field Manual 34–52 are attached to Secretary Rumsfeld's Memorandum for the Commander, US Southern Command; Subject: Counter-Resistance Techniques in the War on Terrorism (S) (April 16, 2003).

23. John McCain, "Torture's Terrible Toll," *Newsweek,* November 25, 2005.

24. Jane Mayer, "Outsourcing Torture," *New Yorker,* February 14, 2007, website, p. 6 of 14.

25. Vikram Dodd and Tania Branigan, "Questioned at Gunpoint, Shackled, Forced to Pose Naked, British Detainees Tell Their Stories of Guantanamo Bay," *The Guardian,* August 4, 2004, posted on TruthOut.org, accessed August 9, 2004. Mayer, "Outsourcing Torture," website, p. 9 of 14. Later, one of the three admitted that he had trained with an AK-47 while in Afghanistan.

26. Josh White, "Interrogation Research Is Lacking, Report Says," *Washington Post,* January 16, 2007, p. A15. Intelligence Science Board, *Educing Information.*

27. Intelligence Science Board, *Educing Information,* p. xxiii.

28. ibid.

29. Quoted in Rejali, *Torture and Democracy,* p. 452.

30. ibid., p. 447.

31. "E-mail between DoD CITF Personnel, Subject: FW: Counter Resistance Strategy Meeting Minutes" [Minutes of an October 2, 2002, meeting at Guantanamo Bay, Cuba [TAB 7] (October 24, 2002. (Note: "All questions and comments have been paraphrased.") Fredman said that "the CIA has employed aggressive techniques on less than a handful of suspects since 9/11."

32. Darius Rejali, *Torture and Democracy,* p. 469.

33. John Conroy, *Unspeakable Acts, Ordinary People: The Dynamics of Torture* (Berkeley: University of California Press, 2000), p. 112, in Jeannine Bess, "'Behind this Mortal Bone': The (In)Effectiveness of Torture," *Indiana Law Journal* 83, p. 355.

34. Department of Defense News Release (June 12, 2005), at http://www.defenselink.mil/releases/2005/nr20050612-3661.html; Department of Defense, Interrogation Log, Detainee 063 (November 23, 2002, to January 11, 2003), at www.time.com/time2006/log/log.pdf; as cited in *Retired Federal Jurists Amici Curiae Brief in support of Petitioners' Supplemental Brief Regarding the Military Commissions Act of 2006* (November 1, 2006), U.S. Court of Appeals for the District of Columbia, *Khaled A.F. AL Odah, et al. vs. U.S.,* pp. 3, 12–13.

35. Matthew Alexander, "My Written Testimony to the Senate Judiciary Committee Hearing," May 13, 2009, posted at: http://www.huffingtonpost.com/matthew-alexander/my-written-testimony-to-t_b_203269.html.

36. Mayer, *Dark Side,* p. 105.

37. See Joseph Margulies, *Guantanamo* (New York: Simon and Schuster, 2006), p. 119.

38. Michael Isikoff, "Forget the 'Poisons and Deadly Gasses,'" *Newsweek,* July 5, 2004, p. 6; Douglas Jehl, "High Qaeda Aide Retracted Claim of Link with Iraq," *New York Times,* July

31, 2004, nytimes.com, accessed July 31, 2004; Dana Priest, "Al Qaeda-Iraq Link Recanted," *Washington Post,* August 1, 2004, p. A20. See also Margulies, *Guantanamo,* p. 119.

39. Mayer, *Dark Side,* p. 138.

40. "Memorandum for John A. Rizzo, Senior Deputy General Counsel, CIA (May 30, 2005) from Steven G. Bradbury, Principle Deputy Assistant Attorney General; Re: 'Application of United States Obligations Under Article 16 of the Convention Against Torture to Certain Techniques that May Be Used in the Interrogation of High Value al Qaeda Detainees,'" p. 5, http://documents.nytimes.com/justice-department-memos-on-interrogation-techniques#p=1.

41. ibid.

42. Dan Eggen and Walter Pincus, "FBI, CIA Debate Significance of Terror Suspect," *Washington Post,* December 18, 2007, p. 1.

43. Ali Soufan, testimony before the Senate Judiciary Committee, May 13, 2009, p. 4. Found at: http://judiciary.senate.gov/hearings/testimony.cfm?id=3842&wit_id=7906. These paragraphs are based on Soufan's testimony.

44. Quoted by Ron Suskind, *The One Percent Solution* (New York: Simon and Schuster, 2006), p. 100. For a longer analysis of the misunderstanding of Abu Zubaida, see Peter Finn and Joby Warrick, "Detainee's Harsh Treatment Foiled No Plots," *Washington Post,* March 29, 2009, p. 1.

45. Scott Shane, "Divisions Arose on Rough Tactics for Qaeda Figure," *New York Times,* April 18, 2009, p. 1.

46. Ali Soufan, testimony before the Senate Judiciary Committee, May 13, 2009, p. 3. Found at, http://judiciary.senate.gov/hearings/testimony.cfm?id=3842&wit_id=7906.

47. Ali Soufan, testimony before the Senate Judiciary Committee, May 13, 2009, p. 8. Found at, http://judiciary.senate.gov/hearings/testimony.cfm?id=3842&wit_id=7906.

48. "Memorandum for John A. Rizzo, Senior Deputy General Counsel, CIA (May 30, 2005) from Steven G. Bradbury, Principle Deputy Assistant Attorney General; Re: 'Application of United States Obligations Under Article 16 of the Convention Against Torture to Certain Techniques that May Be Used in the Interrogation of High Value al Qaeda Detainees,'" p. 5, http://documents.nytimes.com/justice-department-memos-on-interrogation-techniques#p=1.

49. "Memorandum for John A. Rizzo, Senior Deputy General Counsel, CIA (May 10, 2005) from Steven G. Bradbury, Principle Deputy Assistant Attorney General; Re: 'Application of 18 U.S.C. sections 2340-2340A to Certain Techniques that may be used in the Interrogation of High Value al Qaeda Detainee,'" p. 14, http://documents.nytimes.com/justice-department-memos-on-interrogation-techniques#p=1.

50. Darius Rejali, *Torture and Democracy* (Princeton University Press, 2007), p. 506.

51. "Memorandum for John A. Rizzo, Senior Deputy General Counsel, CIA (May 30, 2005) from Steven G. Bradbury, Principle Deputy Assistant Attorney General; Re: 'Application of United States Obligations Under Article 16 of the Convention Against Torture to Certain Techniques that May Be Used in the Interrogation of High Value al Qaeda Detainees,'" pp. 8, 9, http://documents.nytimes.com/justice-department-memos-on-interrogation-techniques#p=1.

52. ibid., p. 10.

53. Soufan, "My Tortured Decision," p. A23.

54. "Memorandum for John A. Rizzo, Senior Deputy General Counsel, CIA (May 30, 2005) from Steven G. Bradbury, Principle Deputy Assistant Attorney General; Re: 'Application of United States Obligations Under Article 16 of the Convention Against Torture to Certain Techniques that May Be Used in the Interrogation of High Value al Qaeda Detainees,'" p. 10, http://documents.nytimes.com/justice-department-memos-on-interrogation-techniques#p=1.

55. ibid., p. 11.

56. On the development of the rules of warfare, see L.C. Green, *The Contemporary Law of Armed Conflict* (Manchester University Press, 1993).

57. Hannah Arendt, *Eichmann in Jerusalem: A Report on the Banality of Evil* (New York: Viking Press, 1963).

58. Guy B. Adams and Danny L. Balfour, *Unmasking Administrative Evil*, rev. ed. (Armonk, NY: M.E. Sharp, 2004). For an insightful analysis of the influence of informal policy on organizational behavior regarding U.S. torture, see Barbara Aramacost, "Interrogation after 9/11: The Law on the Books and the Law on the Ground," University of Virginia Law School Public Law and Legal Theory Working Paper Series, Paper 87 (2008), posted at http://law.bepres.com/uvalwps/uva.publiclaw/art87 (accessed September 5, 2008).

59. Stanley Milgram, *Obedience to Authority* (New York: Harper and Row, 1974). See the detailed description of the experiment and its implications in Adams and Balfour, *Unmasking Administrative Evil*, pp. 36–39, from which this description is taken.

60. Benedict Carey, "Decades Later, Still Asking: Would I Pull That Switch?" *New York Times*, July 1, 2008, p. D1.

61. Philip Zimbardo, *The Lucifer Effect: How Good People Turn Evil* (London: Rider Press, 2007), p. 20.

62. C. Hanley, C. Banks, and P. Zimbardo, "Interpersonal Dynamics in Simulated Prisons," *International Journal of Criminology and Penology* 1 (1974), pp. 69–97. See the detailed description of the experiment and its implications in Adams and Balfour, *Unmasking Administrative Evil*, pp. 27–29, from which this description is taken.

63. Zimbardo, *The Lucifer Effect*, p. 197.

64. Associated Press, *New York Times*, June 9, 2004, p. A10.

65. Zimbardo, *The Lucifer Effect*, pp. 9–11.

66. Guy B. Adams and Danny L. Balfour, "Chapter 7: Administrative Evil in the 21st Century: Abu Ghraib, Moral Inversion and Torture Policy," in *Unmasking Administrative Evil*, 3rd ed. (New York: M.E. Sharpe, 2009, forthcoming).

67. Raul Hilberg, *The Destruction of the European Jews* (New York: Holmes and Meier, 1985), p. 55, in Adams and Balfour, *Unmasking Administrative Evil*, Chapter 7, manuscript of forthcoming 3rd ed.

68. Christopher Browning, *Ordinary Men: Reserve Police Battalion 101 and the Final Solution in Poland* (New York: HarperCollins, 1992), pp. 141–42. Quoted in Adams and Balfour, *Unmasking Administrative Evil*, Chapter 7, manuscript of forthcoming 3rd ed.

69. See S.G. Mestrovic, *The Trials of Abu Ghraib* (Boulder, CO: Paradigm Publishers, 2007), p. 173.

70. Robert J. Lifton, "Doctors and Torture," *New England Journal of Medicine* 351, No. 5 (July 29, 2004), found at http://content.nejm.org/cgi/reprint/351/5/415.pdf (accessed April 9, 2009). See also Robert J. Lifton, *The Nazi Doctors: Medical Killing and the Psychology of Genocide* (New York: Basic Books, 1986).

71. Philip Zimbardo, *The Lucifer Effect* (London: Rider, 2007), p. 17.

72. Quoted in Philip Gourevitch and Errol Morris, *Standard Operating Procedure* (New York: Penguin Press, 2008), p. 48.

73. Bob Brecher, *Torture and the Ticking Bomb* (Oxford: Blackwell, 2007), pp. 60–61.

74. Charles C. Krulak and Joseph P. Hoar, "It's Our Cage, Too," *Washington Post*, May 17 2007, p. A17. John Hutson also commented on the danger of allowing any form of torture: "I know from the military that if you tell someone they can do a little of this for the country's good, some people will do a lot of it for the country's better." Scott Shane, David Johnston, and

James Risen, "Secret US Endorsement of Severe Interrogations," *New York Times,* October 4, 2007, p. 1.

75. Rejali, *Torture and Democracy,* pp. 529, 478.

76. ibid., p. 24.

77. This section is based on Chapter Four of James P. Pfiffner, *Power Play: The Bush Presidency and the Constitution* (Washington: Brookings, 2008).

78. Del Quentin Wilber, "Uighur Detainees May Be Released to U.S.," *Washington Post,* October 5, 2008, p. 3.

79. Mark Denbeaux and Joshua Denbeaux, "Report on Guantanamo Detainees: A Profile of 517 Detainees through Analysis of Department of Defense Data," (April 2005), available at: http://law.shu.edu/aaafinal.pdf. The text of U.S. offers of $4285 and millions at end of Report No. 1.

80. Mark Denbeaux and Joshua Denbeaux, "Report on Guantanamo Detainees," p. 2.

81. ibid., p. 4.

82. Joseph Felter and Jarret Brachman, "An assessment of 516 Combatant Status Review Tribunal (CSRT) Unclassified Summaries," *Combating Terrorism Center, West Point, New York* (July 25, 2007).

83. Mark Denbeaux and Joshua Denbeaux, "Second Report on Guantanamo Detainees: Inter- and Intra-Departmental Disagreements About Who Is Our Enemy," available at: http://law.shu.edu/news/second_report_guantanamo_detainees_3_20_final.pdf, p. 25.

84. ibid., p. 23.

85. Quoted in Margolies, *Guantanamo,* p. 69.

86. Tim Golden, "Administration Officials Split Over Stalled Military Tribunals," *New York Times,* October 25, 2004, p. A1. Margulies, *Guantanamo,* p. 65.

87. Greg Miller, "Many Held at Guantanamo Not Likely Terrorists," *Los Angeles Times,* December 22, 2002, website at: http://www.latimes.com/la-na-gitmo22dec22,0,2294365.story.

88. ibid.

89. ibid.

90. Benjamin Wittes, *Law and the Long War* (New York: Penguin Press, 2008), pp. 79–80.

91. "Report of the International Committee of the Red Cross (ICRC) on the Treatment by the Coalition Forces of Prisoners of War and other Protected Persons by the Geneva conventions in Iraq During Arrest, Internment and Interrogation," (February 2004), Section 1, paragraph 7. Posted at www.globalsecurity.org, accessed July 12, 2004. The report is printed in Karen J. Greenberg and Joshua L. Dratel, eds., *The Torture Papers: The Road to Abu Ghraib* (Cambridge: Cambridge University Press, 2005), pp. 383–404.

92. "Sworn Statement by [blank]," (2004/05/26), 320th MP Bn. Ashley, PA; reprinted in Jameel Jaffer and Amrit Singh, *Administration of Torture* (New York: Columbia University Press, 2007), pp. A-315–A-316.

93. "Sworn statement by [blank]" (2004/05/18), B/CO 470th Military Intelligence Group, Camp Bullis, TX; reproduced in Jaffer and Singh, *Administration of Torture,* p. A-317.

94. Jane Mayer, "Outsourcing Torture," website, p. 1 of 14.

95. See Louis Fisher, *The Constitution and 9/11* (Lawrence, KS: University Press of Kansas, 2008), pp. 346–51.

96. See Louis Fisher, "The State Secrets Privilege: Relying on *Reynolds,*" *Political Science Quarterly* 122, No. 3 (2007), pp. 385–408. See also, Carol D. Leonnig and Eric Rich, "U.S. Seeks Silence on CIA Prisons," *Washington Post,* November 4, 2006, p. 1.

97. Mayer, "Outsourcing Torture," website, p. 12 of 14.

98. Doug Struck, "Cases of Detained Muslims Tarnish Canadian Mounties' Noble Image," *Washington Post*, December 15, 2006, p. A30.

99. Ian Austin, "Canadians Fault U.S. for Its Role in Torture Case," *New York Times*, September 19, 2006, nytimes.com website.

100. Struck, "Cases of Detained Muslims Tarnish Canadian Mounties' Noble Image," p. A30. See also Joseph Margulies, *Guantanamo*, pp. 190–1.

101. This case is based on Neil A. Lewis, "Man Mistakenly Abducted by C.I.A. Seeks Reinstatement of Suit," *New York Times*, November 29, 2006, p. A15.

102. Dana Priest, "The Wronged Man," *Washington Post*, November 29, 2006, p. C1. See the account by Louise Fisher, *The Constitution and 9/11* (Lawrence, KS: University Press of Kansas, 2008), pp. 352–6.

103. Craig Whitlock, "Germans Charge 13 CIA Operatives," *Washington Post*, February 1, 2007, p. A1. Mark Landler, "German Court Challenges C.I.A. Over Abduction," *New York Times*, January 31, 2007, nytimes.com.

104. CNN, "Bush: CIA holds terror suspects in secret prisons," September 7, 2006, found at: http://edition.cnn.com/2006/POLITICS/09/06/bush.speech/index.html, August 1, 2007.

105. Priest, "The Wronged Man," p. C1.

106. This discussion is based on the opinion of the U.S. Court of Appeals for the District of Columbia Circuit in *Parhat v. Gates* (Slip Opinion Number 06–1397) decided on June 20, 2008.

107. Ruth Marcus, "Free This Detainee," *Washington Post*, July 9, 2008, p. A15. Del Quentin Wilber and Josh White, "Judges Cite Need for Reliable Evidence to Hold Detainees," *Washington Post*, July 1, 2008, p. A3.

108. *Parhat v. Gates*, p. 16.

109. ibid., pp. 6–7, 26–27.

110. Wilber, "Uighur Detainees May Be Released to U.S.," p. 3.

111. *Parhat v. Gates*, pp. 5, 7.

112. William Glaberson, "Despite Ruling, Detainee Cases Facing Delays," *New York Times*, October 5, 2008, p. 1.

113. Del Quentin Wilber, "Chinese Detainees' Release Is Blocked," *Washington Post*, October 9, 2008, p. A3. Del Quentin Wilber, "Chinese Muslims Ordered Released From Guantanamo," *Washington Post*, October 8, 2008, p. 1.

114. *Kiyemba, et al. v. Obama*, Court of Appeals of the District of Columbia, No. 08–5424 (February 18, 2009), p. 12.

115. Del Quentin Wilber and Carrie Johnson, "Court Blocks Release of 17 Uighurs into U.S.," *Washington Post*, February 19, 2009, p. A4.

116. *Padilla v. Rumsfeld* (352 F.3rd 695), quoted in Richard M. Pious, *The War on Terrorism and the Rule of Law* (Los Angeles: Roxbury, 2006), pp. 130–7.

117. Dan Eggen, "Padilla Case Raises Questions About Anti-Terror Tactics," *Washington Post*, November 19, 2006, p. A3.

118. Deborah Sontag, "Defense Calls Padilla Incompetent for Trial," *New York Times*, February 23, 2007, nytimes.com.

119. Deborah Sontag, "A Videotape Offers a Window into a Terror Suspect's Isolation," *New York Times*, December 4, 2006, pp. A1, A22.

120. ibid.

121. Deborah Sontag, "Jailers Testify About Padilla's Confinement," *New York Times*, February 28, 2007, website.

122. Sontag, "A Videotape Offers a Window," pp. A1, A22.

123. Eggen, "Padilla Case Raises Questions," p. A3.

124. Peter Whorisky, "Jury Convicts Jose Padilla on Terror Charges," *Washington Post,* August 17, 2007, p. A1.

125. Del Quentin Wilber, "Citing Weak Evidence, Judge Orders Guantanamo Detainee Freed," *Washington Post,* January 15, 2009, p. A11.

126. William Glaberson, "Rulings of Improper Detentions in Cuba as the Bush Era Closes," *New York Times,* January 19, 2009, p. 1

127. See, for example, Pamela Hess, "Officials: Afghanistan Taliban Leader Was at Gitmo," *Washington Post,* March 11, 2009, p. 1.

128. The 1987 Landau Report recommended that "moderate physical pressure" be allowed in limited circumstances, but the coercive methods allowed became so widespread and indiscriminately applied that the Israeli Supreme Court reversed the recommendations in the late 1990s. See the account in Mark Bowden, "The Dark Art of Interrogation," *The Atlantic Online,* October 2003, www.theatlantic.com, accessed July 30, 2004.

129. Rejali, *Torture and Democracy,* p. 478.

Chapter 5: Torture and the Law

1. "President Bush holds press conference following G8 Summit," June 10, 2004, White House website, http://www.whitehouse.gov/news/releases/2004/06/20040610-36.html, accessed December 6, 2008.

2. Mark Mazzetti and Scott Shane, "Notes Show Confusion on Interrogation Methods," *New York Times,* June 18, 2008, website.

3. John Yoo, *The Powers of War and Peace* (Chicago: University of Chicago Press, 2005), p. 172.

4. For a full analysis of the development of habeas corpus, see James P. Pfiffner, *Power Play: The Bush Administration and the Constitution* (Washington: Brookings, 2008), Chapter Four.

5. On POWs, see L.C. Green, *The Contemporary Law of Armed Conflict* (Manchester: Manchester University Press, 1993), pp. 188–206, p. 197.

6. The law was amended by the Military Commissions Act of 2006, discussed later in this chapter.

7. See "LTC Diane E. Beaver, Staff Judge Advocate; to Commander, Joint Task Force 170; Subject: Legal Brief on Proposed Counter-Resistance Strategies" (October 11, 2002). Printed in Karen J. Greenberg and Joshua L. Dratel, eds., *The Torture Papers: The Road to Abu Ghraib* (Cambridge: Cambridge University Press, 2005), p. 229.

8. Army Regulation 190–8, Paragraph 1–5a and 1–5b. Quoted by David E. Graham, "Down a Slippery Slope," *Miller Center Report* (Fall–Winter 2005), p. 31. Graham is executive director of the Judge Advocate General's Legal Center and School of the Department of the Army.

9. Army Field Manual 34–52, "Intelligence Interrogations" (September 1992), Paragraphs 1–7 and 1–8. Quoted by Graham, "Down a Slippery Slope," p. 31.

10. This line of reasoning follows that of Karen Greenberg in "Bush's Criminal Confessions," *Salon.com,* December 11, 2006, accessed March 3, 2007, salon.com.

11. On POWs, see Green, *The Contemporary Law of Armed Conflict,* pp. 188–206.

12. Convention (III) relative to the Treatment of Prisoners of War. Geneva, August 12, 1949. Article 17, paragraph 4 provides that "no physical or mental torture, nor any other form of coercion, may be inflicted on prisoners of war to secure from them information of any kind

whatever. Prisoners of war who refuse to answer may not be threatened, insulted, or exposed to unpleasant or disadvantageous treatment of any kind."

13. Geneva Convention III, Article 4.

14. Alberto Gonzales, "The Rule of Law and the Rules of War," *New York Times,* May 15, 2004, p. A27.

15. U.S. Army Regulation 190–8, quoted in Elsea, "U.S. Treatment of Prisoners in Iraq: Selected Legal Issues," *Congressional Research Service Report for Congress* (RL32395), December 2, 2004, p. 10.

16. Joseph Margulies, *Guantanamo and the Abuse of Presidential Power* (New York: Simon and Schuster, 2006), pp. 71–83.

17. For an argument that the president is bound by treaties, see Derek Jinks and David Sloss, "Is the President Bound by the Geneva Conventions?" *Cornell Law Review* 90, p. 97. They conclude that presidents can terminate or suspend a treaty as long as the provisions of the treaty provide for it and the president's actions are in accord with international law, though he cannot unilaterally abrogate a treaty without congressional approval, pp. 155–60.

18. See "Memorandum from Gordon England, Subject: Application of Common Article 3 of the Geneva Conventions to the Treatment of Detainees in the Department of Defense" (July 7, 2006): "The Supreme Court has determined that Common Article 3 to the Geneva Conventions of 1949 applies as a matter of law to the conflict with Al Qaeda."

19. The law was amended by the Military Commissions Act of 2006, discussed later in this chapter.

20. John Michael Garcia, "U.N. Convention Against Torture (CAT): Overview and Application to Interrogation Techniques," *Congressional Research Service Report for Congress* (RL 32438), January 26, 2009, p. 7.

21. "Memorandum for the President (January 25, 2002) From Alberto R. Gonzales, subject: Decision RE application of the Geneva Convention on Prisoners of War to the Conflict with al Qaeda and the Taliban."

22. "Memorandum for William J. Haynes II, General Counsel, Department of Defence, from Patrick F. Philbin, Deputy Assistant Attorney General, and John C. Yoo, Deputy Assistant Attorney General," (December 29, 2001), p. 1; quoted in Louis Fisher, *Military Tribunals and Presidential Power* (Lawrence, KS: University Press of Kansas, 2005), p. 196. For an argument that the United States and the president are bound by international law, see Jordan J. Paust, *Beyond the Law* (New York: Cambridge University Press, 2007), pp. 20–24.

23. General Assembly Resolution 39/46, Annex, 39 U. GAOR Sup. No. 51, U.N. Doc. A.39/51 (1984).

24. Convention Against Torture and Other Cruel, Inhuman or Degrading Treatment or Punishment, December 10, 1984, S. Treaty Doc. No. 100–20, 1465 U.N.T.S. 85. See also, Jennifer K. Elsea, "Lawfulness of Interrogation Techniques under the Geneva Conventions," *Congressional Research Service Report to Congress* (RL32567), September 8, 2004, p. 9.

25. Robert K. Goldman and Brian D. Tittemore, "Unprivileged Combatants and the Hostilities in Afghanistan: Their Status and Rights Under International Humanitarian and Human Rights Law," (Washington, D.C.: American Society of International Law Task Force Paper, 2002), p. 49.

26. U.S. Law of Land Warfare, Field Manual 27, paragraph 4(b), 7(c), quoted in L.C. Green, *The Contemporary Law of Armed Conflict* (New York: Manchester University Press, 1993), p. 31.

27. Elsea, "Lawfulness of Interrogation Techniques," p. 9. For an argument that Article 75 is part of customary international law, see Goldman and Tittemore, "Unprivileged Combatants," p. 38, 49.

28. See the analysis in *Hamdan v. Rumsfeld*, Slip Opinion, pp. 66–68.

29. ibid., p. 71.

30. ibid., p. 68, note 63.

31. In the Memorandum for the Deputy Attorney General, December 30, 2004, Daniel Levin wrote: "It has been suggested that the prohibition against torture has achieved the status of jus cogens (i.e., a peremptory norm) under international law. See, for example, Siderman de Blake v. Republic of Argentina, 965 F.2d 699, 714 (9th Cir. 1992); Regina v. Bow Street Metro. Stipendiary Magistrate Ex Parte Pinochet Ugarte (No. 3), [2000] 1 AC 147, 198; see also, Restatement (Third) of Foreign Relations Law of the United States § 702 reporters' note 5."

32. "Memorandum for Alberto R. Gonzales, counsel to the president, Standards of Conduct for Interrogation under 18 U.S.C. Sc. 2340–2340A" (August 1, 2002). Reprinted in Greenberg and Dratel, eds., *The Torture Papers*, p. 172. According to *Newsweek*, the memo was written in close consultation with White House lawyers. Daniel Klaidman, "Homesick for Texas," *Newsweek*, July 12, 2004, p. 32.

33. "Memorandum for Alberto R. Gonzales, counsel to the president, Standards of Conduct for Interrogation under 18 U.S.C. Sc. 2340–2340A" (August 1, 2002). Reprinted in Greenberg and Dratel, eds., *The Torture Papers*, p. 172.

34. In the memo printed in Greenberg and Dratel, eds., *The Torture Papers*, p. 44.

35. "Memorandum for Alberto R. Gonzales, counsel to the president, Standards of Conduct for Interrogation under 18 U.S.C. Sc. 2340–2340A" (August 1, 2002). Reprinted in Greenberg and Dratel, eds., *The Torture Papers*, p. 200.

36. Article I, Section 8 also gives Congress the power "to provide for organizing, arming, and *disciplining* [emphasis added] the Militia, and for governing such Part of them as may be employed in the Service of the United States." A significant portion of U.S. troops in Iraq were from state National Guard units, specifically those who were photographed abusing Iraqi prisoners.

37. Jane Mayer, "Outsourcing Torture," *New Yorker*, February 14, 2007, website, p. 8 of 14. John Yoo's belief in the legal right of the president to order torture was quite broad. When asked by Doug Cassel (director of the Notre Dame Law School Center for Civil and Human Rights) if it would be legal for the president to order that the testicles of a child of a suspect be crushed in order to get a suspect to talk, Yoo replied: "I think it depends on why the president thinks he needs to do that." Yoo could have replied that such an act would be morally wrong but that the president had the legal authority to do it, but he didn't. Nat Hentoff, "Don't Ask, Don't Tell," *Village Voice*, January 27, 2006, http://www.villagevoice.com/news/0605,hentoff,71946,6.html.

38. Bybee memo I (August 1, 2002), p. 34.

39. Article VI of the Constitution also provides that "all Treaties made, or which shall be made, under the authority of the United States, shall be the supreme Law of the Land."

40. Jack Goldsmith, *The Terror Presidency* (New York: Norton, 2007), p. 151. Goldsmith revealed that there was a "second August 1, 2002, opinion that still remains classified." This memo approved specific interrogation techniques that were classified.

41. Goldsmith, *The Terror Presidency*, p. 155.

42. "MEMORANDUM OPINION FOR THE DEPUTY ATTORNEY GENERAL, DANIEL LEVIN, Acting Assistant Attorney General, Office of Legal Counsel, December 30, 2004, 'LEGAL STANDARDS APPLICABLE UNDER 18 U.S.C. §§ 2340–2340A *U.S.C. §§ 2340–2340A*.'" The memo: "supersedes in its entirety the August 1, 2002 opinion of this Office entitled Standards of Conduct under 18 U.S.C. §§ 2340–2340A." That statute prohibits conduct "specifically intended to inflict severe physical or mental pain or suffering." This opinion concludes that "severe" pain under the statute is not limited to "excruciating or agonizing" pain or pain "equivalent in

intensity to the pain accompanying serious physical injury, such as organ failure, impairment of bodily functions, or even death." The statute also prohibits certain conduct specifically intended to cause "severe physical suffering" distinct from "severe physical pain."

43. "Memorandum for James B. Comey, Deputy Attorney General, December 30, 2005, RE: Legal Standards Applicable under 18 U.S.C. Sec. 2340–2340A," available at: www.usdoj.gov/olc/18usc23402340a2.htm.

44. Jane Crawford Greenberg and Ariane de Vogue, "Bush Administration Blocked Waterboarding Critic," CBS News website, http://abcnews.go.com/WN/DOJ/story?id=3814076&page=1, accessed November 23, 2007.

45. Goldsmith, *The Terror Presidency,* p. 165. Footnote 8 was inserted into Levin's retraction memo at the insistence of the White House, when Alberto Gonzales was still counsel to the president. See Jan Crawford Greenberg and Ariane de Vogue, "Bush Administration Blocked Waterboarding Critic," ABC News website (November 2, 2007).

46. John Yoo, *War by Other Means* (New York: Atlantic Monthly Press, 2006), pp. 182–83.

47. Excerpted in Richard M. Pious, *The War on Terrorism* (Los Angeles: Roxbury, 2006), pp. 203–5.

48. "Memorandum for John A. Rizzo, Senior Deputy General Counsel, CIA (May 10, 2005) from Steven G. Bradbury, Principle Deputy Assistant Attorney General; Re: 'Application of 18 U.S.C. sections 2340-2340A to Certain Techniques that may be used in the Interrogation of High Value al Qaeda Detainee,'"http://documents.nytimes.com/justice-department-memos-on-interrogation-techniques#p=1.

49. ibid. In a Law Day talk at Fort Meade, home of the National Security Agency, Comey said, "We are likely to hear the words: 'If we don't do this, people will die.' ... It takes far more than a sharp legal mind to say 'no' when it matters most ... it takes moral character."

50. "Memorandum for John A. Rizzo, Senior Deputy General Counsel, CIA (May 10, 2005) from Steven G. Bradbury, Principle Deputy Assistant Attorney General; Re: 'Application of 18 U.S.C. sections 2340-2340A to the Combined Use of Certain Techniques in the Interrogation of High Value al Qaeda Detainees,'" http://documents.nytimes.com/justice-department-memos-on-interrogation-techniques#p=1.

51. In a public statement, Senator McCain said that "the intelligence we collect must be reliable and acquired humanely.... To do differently not only offends our values as Americans, but undermines our war effort, because abuse of prisoners *harms*—not helps—us in the war on terror.... Mistreatment of our prisoners endangers U.S. troops who might be captured by the enemy—if not in this war, then in the next. And third, prisoner abuses exact on us a terrible toll in the war of ideas." From "Statement of Senator John McCain Amendment on (1) the Army Field Manual and (2) Cruel, Inhumane, Degrading Treatment," November 4, 2005. Posted at: http://www.humanrightsfirst.info/pdf/05117-etn-mccain-stat-detain-amdts-auth.pdf. See also his article, "Torture's Terrible Toll," *Newsweek,* November 22, 2005.

52. The act defines cruel, inhuman, or degrading treatment as "the cruel, unusual, and inhumane treatment or punishment prohibited by the Fifth, Eighth, and Fourteenth Amendments to the Constitution, as defined in the United State Reservations, Declarations and Understandings to the United Nations Convention Against Torture and Other Forms of Cruel, Inhuman or Degrading Treatment of Punishment done at New York, December 10, 1984." Source: "H.R. 2863, Department of Defense Appropriations Act, 2006 (Enrolled as Agreed to or Passed by Both House and Senate), P.L. 109–148, Title X," found at http://thomas.loc.gov/cgi-bin/query/F?c109:7./temp/~c109yVTxt7:e189414.

53. Josh White, "President Relents, Backs Torture Ban," *Washington Post,* December 16, 2005, p. 1.

54. That is, if the U.S. person undertakes interrogation practices that "were officially authorized and determined to be lawful at the time that they were conducted, it shall be a defense that such officer, employee, member of the Armed Forces, or other agent did not know that the practices were unlawful and a person of ordinary sense and understanding would not know the practices were unlawful." Source: "H.R. 2863, Department of Defense Appropriations Ace, 2006 (Enrolled as Agreed to or Passed by Both House and Senate)," found at http://thomas.loc.gov/cgi-bin/query/F?c109:7:./temp/~c109yVTxt7:e189414.

55. Dan Froomkin, "Bush Demands Freedom to Torture," *White House World, washingtonpost.com*, December 14, 2007, http://www.washingtonpost.com/ac2/wp-dyn/NewsSearch?sb=-1&st=froomkin&. See the letter by former generals urging Congress to ignore Bush's veto threat, *Huffington Post*, http://www.huffingtonpost.com/2007/12/13/military-leaders-ignore-_n_76656.html?view=print. Steven Lee Myers, "Bush Vetoes Bill on C.I.A. Tactics, Affirming Legacy," *New York Times*, March 9, 2008, p. A1. See Louis Fisher, *The Constitution and 9/11* (Lawrence, KS: University Press of Kansas, 2008), p. 359.

56. The White House, "President's Statement on Signing of H.R. 2863, the 'Department of Defense, Emergency Supplemental Appropriations to Address Hurricanes in the Gulf of Mexico, and Pandemic Influenza Act, 2006,'" December 30, 2005, found on White House website, http://www.white house.gov.

57. For further analysis of these constitutional issues, see James P. Pfiffner, "Torture and Public Policy," *Public Integrity* 7, no. 4 (Fall 2005), pp. 313–30; *Power Play* (Washington: Brookings, 2008), Chapter Six; and "Presidential Signing Statements and Their Implications for Public Administration," *Public Administration Review* 69, No. 2 (March/April 2009), pp. 249–55.

58. "Memorandum for the Vice President, et al., Subject: Humane Treatment of al Qaeda and Taliban Detainees" (February 7, 2002), signed by President Bush. The memorandum is reproduced in Greenberg and Dratel, eds., *The Torture Papers*, pp. 134–35.

59. Even though Iraq was officially covered by the Geneva Conventions, the Schlesinger Report concluded that the techniques used at Guantanamo migrated to Abu Ghraib.

60. Peter Baker, "GOP Infighting on Detainees Intensifies," *Washington Post*, September 16, 2006, p. 1. See the transcript of President Bush's press conference of September 15, 2006, at: http://www.whitehouse.gov/news/releases/2006/09/20060915-2.html.

61. R. Jeffrey Smith, "Behind the Debate, CIA Techniques of Extreme Discomfort," *Washington Post*, September 16, 2006, p. A3; R. Jeffrey Smith, "Detainee Measure to Have Fewer Restrictions," *Washington Post*, September 26, 2006, p. 1; Charles Babington and Jonathan Weisman, "Senate Approves Detainee Bill Backed by Bush," *Washington Post*, September 29, 2006, p. 1.

62. According to Judge Evan Wallach, "to be effective, waterboarding is usually *real* drowning that simulates death. That is, the victim experiences the sensations of drowning; struggle, panic, breath-holding, swallowing, vomiting, taking water into the lungs." Evan Wallach, "Waterboarding Used to Be a Crime," *Washington Post*, November 4, 2007, p. B1. According to Malcom Nance, former master instructor and chief of training at the U.S. Navy Survival, Evasion, Resistance, and Escape School in San Diego: "Waterboarding is not simulation ... Waterboarding is a controlled drowning ... as the lungs are actually filling with water ... the victim is drowning." Malcom Nance, blog (no title) in *Small Wars Journal* online at www .smallwarsjournal.com, available at: www.smallwarsjournal.com/blog/2007/10/waterboarding-is-torture-period/. A Japanese officer, Yukio Asano, was sentenced to fifteen years at hard labor for waterboarding an American in World War II. Walter Pincus, "Waterboarding Historically Controversial," *Washington Post*, October 5, 2006, p. 17.

63. See Scott Shane and Adam Liptak, "Shifting Power to a President," *New York Times*, September 30, 2006, p. 1.

64. "Candidates on Use of Torture to Interrogate Detainees," *New York Times*, November 3, 2007, p. A13.

65. Tim Golden, "Detainee Memo Created Divide in White House," *New York Times*, October 1, 2006, p. 1.

66. The letter was posted on *TimesOnLine* on September 15, 2006, www.timesonline .co.uk.

67. The letter is dated September 12, 2006, and is available at: http://www.humanrightsfirst .info/pdf/06920-etn-krulak-ltr-mccain-ca3.pdf.

68. The letter is dated September 20, 2006 and is posted at: http://www.humanrightsfirst .info/pdf/06920-etn-krulak-ltr-mccain-ca3.pdf. On the same website, see also a letter to John McCain from former Chairman of the Joint Chiefs of Staff John Vessey, dated September 12, 2006.

69. Elsea, "Lawfulness of Interrogation Techniques," p. 5. Smith, "Behind the Debate, CIA Techniques of Extreme Discomfort," p. A3.

70. See Michael John Garcia, "The War Crimes Act: Current Issues," *Congressional Research Service Report* (RL33662), January 22, 2009.

71. Mark Mazzetti and Neil A. Lewis, "Military Lawyers Caught in the Middle on Tribunals," *New York Times*, September 16, 2006, p. 1.

72. "Executive Order: Interpretation of the Geneva Conventions Common Article 3 as Applied to a Program of Detention and Interrogation Operated by the Central Intelligence Agency," July 20, 2007, posted on White House website: http://www.whitehouse.gov.news/ releases/2007/07/20070720-4.html.

73. Mark Mazzetti, "C.I.A. Allowed to Resume Interrogations," *New York Times*, July 20, 2007.

74. See particularly Marty Lederman, "The CIA Interrogation Executive Order: Well, Did You Really Expect Anything Better?" July 20, 2007, *Balkinization Blog*, http://balkin.blogspot .com/.

75. P.X. Kelley and Robert F. Turner, "War Crimes and the White House," *Washington Post*, July, 26, 2007, p. A21.

76. Quoted by Nat Hentoff, "Gitmo: The Worst of the Worst?" *Village Voice*, March 23, 2006, villagevoice.com.

77. Claire Breay, *Magna Carta* (London: the British Library, 2002), p. 52. The two phrases "law of the land" and "due process of law" "are employed interchangeably in constitutional law, and mean the same thing." See William Blackstone, *Commentaries on the Laws of England* Vol. 1 (Chicago: Callaghan and Company, 1899), facsimile of the Fourth Edition, pp. 134–5, footnote 1.

78. Associated Press, "No Legal Rights for Enemy Combatants, Scalia Says," *Washington Post*, March 27, 2006, p. A3.

79. MSNBC.com, "Government Argues for Holding Detainees," December 1, 2004, at: http://www.msnbc.msn.com/id/6631668/print/I/displaymode/1098/.

80. See the analysis in Howard Ball, *Bush, the Detainees, and the Constitution* (Lawrence, KS: University Press of Kansas, 2007), pp. 90–124.

81. *Johnson v. Eisentrager* 399 U.S. 763 (1950).

82. See Brief for the Respondents in Opposition, *Rasul v. Bush*, Nos. 03–334 and 03–343, pp. 10–13, posted on FindLaw.com.

83. Brief for the Respondents, quoted in Ball, *Bush, the Detainees, and the Constitution*, p. 92.

84. *Johnson v. Eisentrager*, 339 U.S. 763 (1950).

85. ibid.

86. 542 U.S. 466 (2004).

87. *Rasul v. Bush*, 542 U.S. 466 (2004).

88. Excerpt in Pious, *The War on Terrorism*, p. 173.

89. *Rasul v. Bush*, 542 U.S. 466 (2004).

90. The Habeas Corpus Statute, 28 U.S. C. Sec. 2241, gives federal courts the jurisdiction to hear habeas corpus appeals.

91. Brief for the Respondents, *Hamdi V. Rumsfeld*, No. 03–6696, p. 10, posted on FindLaw .com.

92. *Hamdi vs. Rumsfeld* 542 U.S. 507 (2004).

93. ibid.

94. ibid.

95. ibid. See Ronald Rotunda, "Federalism and the Separation of Powers," *Engage* 8, No. 3 (2006), pp. 54–62 and "The Detainee Cases of 2004 and 2006 and Their Aftermath," *Syracuse Law Review* 57, No. 1 (2006), pp. 1–62.

96. In remarks after she had retired from the Supreme Court, Justice O'Conner said about the intimidation of federal judges, "We must be ever-vigilant against those who would strong-arm the judiciary into adopting their preferred policies. It takes a lot of degeneration before a country falls into dictatorship, but we should avoid these ends by avoiding these beginnings." Her remarks were reported by Nina Totenberg of National Public Radio according to Raw Story, "Retired Supreme Court Justice Hits Attacks on Courts and Warns of Dictatorship," March 10, 2006, website: rawstory.com.

97. Pious, *The War on Terrorism and the Rule of Law*, p. 153.

98. "Detention, Treatment, and Trial of Certain Non-Citizens in the War Against Terrorism," November 13, 2001, found at: http://www.whitehouse.gov/news/releases/2001/11/20011113-27 .html.

99. See Fisher, *Military Tribunals*, p. 168.

100. ibid., p. 173.

101. "Department of Defense, Military Commission Order No. 1" (March 21, 2002), signed by Donald Rumsfeld, available at: http://www.defenselink.mil/news/Mar2002/d20020321ord .pdf.

102. Public Law 109–148, 119 Stat. 2739.

103. 28 U.S.C Sec. 2241 (e).

104. The Court noted that Congress explicitly rejected language that would have made the law apply to previous appeals and that Senators Graham and Kyl inserted language into the Congressional Record after the Senate debate and tried to make it appear that their words were spoken during the debate over the bill. *Hamdan vs. Rumsfeld* (2006), No. 05–184, Slip Opinion, p. 15, note 10.

105. *Hamdan v. Rumsfeld* (2006), No. 05–184, Slip Opinion, pp. 27, 60–61.

106. ibid., pp. 2–4.

107. Military Commission Order No. 1, March 21, 2002, found at: http://www.defenselink .mil/news/Mar2002/d20020321ord.pdf.

108. See Michael C. Dorf, "A Federal Appeals Court Upholds ... Jurisdiction-Stripping of MCA," FindLaw: http://writ.news.findlaw.com/dorf/20070228.html, February 28, 2007, p. 4 of 5.

109. *Hamdan v. Rumsfeld* (2006), No. 05–184, Slip Opinion, pp. 4, 6.

110. *Law of War Handbook* (2004), p. 144, Slip Opinion, p. 68, note 63.

111. *Hamdan v. Rumsfeld* (2006), No. 05–184, Slip Opinion, p. 7.

112. 28 U.S.C. Section 2241(e).

113. See Jennifer K. Elsea and Kenneth R. Thomas, "Enemy Combatant Detainees: Habeas Corpus Challenges in Federal Court," *Congressional Research Service* (RL33180), April 6, 2007, pp. 20–21.

114. 476 F.3d 981.

115. *Boumediene v. Bush*, No. 06–1195, (2008) Slip Opinion, p. 3.

116. See Michael C. Dorf, "A Federal Appeals Court Upholds the Jurisdiction-Stripping Provisions of the MCA...." FindLaw, February 28, 2007, writ.news.findlaw.com/dorf/20070228 .html.

117. *Boumediene vs. Bush*, 476 F.3rd, 981, 989 (2007 D.C. Circuit); see the analysis by Louis Fisher in *The Constitution and 9/11: Recurring Threats to America's Freedoms*, pp. 245–7.

118. This account is based on the "Declaration of Stephen Abraham, Lieutenant Colonel, United States Army Reserve," found at: http://www.scotusblog.com/movabletype/archives/ Al%20Odah%20reply%206-22-07.pdf; and Susan Schmidt, "Trail of an 'Enemy Combatant': From Desert to U.S. Heartland," *Washington Post*, July 20, 2007, pp. 1, 16.

119. Susan Schmidt, "Trail of an 'Enemy Combatant,'" pp. 1, 16.

120. "Declaration of Stephen Abraham, Lieutenant Colonel, United States Army Reserve," p. 5.

121. Susan Schmidt, "Trail of an 'Enemy Combatant,'" pp. 1, 16.

122. Morris D. Davis, "AWOL Military Justice," *Los Angeles Times*, December 10, 2007.

123. ibid.

124. Morris Davis, "Unforgivable Behavior, Inadmissible Evidence," *New York Times*, February 17, 2008, p. 12.

125. Josh White, "Colonel Says Speaking Out Cost a Medal," *Washington Post*, May 29, 2008, p. A9.

126. Peter Finn, "Guantanamo Trials' Overseer Reassigned," *Washington Post*, September 20, 2008, p. 2.

127. Peter Finn, "Guantanamo Prosecutor Quits, Says Evidence Was Withheld," *Washington Post*, September 25, 2008, p. A6; William Glaberson, "Guantanamo Prosecutor Is Quitting in Dispute Over a Case," *New York Times*, September 25, 2008, p. A18.

128. Bob Woodward, "Detainee Tortured, Says U.S. Official," *Washington Post*, January 14, 2009, p. 1.

129. Bob Woodward, "Detainee Tortured, Says U.S. Official," *Washington Post*, January 14, 2009, p. 1.

130. "From John C. Yoo To Deputy Counsel to the President (September 25, 2001), The President's Constitutional Authority to Conduct Military Operations Against Terrorists and Nations Supporting Them," reprinted in Greenburg and Dratel, eds., *The Torture Papers*, pp. 3–24.

131. "From Alberto Gonzales to The President, 'Decision RE Application of the Geneva Conventions on Prisoners of War to the Conflict with "Al Qaeda and the Taliban,"'" (January 25, 2002). Reprinted in Greenberg and Dratel, eds., *The Torture Papers*, p. 118.

132. Justice Jackson dissenting in *Korematsu v. U.S.* 323 U.S. 214 (1944).

Chapter 6: Command Responsibility

1. Department of Defense briefing, December 3, 2002, quoted in Philippe Sands, *Torture Team* (New York: Palgrave Macmillan, 2008), p. 14.

2. Condoleezza Rice at Stanford University, April 30, 2009. Video found at: http://www
.cbsnews.com/stories/2009/05/01/national/main4983736.shtml. http://blog.foreignpolicy.com/
posts/2009/04/30/condi_rice_defends_torture_as_legal_and_right

3. Quoted by Nat Hentoff, "Gitmo: The Worst of the Worst?" *Village Voice*, March 23,
2006, villagevoice.com.

4. "President Bush, Prime Minister Blair Discuss War on Terror," Press Conference, July
17, 2003, at: http://www.whitehouse.gov/news/releases/2003/07/20030717-9.html. President
Bush continued to condemn detainees in Guantanamo even after it had been demonstrated that
many of them were innocent or posed no threat to the United States. See Donna Miles, "Bush:
Guantanamo Detainees Receiving Humane Treatment," Department of Defense, American
Forces Press Service, June 20, 2005, available at http://www.defenselink.mil/news/newsarticle
.aspx?id=16359, accessed April 2, 2005.

5. Fox News, "Rumsfeld: Afghan Detainees at Gitmo Bay Will Not Be Granted POW
Status," January 28, 2002, available at: http://www.foxnews.com/story/0,2933,44084,00.html.

6. News Conference of Secretary of Defense Rumsfeld, January 27, 2002, available at:
http://www.defenselink.mil/transcripts/2002/t01282002_t0127enr.html.

7. According to the Schlesinger Report, "Interrogators and list of techniques circulated
from Guantanamo and Afghanistan to Iraq," p. 7.

8. Schlesinger Report, p. 69. "Despite the number of visits and the intensity of interest
in actionable intelligence, however, the 'Panel found no undue pressure exerted by senior officials. Nevertheless, their eagerness for intelligence may have been perceived by interrogators
as pressure.'"

9. R. Jeffrey Smith, "Bush Adviser Toured Abu Ghraib," *Washington Post*, June 19, 2004;
CBS News report "Prison Officer Says He Felt Heat," June 18, 2004.

10. Interview of the vice president by Jonathan Kar, ABC News (December 15, 2008),
Vice President's Ceremonial Office, Executive Office Building. White House website: www
.whitehouse.gov/news/releases/ 2008/12/print/2008 1215-8, accessed December 22, 2008.

11. "William H. Parks, Command Responsibility for War Crimes, 62 Mil. L. Rev. 1 at
5" (quoting from Articles of War, Provisional Congress of Massachusetts Bay, April 5, 1775).
Quoted in Stuart E. Hendin, "Command Responsibility and Superior Orders in the Twentieth
Century—A Century of Evolution," *Murdoch University Electronic Journal of Law* (March 2003),
paragraph 8 [no page numbers in text, but all paragraphs are numbered]. Available at: http://
www.murdoch.edu.au/elaw/issues/v10n1/hendin101_text.html. These historical paragraphs
are based on Hendin's article cited in this note.

12. Andrew D. Mitchell, "Failure to Halt, Prevent or Punish: The Doctrine of Command
Responsibility for War Crimes," (2000) Sydney L. Rev. 381, 383. Quoted in Hendin, "Command
Responsibility and Superior Orders in the Twentieth Century," paragraph 14. Available at: http://
www.murdoch.edu.au/elaw/issues/v10n1/hendin101_text.html.

13. Hendin, "Command Responsibility and Superior Orders in the Twentieth Century,"
paragraphs 53–60.

14. "Activities of the Far Eastern Commission, Report by the Secretary General," separate
26-Jul 10, 1947, 16DEP't St. Bull. 804–806 (1947) Article 6 (a). Quoted in Hendin, "Command
Responsibility and Superior Orders in the Twentieth Century," paragraph 96.

15. General Headquarters United States Army Forces, Pacific Office of the Theatre Judge
Advocate, Review of the Record of Trial by a Military Commission of Tomoyuki Yamashita,
General Japanese Army (December 26, 1945), reprinted in Courtney Whitney, "The Case of
General Yamashita: A Memorandum" 60 (1950). Quoted in Hendin, "Command Responsibility
and Superior Orders in the Twentieth Century," paragraph 101.

16. YAMASHITA v. STYER, Commanding General, U.S. Army Forces, Western Pacific. 327 U.S. 1 (1946), http://caselaw.lp.findlaw.com/scripts/getcase.pl?court=US&vol=327&invol=1. Passages quoted in Hendin, "Command Responsibility and Superior Orders in the Twentieth Century," paragraph 102.

17. Ibid.

18. In RE Yamashita 327 U.S. 1 (1946), p. 16.

19. Human Rights Watch, "Getting Away with Torture? Command Responsibility and the U.S. Abuse of Detainees," *Human Rights Watch* 17, No. 1(G), Annex, p. 88.

20. *Prosecutor v. Sefer Halilovic,* Judgment (Case No. IT-01-48-T), November 16, 2005, found at: http://www.un.org/icty/halilovic/trialc/judgement/tcj051116e.htm#IIIB, accessed February 14, 2009, paragraphs 63 and 65.

21. See U.S. Department of the Army, The Law of Land Warfare (FM 27–10), paragraph 501 (July 1956), quoted in Human Rights Watch, "Getting Away with Torture?" p. 88; also cited in William G. Eckhardt, "Command Criminal Responsibility: A Plea for a Workable Standard," *Mililtary Law Review* 97 (1982), p. 31; and in Martha Minow, "Living Up to Rules: Holding Soldiers Responsible for Abusive Conduct and the Dilemma of the Superior Orders Defence," *McGill Law Journal* 52 (2007), p. 15.

22. Quoted by John D. Hutson and James Cullen in "From the Top Down." Rear Admiral Hutson (Ret.) served as the judge advocate general for the U.S. Navy from 1997 to 2000. Brigadier General Cullen (Ret.) served in the U.S. Army's Reserve Judge Advocate General's Corps and last served as the chief judge of the U.S. Army's Court of Criminal Appeals, found at: http://humanrightsfirst.org/us_law/commentary/hutson-cullen-041805.pdf.

23. Quoted in Jameel Jaffer and Amrit Singh, *Administration of Torture* (New York: Columbia University Press, 2007), p. 43.

24. *AR 15-6 Investigation of the Abu Ghraib Detention Facility and 205th MI Brigade,* (hereinafter Jones Report), LTG Anthony R. Jones. Reprinted in Karen J. Greenberg and Joshua L. Dratel, eds., *The Torture Papers: the Road to Abu Ghraib* (New York: Cambridge University Press, 2005), pp. 991–1018.

25. Jones Report, pp. 3, 4, 5, 17.

26. ibid., p. 17.

27. *Investigation of the Abu Ghraib Detention Facility and 205th Military Intelligence Brigade.* Major General George R. Fay, Investigating Officer, in Steven Strasser, ed., *The Abu Ghraib Investigations* (New York: Public Affairs, 2004), pp. 109–71. Fay Report, p. 110–11.

28. *Final Report of the Independent Panel to Review Department of Defense Detention Operations,* chaired by James R. Schlesinger, in Strasser, *The Abu Ghraib Investigations,* p. 33. (Hereinafter the Schlesinger Report.)

29. Schlesinger Report, p. 81.

30. ibid., pp. 8–9.

31. ibid., p. 9.

32. ibid., p. 69. Schlesinger found "no undue pressure exerted by senior officials. Nevertheless, their eagerness for intelligence may have been perceived by interrogators as pressure."

33. ibid., p. 33.

34. Amnesty International to the U.S. government, "Memorandum to the US Government on the Rights of People in US Custody in Afghanistan and Guantanamo Bay," April 15, 2002, http://webamnesty.org/library/index/ENGAMR50532002. Quoted in Human Rights Watch, "Getting Away with Torture?" p. 46.

35. Jane Mayer, *The Dark Side* (New York: Doubleday, 2008), pp. 184–5.

36. Interview with Spike Bowman, Washington, February 26, 2009.

37. ICRC, "Report of the International Committee of the Red Cross on the Treatment by the Coalition Forces of Prisoners of War and Other Protected Persons by the Geneva Conventions in Iraq during Arrest, Internment and Interrogation," February 2004, paragraphs 33–34. Quoted in Human Rights Watch, "Getting Away with Torture?" p. 44.

38. Peter Slevin and Robin Wright, "Pentagon Was Warned of Abuse Months Ago," *Washington Post,* May 8, 2004, p. A12; "Early Warnings Missed: a Prison-Abuse Timeline," *Los Angeles Times,* May 16, 2004, http://articles.latimes.com/2004/may/16/opinion/op-soller16.

39. For a list of citations, see Human Rights Watch, "Getting Away with Torture?" p. 46.

40. Army Times Editorial, "A Failure of Leadership at the Highest Levels," May 17, 2004, ArmyTimes.com.

41. Ian Fishback, "A Matter of Honor," *Washington Post,* September 28, 2005, p. A21.

42. ibid.

43. Eric Schmitt, "Officer Criticizes Detainee Abuse Inquiry," *New York Times,* September 28, 2005, website.

44. Eric Schmitt, "3 in 82nd Airborne Say Beating Iraqi Prisoners Was Routine," *New York Times,* September 24, 2005, website.

45. Schmitt, "Officer Criticizes Detainee Abuse Inquiry," website.

46. Alexander, "Torture's the Wrong Answer," p. B1.

47. Mayer, *The Dark Side,* pp. 307–11.

48. ibid., p. 310.

49. This account is based on ibid., pp. 316–19.

50. Quoted in ibid., pp. 317–18.

51. ibid., pp. 318–19.

52. Jane Mayer, "The Memo," *The New Yorker,* February 27, 2006 (online version posted February 20), p. 13 of 14 on webpage.

53. Sands, *Torture Team,* p. 225.

54. Department of the Army, *Human Intelligence Collector Operations,* Field Manual 2–223 (replacing FM 34–52), found at: http://www.army.mil/institution/armypublicaffairs/pdf/fm2-22-3.pdf.

55. Dan Froomkin, "Bush Demands Freedom to Torture," *White House World, washingtonpost.com,* December 14, 2007, http://www.washingtonpost.com/ac2/wp-dyn/NewsSearch?sb=-1&st=froomkin&. See the letter by former generals urging Congress to ignore Bush's veto threat, *Huffington Post,* http://www.huffingtonpost.com/2007/12/13/military-leaders-ignore-_n_76656.html?view=print. Steven Lee Myers, "Bush Vetoes Bill on C.I.A. Tactics, Affirming Legacy," *New York Times,* March 9, 2008, p. A1. See Louis Fisher, *The Constitution and 9/11* (Lawrence, KS: University Press of Kansas, 2008), p. 359.

56. Greg Miller, "Cheney was Key in Clearing CIA Interrogation Tactics," *Los Angeles Times,* December 16, 2006, at: http://articles.latimes.com/2008/dec/16/nation/na-cheney16.

57. For accounts of Cheney's influence in the Bush administration, see Barton Gellman, *Angler* (New York: Penguin Press, 2008). See also James P. Pfiffner, "Decision Making in the Bush White House," *Presidential Studies Quarterly* (forthcoming 2009).

58. Communication from David Kay to the author, August 13, 2008: "The interrogation episode remains for me a very unhappy memory. John Abizaid was unhappy that I was not finding WMD because he wanted to turn ISG resources over to the military to use against the growing insurgency. He went behind my back to argue in Washington that I needed to use more 'robust' interrogation methods. I was very unhappy when I learned this and refused. What we need was more people who spoke Arabic, not more 'forceful' tactics."

59. Seymour M. Hersh, "Chain of Command," *New Yorker,* May 17, 2004, p. 42.

60. Taguba Report, "Other Findings/Observations," 4a.

61. Jennifer K. Elsea, "Lawfulness of Interrogation Techniques under the Geneva Conventions," Washington: Congressional Research Service Report to Congress (RL32567), September 8, 2004, p. 5. R. Jeffrey Smith, "Behind the Debate, CIA Techniques of Extreme Discomfort," *Washington Post*, September 16, 2006, p. A3.

62. Mayer, *The Dark Side*, pp. 164–5.

63. Physicians for Human Rights, *Broken Laws, Broken Lives: Medical Evidence of Torture by US Personnel and Its Impact* (June 2008), available at: http://brokenlives.info/?page_id=69.

64. See the argument in Chapter 28 of Sands, *Torture Team*, pp. 224–32. Lawrence Wilkerson, chief of staff to Secretary of State Colin Powell, concluded that the top Bush administration lawyers who helped create U.S. torture policy (Gonzales, Haynes, Yoo, and Addington) may be guilty of war crimes. See Sands, p. 203.

65. See Eric Lichtblau and Scott Shane, "Report Detains Dissent On Guantanamo Tactics," *New York Times*, May 21, 2008, p. A17.

66. P.X. Kelley and Robert F. Turner, "War Crimes and the White House," *Washington Post*, July 26, 2007, p. A21.

67. Steven M. Kleinman, Colonel, US Air Force, "Statement before the United States Senate Committee on Armed Services, Hearing on the Treatment of Detainees in U.S. Custody," (September 25, 2008), found on the Senate Armed Services Committee website: http://armed-services.senate.gov/statemnt/2008/September/Moulton%2009-25-08.pdf.

68. Hearing on the Treatment of Detainees in U.S. Custody Before the Senate Committee on Armed Services, 110th Congress 5 (2008), Statement of Alberto Mora, http://armed-serevices.senate.gov/statement/2008/June/Mora%2006-17-08.pdf, quoted in Amicus Brief of Former National Security Officials and Counterterrorism Experts in Support of Petitioner, *Al-Marri v. Spagone* (No. 08–368).

69. Mike Mullen, "Building Our Best Weapon," *Washington Post*, February 15, 2009, p. B7.

70. Bob Woodward, "Detainee Tortured, Says U.S. Official," *Washington Post*, January 14, 2009, p. 1.

71. Quoted by Roger Cohen, "A Command of the Law," *New York Times*, November 27, 2008, *New York Times* website, accessed November 30, 3008.

72. John F. Harris, Mike Allen, and Jim VandeHei, "Cheney Warns of New Attacks," *Politico*, February 4, 2009, http://dyn.politico.com/printstory.cfm?uuid=3F1CDAB1-18FE-70B2-A815919AC2807E4.

73. Greg Miller, "Departing CIA Chief Hayden Defends Interrogations," *Los Angeles Times*, January 16, 2009, http://www.latimes.com/news/nationworld/worldlatinamerica/la-nacia16,0,1817803.story.

74. Harris, Allen, and VandeHei, "Cheney Warns of New Attacks," http://dyn.politico.com/printstory.cfm?uuid=3F1CDAB1-18FE-70B2-A815919AC2807E4. Cheney's attitude toward the use of harsh interrogation techniques seemed to echo what Caligula is said to have declared: "oderint dum metuant," which means "let them hate so long as they fear."

75. White House, Office of the Press Secretary (January 22, 2009), Executive Order, "Ensuring Lawful Interrogations."

76. White House, Office of the Press Secretary (January 22, 2009), Executive Order, "Review and Disposition of Individuals Detained at the Guantanamo Bay Naval Base and Closure of Detention Facilities." The closing of Guantanamo was complicated by the presence of genuine terrorists who continued to want to harm the United States and the return to the battlefield of some who had already been released. The challenge was convicting those guilty of crimes

without using evidence obtained through torture. See Pamela Hess, "Officials: Afghanistan Taliban Leader Was at Gitmo," *Washington Post,* March 11, 2009, p. 1.

77. See, for example, Dahlia Lithwick, "Forgive Not," *New York Times,* January 11, 2009, http://www.nytimes.com/2009/01/11/opinion/11lithwick.html?pagewanted=print.

78. Mark J. McKeon, "Why We Must Prosecute," *Washington Post,* April 28, 2009, p. A23. McKeon also made clear that any crimes the United States may have committed in the war on terror are in no way comparable to those committed by Milosevic or Saddam Hussein.

79. See Michael John Garcia, "The War Crimes Act: Current Issues," *Congressional Research Service* (RL33662), January 22, 2009, p. 8.

80. "Amicus Curiae Brief of Former National Security Officials and Counterterrorism Experts in Support of Petitioner, *Al-Marri v. Spagone,* No. 08-368" (2008, no date provided), p. 21.

81. Jack M. Balkin, "A Body of Inquiries," *New York Times,* January 11, 2009, http://www.nytimes.com/2009/01/11/opinion/11balkin.html?_r=1&pagewanted=print.

82. *The Writings of Abraham Lincoln,* V01, p. 01, Free Public Domain E-Books, found at: http://www.classic-literature.co.uk/american-authors/19th-century/abraham-lincoln/the-writings-of-abraham-lincoln-01/.

83. The White House, Office of the Press Secretary, "Statement of President Barack Obama on Release of OLC Memos," April 16, 2009, http://www.whitehouse.gove/the-press_office/Statement-of-President-Barack-Obama-on-the-Release-of-OLC-Memos/.

84. Friedrich Nietzsche, *The Philosophy of Nietzsche* (New York: The Modern Library, 1927, 1954), p. 466.

85. Alexander (a pseudonym), "Torture's the Wrong Answer," p. B.1.

Index

About the Author

James P. Pfiffner is University Professor in the School of Public Policy at George Mason University. His major areas of expertise are the presidency, American national government, and public management. He has written or edited twelve books on the presidency, including *Power Play: The Bush Administration and the Constitution* (2008), and he has published more than 100 articles and chapters in books, professional journals, reference works, and the popular press. While serving with the 25th Infantry Division (1/8 Artillery) in 1970 he received the Army Commendation Medal for Valor in Vietnam and Cambodia.